The *Bildungsroman* – the story of the development or formation of a young man – is the most famous German contribution to the European novel. Most studies of the *Bildungsroman* have concentrated on its underlying philosophy; Michael Minden addresses it as literature. He offers detailed readings of some of the best-known novels in the German language, from Goethe to Mann, including *Wilhelm Meisters Lehrjahre*, *Agathon*, *Anton Reiser*, *Hyperion*, *Heinrich von Ofterdingen*, *Der grüne Heinrich*, *Der Nachsommer* and *Der Zauberberg*. Looking at the novels from the points of view of gender, subjectivity and ideology of the aesthetic, and taking account of late-twentieth-century literary theory, Minden uncovers aspects and motifs which subvert traditional ideas of the *Bildungsroman* and raise questions about the function and status of literature.

CAMBRIDGE STUDIES IN GERMAN

THE GERMAN *BILDUNGSROMAN*

CAMBRIDGE STUDIES IN GERMAN

General editors: H. B. NISBET and MARTIN SWALES
Advisory editor: THEODORE J. ZIOLKOWSKI

Also in the series

ANNA K. KUHN
Christa Wolf's Utopian Vision
From Marxism to Feminism

LESLEY SHARPE
Friedrich Schiller: Drama, Thought and Politics

PETER HUTCHINSON
Stefan Heym: The Perpetual Dissident

ERNST BEHLER
German Romantic Literary Theory

MICHAEL BUTLER (editor)
The Narrative Fiction of Heinrich Böll
Social Conscience and Literary Achievement

J. P. STERN
The Dear Purchase: A Theme in German Modernism

SEÁN ALLAN
The Plays of Heinrich von Kleist: Ideals and Illusions

W. E. YATES
Theatre in Vienna: A Critical History 1776–1995

THE GERMAN BILDUNGSROMAN

Incest and Inheritance

MICHAEL MINDEN

University of Cambridge

CAMBRIDGE
UNIVERSITY PRESS

Published by the Press Syndicate of the University of Cambridge
The Pitt Building, Trumpington Street, Cambridge CB2 1RP, United Kingdom

Cambridge University Press
The Edinburgh Building, Cambridge CB2 2RU, United Kingdom
40 West 20th Street, New York, NY 10011-4211, USA
10 Stamford Road, Oakleigh, Melbourne 3166, Australia

First published 1997

Printed in United Kingdom at the University Press, Cambridge

Typeset in Monotype Baskerville 11/12½pt

A catalogue record for this book is available from the British Library

Library of Congress cataloguing in publication data

Minden, Michael.
The German Bildungsroman: incest and inheritance / Michael Minden.
p. cm. – (Cambridge studies in German)
Includes bibliographical references and index.
ISBN 0 521 49573 3 (hardback)
1. Bildungsroman. 2. German fiction – History and criticism.
3. Goethe, Johann Wolfgang von, 1749–1832. Wilhelm Meisters Lehrjahre. I. Title. II. Series.
PT747.E6M56 1997
833.009 – dc20 97-31666 CIP

ISBN 0 521 49573 3 hardback

SE

To my mother and the memory of my father
and my grandmother

Contents

Acknowledgements

Versions of what follows (but never in unamended form) have appeared in the *Deutsche Vierteljahresschrift für Literatur und Geistesgeschichte*, *London German Studies*, *Publications of the English Goethe Society*. This book has taken a long time to write and many friends and colleagues have given me the benefit of their advice and attention. Thanks are due to Ian Roe and Helen Watanabe a long time ago; to Andrew Bowie, Peter Hutchinson, Ben Morgan, Roger Paulin, Ritchie Robertson, Martin Swales, Elizabeth Wright, who all read parts of drafts and gave help and encouragement; and especially to Nicholas Boyle, who has been so generous with his kindness, knowledge and wise scholarship. Paul Connerton and Dave Russell have been exceptionally stimulating friends. Several anonymous publisher's readers have offered careful and considered criticism of various drafts. Peter Schnyder gave me invaluable help in the latter stages of preparing the manuscript. My wife Mary and son Joseph have given the book its real meaning. The mistakes and idiosyncrasies are my own.

Introduction

Vom Vater hab' ich die Statur,
Des Lebens ernstes Führen,
Von Mütterchen die Frohnatur
Und Lust zu fabulieren.

(Goethe)

Sei ein Mann und folge mir nicht nach.

(*Werther*)

Dichter will so gerne Knecht sein,
Weil die Herrschaft draus entspringt.

(*Westöstlicher Divan*)

This is a study of the German *Bildungsroman* as a series of variations on Goethe's *Wilhelm Meisters Lehrjahre* (1795–1796). It offers a definition of the genre based on the peculiarities of the texts themselves, not on the idea of *Bildung*.[1]

The idea of *Bildung* – the development or formation of a young man – is basically linear. I shall argue that these novels are in fact circular. The answer to the question, 'Where is this journey of maturation and discovery leading?' is Novalis's 'immer nach Hause': the destination is always home.[2]

The circularity of this return has both a feminine and a masculine aspect. The thematic motifs in which these two guarantees of development are expressed in the *Bildungsroman* are incest and inheritance.

By 'incest' I mean generally a motif expressing the quintessence of desire, with its logical end in the collapse of all differences. It is not surprising that the desire of the masculine protagonists of the *Bildungsroman* should be embodied in women figures, who often have a structural function as well as a thematic one. The most obvious example of this sort of structural function is the ending in marriage, a motif from which the *Bildungsroman* has deviated in a rich variety of ways, ever since its inception with Wieland's *Die Geschichte des Agathon* in 1767. Yet behind this basic masculine heterosexual determination there lies a fundamental orientation upon the mother. This is at its clearest in the *Lehrjahre* and Novalis's *Heinrich von Ofterdingen* (1802), but it has effects everywhere.

As for the masculine determination, 'inheritance', there is first a word to be said about the sort of construction of masculine identity that the *Bildungsroman* avoids.

In modern psychoanalysis and literary criticism (as the famous theory of Harold Bloom attests), rivalry is sometimes evoked as the essence of relations between men. For the influential post-Freudian psychoanalyst Lacan (deriving his idea from Hegel) rivalry is the matrix of the psyche.[3] Any rivalry model, however, will disturb the clear focus upon the individual to which the *Bildungsroman* is committed. For rivalry you need two individuals. The *Bildungsroman*, while certainly containing instances of rivalry, actually tends to avoid it as a structural principle. It is interesting how the catastrophe at the end of the first book of the *Lehrjahre* is precisely Wilhelm Meister's physical and mental breakdown at the discovery that he has a successful rival for the affections of Marianne. This catastrophe supplies the key to progression beyond the problems of subjectivity that had remained unresolved in Goethe's earlier novel, *Werther*. It is as though the model of development proposed in the *Lehrjahre* depends on the *refusal* of rivalry, and with it on the refusal of a certain heroic masculine form of establishing authority and meaning. The crisis at the end of the first book, and the regeneration at the start of the second, confirm how the *Bildungsroman* is seeking to define new forms of masculine authority.

Confirmation for this understanding of the genre, as subverting what were once received gender definitions, comes from the scholar credited with coining the term *Bildungsroman* in the first place.[4] Professor Karl Morgenstern, a rather belated *Aufklärer*, in a lecture given in 1810, was uneasy about the lack of moral rigour and masculine character displayed by the heroes of the novels for which he had just found a name.[5] He recognised that here was a new kind of hero and a kind of novel worthy of the advocacy of an academic aesthetician like himself. Yet he nevertheless found the fact that Wilhelm Meister is represented with unalloyed sympathy, rather than framed within a judgement about his acts and achievements, somehow offensive to his sense of the manliness expected of a proper hero. He may have been a hero fit for a *novel*, but not a real hero. For Morgenstern, Wilhelm Meister was a character disconcertingly lacking in 'personal energy and distinct direction', und thus 'unmanly'.[6]

Nevertheless, despite this significant redefinition of the masculine, there is also a fundamentally traditional, feudal, aspect to the way in which the continuity of masculine identity is guaranteed: the principle of primogeniture. The laws of inheritance guarantee the eldest son his name and power. The protagonists of these novels tend correspondingly to be the only children of their parents, and there is no example among them of a *younger* son. They inherit, materially, spiritually or both, from fathers and father figures. This is the masculine circularity which corresponds to the feminine one grounded in the love of the mother.

Much of the variation we observe within the unified model of the *Bildungsroman* is the result of the differing ways in which, in each work, the two circularities just described are related to one another. The decisive unifying factor for the model as a whole is not how they are linked, but *that* they are linked. Compatibility between the two circularities, between the feminine and the masculine dimensions, is constitutive of the model.

This explains the importance of the theme of androgyny in the genre which surfaces in the *Lehrjahre* and *Der Zauberberg* (1926). In the *Bildungsroman* in general the masculine protagonist is strongly marked by feminine traits. Thomas Mann, talking about artists, suggested: 'There is always something feminine in the essence of the beautiful. Look at the example of the artist, who has never been simply or brutally masculine (der nie und nirgends ein reiner und roher Mann gewesen ist).'[7]

Mann's application of the idea of androgyny to the sphere of art is not fortuitous. Terry Eagleton, in *The Ideology of the Aesthetic,* remarks aptly that the aesthetic is 'a fantasy of father and mother in one',[8] and the relation of incest and inheritance to the sphere of art and the aesthetic is indeed central to the *Bildungsroman*. This emerges most clearly when we look at two novels which, together, play a pivotal part in this book: *Heinrich von Ofterdingen* (1802) and *Der Nachsommer* (1857). In these two texts the play, both enigmatic and urbane, made by Goethe with the combination of masculine and feminine is dramatically polarised. In the former the feminine predominates but enfolds within itself the masculine, while in the latter the converse happens. In Novalis and Stifter respectively the *Bildungsroman* themes of incest and inheritance emerge in their clearest forms.

Novalis's protagonist, in his incestuous journey towards the maternal source, is unambiguously a creative person, a poet. In Stifter's *Der Nachsommer* the protagonist is not a creative personality, but art plays no smaller a role than it does with Novalis. The difference is that in Stifter art is represented from the point of view of its products, not its source. These products are passed on from father to son. They imbue the ancient law of primogeniture with all the modern values of a Novalis. Historically, it took private collectors as well as original geniuses to create what modernity understands as art.[9]

The protagonists of Novalis and Stifter are extremes. The typical *Bildungsroman* hero does not know whether he is an artist or not. This may seem simply a character weakness, but it is thematically crucial. The combination of masculine and feminine attitudes to art is expressed in this *hesitation* in the realm of characterisation.

Incest and inheritance also have their expression on the level of narrative technique. The *Bildungsroman*, as we have said, relies upon the co-operation of these two principles. The hero, hesitant about his creativity, relies upon the confident offices of one in no such doubt: the narrator. To that extent, this is the configuration of autobiography, in which a mature and accomplished voice recounts the vicissitudes of the less complete person he once was. Yet the *Bildungsroman* enjoys a peculiar, though important, relationship with the genre of modern autobiography. The relation between them can be expressed by saying that the *Bildungsroman* is invariably *not quite* autobiographical. The clearest example of this is Gottfried Keller's *Der grüne Heinrich* (1854–1855, 1879–1880).

The *Bildungsroman* proceeds by disowning personal experience, and making this the first step towards universalising it. Instead of seeking ways of making personal experience historically significant (as Goethe did in his own autobiography, *Dichtung und Wahrheit*) or asserting with all the force of a subjective revolution that personal experience is important *because* it is personal (as Rousseau did in his *Confessions*) the *Bildungsroman* makes the shortcomings of the individual – the very 'false starts and wrong choices' of the dictionary definition of the genre[10] – the driving force of its narratives. In the case of Goethe's seminal novel the hero is ironically called *Meister* (master), while represented as perpetually making mistakes. Wilhelm is decentred, but only to become central again by virtue of his decentredness.

In the essay 'Goethe und Tolstoy' (1921) Thomas Mann writes as follows about the genesis of the *Bildungsroman*. He cites Goethe as saying somewhere that in Wilhelm Meister he sees his own 'beloved image' ('geliebtes Ebenbild'). This relationship between author and protagonist, Mann explains, is not one of blank narcissism, but is informed by an urge to self-improvement and self-formation:

> And precisely . . . this sense of one's own 'I' as a duty to be performed, a moral, aesthetic and cultural commitment, is objectified in the hero of the autobiographical novel of formation and development (Bildungs- und Entwicklungsroman). It is embodied in a 'thou', in relation to whom the poetic 'I' assumes the role of guide, teacher, educator; identical with him, but at the same time superior to the degree that Goethe at one point refers to [Wilhelm] with paternal affection as 'a poor dog', a designation as full of feeling for himself as for his 'other'.[11]

In the light of Mann's remarks we can reformulate the co-operating principles of incest/inheritance, Novalis/Stifter, in terms of two types of authorship. In the character of the protagonist, in his 'false starts and wrong moves', there is an open-ended idea of *self*-authorship, an individual's own attempts to realise his own potential. To represent a protagonist as striving to author *himself* is the positive reinterpretation Goethe and the others find for the psychological dilemma of Karl Philipp Moritz's *Anton Reiser* (first three volumes 1785–1786, final volume 1790), the eponymous hero of which flounders in attempts to firm up an identity by misconceived acts of authorship, or by acting up a version of a self in the form of a dramatic role.

The other type of authorship is implied by the existence of the text itself, because the text is evidence of the act of authorship responsible for it. The thematic-formal closure of the artefact has its proper voice in the assured voice of the narrator. The first-person novels *Der Nachsommer* and *Der grüne Heinrich* do not, as one might be tempted to object, negate this model but provide highly instructive variations upon it.

These two kinds of author are not identified with one another. The writer of the text does not represent his own subjectivity in formal completion. That would be narcissism or autobiography or both. The link between the subject represented and the subject representing, which is the *raison d'être* of autobiography, remains, in the *Bildungsroman*, covert. The 'not quite' is an act of hiding, of veiling the link between the self-authoring hero, the completion of whose work lies in the future, and the author of the finished text, whose act of authorship is in the past. (Here again Novalis and Stifter respectively offer the purest examples.)

The *Bildungsroman*, in the form of *Wilhelm Meisters Lehrjahre*, came about at an historical juncture at which two complex issues were joined. The structure we have seen variously realised in terms of incest and inheritance, Novalis and Stifter, and disguised autobiography can also be seen in their terms. They are named in the title of Andrew Bowie's recent study of German philosophy from Kant to Nietzsche: *Aesthetics and Subjectivity*.[12] The argument of Bowie's book is that the development of what had come by the time of Kant's great critical philosophy (but not by him) to be called 'aesthetics', that is the part of philosophy dedicated to the theory of beauty, answered the question posed by subjectivity in the secularised world of post-Enlightenment Europe. Subjectivity posed a question for two reasons: first because in a post-theological environment the human subject is at once liberated and disoriented, and second, because the realm of subjectivity as the site of the free agency of reason needed to be defended against the modern scientific view which subordinates nature to the law of causality, and threatens to leave no place for moral self-determination.[13]

Kant himself left the subject 'divided between an autonomous – but impersonally rational – and an individual – but heteronomous – self'.[14] The former 'transcendental' subject has given encouragement to the modern myth of the fully self-present subject and hence to its deconstruction.[15] But the modern subject has to be thought of against the background of these *two* determinations, an abstract sovereign on one hand and, on the other, an impoverished slave to the senses. At once universal, as the seat and agent of reason (and thus freedom), and irredeemably partial.

It is precisely this *double* determination that is reflected in the *Bildungsroman*: the (secret) alliance between an assured narrative voice, equipped with general maxims – 'Herr der Gegensätze' ('master of contradictions'), as Mann's narrator puts it in *Der Zauberberg* – and the 'poor dog' of an empirical subject who has to make his way amid the vicissitudes of concrete circumstances. Similarly, the union of incest and inheritance, of Novalis and Stifter, in the *Bildungsroman* genre can be understood as a reflection of the attempt to unite in a single discourse the potentially infinite but perpetually partial subject and a form of objectification which does not negate it. This form is the privileged and special sort of non-instrumental objectification which modernity understands as art.

Bowie's exposition of the role aesthetics plays in relation to the modern problems of subjectivity is therefore relevant to the literary context of the *Bildungsroman*. All the more so in light of the fact that two of the writers whose literary work features in this book, Hölderlin and Novalis, also occupied themselves in theory with the post-Kantian problem of the subject.

The philosophical context was set by Johann Gottlieb Fichte, who, in the wake of Kant, sought to do more than Kant had done to defend the human subject against the threat of objectification among the other 'things' of the causally determined world. Although Fichte's system absolutises the notion of the subject in a way that subsequent thinkers have deemed flawed, it is nevertheless to him that we owe the still-valid insight 'that reflection on the subject by the subject reveals a reality which will never exhaust itself in what could be known objectively'.[16]

For Fichte the way out of the philosophical impasse – that the I cannot know the I without at the same time attesting to the prior *possibility* of that knowledge (which it therefore does *not* know) – is to claim that we do nevertheless have access to the ground of subjectivity in the realisation in thought of the moral freedom which has its – unknowable – source within subjectivity. In positing an absolute subject as its own ground, a unification of knowing, being and doing, a pure self-realisation, philosophy is itself an act of self-realisation for human subjectivity.

Both Hölderlin and Novalis take up the challenge of giving an account of something – subjectivity – which they know will always resist having an account given of it. Yet they are not content with Fichte's *philosophical* resolution of the question. For Novalis, it is this very partialness which is a token of the wholeness against which the partialness *is* partial: 'we feel ourselves as a part and are precisely for that reason the whole'.[17] 'Instead of thinking that philosophy could reach the fundamental ground, the "initial impulse" of freedom that Fichte posits as the absolute beginning, philosophy must realise its own inherent failure to be complete.'[18] And when it is the site of the realisation of a failure, philosophy becomes very difficult to distinguish from poetry.

Hölderlin also resists Fichte's claim to be able in philosophy to go back to the originary self-founding act of subjectivity.[19] Instead he overcomes the formal aporias of the I's attempts to unify itself in the face of the division of self-consciousness by turning away from thought to action, in the quest for a form of true self-knowledge. The I must exercise 'its free spontaneity in the choice of an external object, which will reveal the I's "poetic individuality"'.[20] 'Reveal' has here the sense of furnishing the subject with a way of knowing itself via the detour through an external sphere which bears the marks of the subject, yet lies outside narcissistic circularity, enabling the subject 'to grasp what it would be like to realise its most fundamental self'.[21] At the same time, and like the subject itself, this external sphere or object demonstrates the fundamental indivisibility of subject and object. This sort of activity, in which the secret harmony of inner and outer is enacted, is *aesthetic* activity, the only free activity available to Man. Once more, in the case of Hölderlin, the struggle with the philosophically recalcitrant problem of how subjectivity can be known (i.e. know itself) leads towards a form of knowing which is in fact doing, and that doing is aesthetic activity.

The philosopher Friedrich Wilhelm Joseph Schelling, the thinker in whose work the idea of art assumed especially great importance,[22] brings together the systematic impulse of Fichte and the huge importance attached to art by Novalis and Hölderlin and produces a solution which is a philosophical version of the literary solution achieved by the *Lehrjahre*.[23] While cognitive philosophy can never show us the true nature of our subjectivity, can never turn upon its own knowing and know *it*, *art* can reveal to our intuition the way in which consciousness is part of nature because art is 'the *unity* of conscious and unconscious activity';[24] 'the conscious intention of the artist coincides with the unconscious compulsion of the artist's genius'.[25]

Schelling's attempt to understand art as the point of convergence and mutual confirmation of human rational determination and human nature as unconscious genius is thus a close relative to the *Lehrjahre*, where an 'unconscious' hero (a hero whose consciousness always lags behind his actions) is in the process of authoring or producing himself, and a narrator assumes the conscious responsibility of giving an account of this significant indeterminateness within a finished product, the novel itself, of which he, the narrator, is understood as the author.

The development of the relation between subjectivity and aesthetics in the phase after Kant exhibits an increasing blurring of the distinction between literature and philosophy. While the *Lehrjahre* can be seen to be informed by the same impulses as informed Schelling, its status as a work of literature and not a system of ideas provides it and its cognate texts with possibilities less easily accessible to philosophy. If this study is able to make a contribution to the debate about modern subjectivity, it is because it takes seriously the particularities of these novels as literary texts, rather than as vehicles for the *idea* of Bildung.

The particular advantage literature has over philosophy is the possibility of a play with genre, and with its own form. What happens with the *Lehrjahre* is as follows. In the wake of Blanckenburg's *Versuch über den Roman* (1774), the first German 'theory of the novel', and Wieland's *Agathon*, Goethe's novel played the decisive role in bringing the German novel under the jurisdiction of the aesthetic. This was a time in literary debate at which the novel was by no means assured of its status as serious literature. From then on, Goethe's adoption of the novel form supplied a reference point for those who wished to urge the aesthetic pedigree of the novel form.[26]

What Goethe did was to transform a popular form into an aesthetic artefact. This transformation is clear in the change from the early autobiographical, realistic and comic fragment, now known as the *Theatralische Sendung*, into the finished version of the novel, which universalises the particular experience it encloses. Readers have often complained about the artificiality of the *Lehrjahre* as opposed to the spontaneity of the *Sendung*. But this misses the point. Goethe gave a demonstration of how the aesthetic produces its effects: by enhancing artifice. By ironically disclosing its artificiality, acknowledging its limits, it produces an allegorical aura. It knows more than it can show. Individual experience does have universal significance, yet the rules for this consonance cannot be set down as knowledge, they can only be lived, just as a novel is never reducible to its 'ideas' and must be read with an eye to sensuous particularity as well as cognitive grasp. In pratice, this meant that Goethe reinvented existing popular novel discourses, realism and fantasy, but with the quality of universality added.

The closure or evident artificiality of the novel is *at once* organically pleasing *and* points beyond itself to truths to which it has no immediate access. This is thematically displayed in the contrast between Mignon and Natalie, to which we shall return in the next chapter.

Hence a sense of infinite subjective potential – incest – can be played off against a closure or limit – inheritance – which it informs and transcends but does not disrupt. The infinite regress of any attempt to represent subjectivity can be halted by expressing the limitedness of all subjective experience, while preserving a sense of the unboundedness of subjectivity itself. This is the juxtaposition of 'Nacheinander' and 'Nebeneinander' of which Martin Swales speaks in his study of the *Bildungsroman*.[27] By embodying closure, the work of art gives something to be transcended. Without this limit it would not be possible to intimate the unlimited. Novalis certainly grasped this both passionately and theoretically; but his desire to articulate this insight, not only in his theoretical writing but also in *Heinrich von Ofterdingen*, is impatient to go beyond itself.[28] This urgency is nowhere better expressed than in Novalis's furious objections to the *Lehrjahre*, a text he also revered.[29] The attempt in Klingsohr's *Märchen* (at the end of the first book of *Ofterdingen*) to bind together narrative and ideas, the sensuous and the abstract, by trying to make explicit the inner incestuous implication of the Goethean model, the collapse of all differences, falls at the very limit of the charmed circle of that model, and arguably fails both in respect of narrative and in respect of ideas.

Hölderlin, on the other hand, feels more immediately than Novalis the challenge posed by the world of practical reason to the inner world of the poet, and is resolved to meet it, even if this means exchanging the pen for the sword.[30] What makes for the incomparable poetic power of Hölderlin is the perpetual defeat of this resolve. His words are always also deeds, and as such doomed to frustration. The limitation of his texts is radical and completely uncompromising. It is certainly a significant limitation, but its significance is a tragic one, and thus in the end foreign to the circularities of the *Bildungsroman*. His commitment to an ideal of the consonance between inner and outer is such that a conscious and ironic exploitation of artifice like that of the contemporaneous *Lehrjahre* is out of the question. Whereas, therefore, *Heinrich von Ofterdingen* is included in this study as a variation upon the *Lehrjahre*, *Hyperion* is included in it as a significant *contrast* to the Goethean model.

Thus the *Lehrjahre* is part of the preoccupation with subjectivity and aesthetics of the time, but has the advantage of particularity on its side. It is itself a version of the aesthetic, but, unusually, in artistic *practice* rather than in theory, or even the theory-cum-practice of the Romantic sort.

One of the most persistent themes of the *Bildungsroman* is that the form of the novel and the form of a well-lived life, though not identical, are mutually confirming. Already at the time Morgenstern was writing, the accepted assumption was that the best novels – those which were the formally most successful and valid – were those which dealt with the development of an individual person.[31] Morgenstern himself saw the value of *Bildungsromane* in giving literary form to the artist's *own* development, thus offering exemplary representations of Man himself. For Moritz, the hope of a 'Roman eines Lebens' (the novel of a life) animates his own fragmented discourse.[32] The Romantics were as positive as Moritz was negative, implying almost that there is an absolute identity between life and novel. On one hand, the best novels are direct expressions of real subjectivity: Friedrich Schlegel valued only those works which offered 'a more or less disguised confession on the part of the author, the yield of his experiences, the quintessence of his particular nature'.[33] On the other, the best lives are novels. For Novalis, 'life should be a novel (Roman) not given to us, but made by us',[34] or elsewhere, 'A novel is a life as a book.'[35] Once more on the negative side, Keller dreamed of a coincidence of life and novel which eluded him in his labours to make a novel out of his failed development as an artist.[36] And Thomas Mann approved Novalis's notion of lives as novels thought [*sic*] by ourselves.[37] For him the positive autobiographical impulse was the key both to a successful life and to literary composition: 'Love for oneself is always the start of a life resembling a novel (eines romanhaften Lebens).'[38]

This persistent link between the form of a life and the form of the novel bears witness to the proximity of the construction of art in the *Bildungsroman* to the philosophical/aesthetic debate which was its background. There is an unspoken affinity between the aesthetic work and the individual life. A self-authoring converges with a shaping from without: this is the ideal, at the centre of Fichte and the whole post-Kantian project, of a knowing, a being and a doing which are one. Terry Eagleton observes that: 'the aesthetic artefact is a covert trope of the humanist subject'.[39] This is true of the *Bildungsroman*, except that the *Bildungsroman* is not covert but, as a *Roman* about *Bildung*, overt in its representation of the humanist subject. But it would be wrong to assume, as Eagleton sometimes appears to do, that this subject is unproblematically self-present. The whole complex and precarious balancing of incest and inheritance in the *Bildungsroman* is necessary precisely because it is not.

Over a hundred years after the Romantic confluence of aesthetics and subjectivity came another massively influential formulation of how subjectivity is determined, Freud's theory of the Oedipus Complex. Freud, as a cultured Austrian, owed much to the German cultural tradition which includes Romanticism and the *Bildungsroman* tradition, so that the leap from Romanticism to psychoanalysis is by no means as unexpected as it might appear at first sight. What is at stake in the Oedipus Complex is also a harmonisation of incest with inheritance, of law with desire. Although Freud, despite his literary style and culture, had a scientific view of what lay behind subjective partialness (in that sense he was closer to Moritz than to Goethe), the *successful negotiation* of the Oedipal stage is nevertheless a sort of *Bildungsroman*. The Oedipus Complex is also, after all, the story of how a middle-class European male can combine the love of the mother with succession to the father without ultimately destructive rivalry or re-absorption into a pre-individuated state. Just like the *Bildungsroman*, it is a highly precarious compromise which strives at the same time to establish itself as a norm.

If the Oedipal pattern provides a recurrent point of reference in the pages which follow, this is not to reduce the texts under discussion to a well-known and predictable Freudian paradigm as though this were a discovery. Rather, it is a co-optation of Freud for my argument, to the extent that he belongs to the same 'episteme' as the corpus of work with which we are concerned. That Goethe and Freud tell roughly the same story is an indication of the endurance of a certain model across a long time. The word 'episteme' comes from Michel Foucault's *The Order of Things*, and designates the 'discursive regularities' which define and produce periods of historical time. The relevance of Foucault's term to my concern is, first, that his 'modern' episteme begins at the same time as the composition of *Wilhelm Meisters Lehrjahre*, and second, that the definition of what Foucault calls the 'Age of Man' corresponds precisely to my view of the paradox upon which these texts are based. For Foucault 'modernity begins with the incredible and ultimately unworkable idea of a being who is sovereign precisely by virtue of being enslaved'.[40]

At all events, the centring of partialness in the *Lehrjahre* model, the specific union of two sorts of authorship, the spinning of an authority out of the very lack of it, all accord perfectly with Foucault's characterisation of the Modern Age, the Age of Man, in which Man occupies 'an ambiguous position as an object of knowledge and as a subject that knows'.[41] 'Man becomes the subject and the object of his own understanding.'[42] The same determining epistemological paradox still has its place in the humanistic theology of *Der Zauberberg*, with its reflections upon the *Homo Dei*, a concept which Mann elsewhere glossed as 'der Mensch selbst mit seiner religiösen Frage nach sich selbst . . . der ewigen Rätsel-Aufgabe der Humanität' ('Man himself with his religious quest for himself . . . the eternal puzzle of humanity').[43]

The findings of this study thus conform to Foucault's grand periodisation. Yet effects of a more conventionally conceived history also claim attention where, as in the analyses that follow, literary detail is as important as broad historical development. These effects are felt in three ways.

First, historical development, and particularly the consciousness of it, produces, in *Der grüne Heinrich*, a peculiar tension, which amplifies a productive tension already exploited within the *Lehrjahre* to the point at which the *Lehrjahre* model is itself threatened. Second, the ideal of aesthetic representation, the system in which the authenticity of subjectivity passes into the public domain, and can thus be objectively ownable as well as subjectively authentic, comes under increasing pressure from another view of the world. This view, again, is contained (in both senses of the word) in the *Lehrjahre*, but increases its influence to the point where it affects the objective status, and thus the possibility of meaning, of the artefacts we are examining: namely, that specifically industrial and capitalistic view of the world which sees everything (including, in the end, the human subject) in terms of mobility, substitution and exchange. Third, and this is the concrete manifestation of the second, it is clear that many of the historical vicissitudes of the *Bildungsroman* are in fact related to those of the ideal of the aesthetic, which, as Franco Moretti observes, rapidly became what, from the second half of the nineteenth century, was known as Kitsch.[44] At the heart of the phenomenon of Kitsch is the false claim that individual desires and the objective world can overlap in certain ownable objects. Many, if not all, of the commodities of consumer culture are the products of this claim. It is what becomes of the great aesthetic ideal in the age of capitalist commodification, and is why the post- or anti-*Bildungsroman* ethos of the *avant-garde* rises against that ideal. The variations in these texts are in part the result of the different means they employ in order both to remain faithful to the Goethean paradigm, and to fend off the dire threat of Kitsch, which, once more, is germinating in the *Lehrjahre* itself (in the problem of how to 'represent' Mignon's funeral).

Thomas Mann was the master of the exploitation – both artistic and commercial – of cultural liminality, and his ironic version of the *Lehrjahre* model in my opinion also marks its end. My concluding brief reference to Kafka is intended as an incisive and relevant contrast to the literary model discussed in this book. Kafka's understanding and practice of writing point towards the different combinations of autobiography and literature which, after Nietzsche and Proust, have proved determining in the twentieth century.

The first two chapters of this book, on the *Lehrjahre* and on three cognate texts not directly influenced by Goethe's novel, have an introductory function. In Chapter One, some of the terms are generated which will be used in the succeeding chapters. The second chapter, on novels by Wieland, Moritz and Hölderlin, maps an historical and intellectual context for Goethe's novel, using literary texts rather than abstract terms. The remaining three chapters offer analyses of four other major novels associated with the *Bildungsroman* genre. In place of a discursive conclusion there is the short section on Kafka, to which I have just referred, as an 'other' to the humanist novel of development.

The organisation of the eight analyses is a reflection of a *context*, and not subordinate to any principle imposed from elsewhere, not even chronology. The treatment in tandem of Novalis and Stifter (Chapter Four) might seem at first sight to be the oddest effect of this method. However, it is indispensable for my overall sense of this context that these two extraordinary texts should appear removed from their respective, more usual, contexts. The defamiliarisation is thus intentional and strategic. On the other hand, with this one limitation the analyses can stand for themselves and be consulted independently, as well as for their place in a configuration.

CHAPTER ONE

Wilhelm Meisters Lehrjahre

Wilhelm Meisters Lehrjahre is divided into eight Books. The first five deal with the early history and adventures of the character who gives the work its name, Wilhelm Meister, the son of a wealthy merchant at an unspecified date somewhere in eighteenth-century Germany. Wilhelm Meister is enthusiastic about the theatre. After an unhappy love affair with an actress, he joins a troupe of players himself. The early Books chronicle his eventful theatrical career culminating, in Book Five, in a production of *Hamlet.* The reader encounters many subsidiary characters in the course of this theatrical life, notably the mysterious child Mignon and the anonymous melancholy Harpist. After the production of *Hamlet*, Wilhelm's progress tends away from the theatre and falls under the influence of a noble family and a secret society with which some of the family members are associated. Book Six is an interruption of the main narrative. It is the spiritual autobiography of a pious woman who eventually turns away from the profane world to espouse a life of religious devotion. Although it does not move Wilhelm's story forward, it does introduce the noble family with which he is to become involved, and this involvement is played out in the final two Books of the novel. In these last two Books various secret relationships hinted at in the course of the narrative are brought into the open. Wilhelm is initiated into a secret society, which, as it turns out, has watched over him, and the novel ends with his engagement to the noble family's most beautiful and spiritually accomplished daughter.

Like *Faust*, *Wilhelm Meister* accompanied Goethe throughout his life. It had always been known that the *Lehrjahre* (1795–1796) was the revision of an earlier work, written between 1777 and 1786, and referred to as the *Theatralische Sendung*. In 1910 a copy of this fragment was discovered. It is a 'remarkably realistic', 'semi-autobiographical' work,[1] concerned with the theatre, its actual contemporary condition, its possible role in the national cultural development of Germany, and Wilhelm Meister's personal and passionate involvement with these things. The protagonist of this early novel is more prominently depicted as a creative artist than his later counterpart. The family from which he springs is less blandly typical than that of the later Meister: his father worries, his mother is unfaithful, his sister speaks, his grandmother is generous but thrifty. It is a novel closely associated with the drama, and is correspondingly more lively than the *Lehrjahre*, which has a wider range of styles.

In both versions Wilhelm Meister comes upon a copy of a David and Goliath play hidden away in the pantry, and hoards it himself as a forbidden pleasure to which he takes every secret opportunity to return: 'Wilhelm laboured to stamp the whole piece upon his mind; laid hold of all the characters, and learned their speeches by heart, most commonly, however, taking up the parts of the chief personages, and allowing all the rest to move along with them, but as satellites, across his memory.'[2]

The shift from the early version to the revision can be said to repeat Wilhelm's original tendency to place himself at or near the centre of a configuration around which everything else finds its orbit. In the case of the *Lehrjahre*, however, it is a sense of Wilhelm Meister as a representative subject, rather than as just another character, which moves into the centre of the work as a whole.

Schiller was extremely perceptive in his analysis of the uniqueness of Goethe's novel hero:

> Wilhelm Meister is the most necessary, but not the most important, character. One of the peculiarities of your novel is precisely that it neither has nor needs such an 'important' character. Everything happens around him or to him, but not strictly *because* of him. The things around him represent the energies in play, while he represents and expresses that which is to be developed and formed by them, and for this reason he is bound to enjoy a different relationship with the other characters than the hero in a novel usually does. (eben weil die Dinge um ihn her die Energien, er aber die Bildsamkeit darstellt und ausdrückt, so muß er ein ander Verhältnis zu den Mitcharakteren haben, als der Held in andern Romanen hat.)[3]

This sense of a subjectivity set apart from, but at work in, the world is sustained by a pervasive but elusive ironic tone (recognised by Friedrich Schlegel in his famous essay on the novel).[4] The words about the David and Goliath play just quoted reappear almost verbatim in the *Lehrjahre*, but spoken by Wilhelm in the first person, rather than by a narrator. He therefore becomes their subject in a double and ironic sense (he speaks them about himself; we as readers become acquainted with his own sense of himself, his subjective life) rather than simply their object. The protagonist's move into the centre (and the associated pervasive narrative irony) are among the most marked differences between the two versions.

Work on the composition of the *Theatralische Sendung* was interrupted by a profound re-orientation in the author's life. When he returned to the project in the 1790s (after his reading of Kant, and after the French Revolution), he worked the original material into a symbolic organisation more in accord with his new concern with formulating universally valid statements. Goethe's mature desire was to 'convey general insights without usurping the primary status of specific experiences',[5] and maxims and aphorisms provided an efficient means of doing this. The *Sendung* provided the bulk of the 'specific experiences' against which the *Lehrjahre*'s many aphorisms and aphoristic, generalising devices (notably the *Turmgesellschaft*) achieve the appropriate effect.

Starting in 1807, Goethe wrote a sequel to the *Lehrjahre*, called *Wilhelm Meisters Wanderjahre*, which was first published in 1821 and again, in substantially expanded form, in 1829. In it, the character Wilhelm Meister functions as a link for a range of formally disparate material. The reader rejoins Meister after the happy ending in the previous work, engaged in a series of journeys and subject to certain strange conditions of behaviour laid down by the society with which he had become involved at the end of the earlier novel. An account of his wanderings, of his decision to become a surgeon, and of the development of his son, Felix, together with contributions from other members of the society and many maxims, are interspersed with *Novellen* which offer a formal and thematic contrast to the heterogeneous material surrounding them. The work as a whole is informed by a detachment which allows it to play over a whole range of historical and timeless issues in a spirit of contemplation, renunciation and mystical spirituality, resigned to the inability of any one coherent aesthetic model to embrace the divergent realities of the contemporary historical circumstances.

In a sense the *Lehrjahre* and the *Wanderjahre* belong together, but it is beyond the scope of my argument to address the later work. The authors who wrote with Goethe in mind will often have been thinking of the *Wanderjahre* when they wrote, as well as of the *Lehrjahre*. But it is the specific dynamics of the *Lehrjahre* model and the very problems inherent in attempting to put such a model together which are at issue here, rather than the development which the Meister theme underwent in Goethe's own later work, and it is therefore necessary to impose what in a way is an artificial limitation.

Within Goethe's biography, then, the *Lehrjahre* satisfies a desire for symmetry by offering a point of balance between the autobiographically inspired *Sendung* and the Olympian, detached *Wanderjahre*. It is a point in Goethe's production where the individual and the world are grasped in a vital and positive interrelation, and as such one of the most unambiguously optimistic and harmonious moments in his work.

That triumphant centrality has certainly also been taken up by literary history. This is connected with the fact that the composition of the *Lehrjahre* coincided with Goethe's co-operation with Schiller. Their collaboration was basically an attempt to give aesthetic expression to the neo-humanist thought of Kant, Humboldt and Herder, to seek a literature both timeless and contemporary, and thereby to contribute a classical style and corpus to German culture. The *Lehrjahre* can be read as the culmination of the development of, and itself the expression of, a philosophical line of thought which established a specific, secular, organic view of the connection between individual and world, articulated in the concept of the process of *Bildung*.[6] Meister's story is the exemplary embodiment of a process of *Bildung*, since it is the product of inner and outer laws in an interaction which, although subject to the effects of chance, is nevertheless itself at some level regular rather than random. With Schiller's *Briefe über die ästhetische Erziehung des*

Menschen (1795), it is the most important document of the aesthetic humanism associated with Weimar Classicism.

The literary-historical situation of the *Lehrjahre* comes into clearer focus when we move from intellectual history (what in German is called *Geistesgeschichte*) to the more sociologically and historically anchored history of genres. The *Lehrjahre* is certainly a document of Weimar Classicism, but it is also a novel, and needs to be seen against the background of the history of the genre. One of the most striking things about it is how unlike a novel it actually is. It is ponderous and contrived in ways one does not associate with the novel genre. This is all the more surprising when one compares the *Lehrjahre* with the *Theatralische Sendung*, which, with its brawls and farces, its comic pleasure in details of contemporary life, is really not that far from Fielding.[7]

The background to this marked and programmatic shift is the popularity of the genre at the time of Goethe's collaboration with Schiller. The novel could not be ignored in debates about literary matters, but it was far too vulgar for unqualified approval. It had to be assimilated into the established system of genres, but at the same time it posed a threat to the clarity and authority of that system, being itself heterogeneous in origin and content, and not easily sanctioned by reference to antiquity. Whilst posing a distinct threat to traditional literary values, it repeatedly attracted comment and speculation because of the perspectives it opened on a more 'modern' form of literature.[8]

This debate has left its mark in the text itself, where a highly self-conscious and sophisticated genre tussle is conducted around the personality of Wilhelm Meister. The theme is elaborated by reference to Wilhelm's production of *Hamlet*, so that instead of the play within a play, we have a play within a novel. The different characteristics of novel and dramatic heroes are played off against each other. Hamlet and Wilhelm mirror each other: Hamlet is a novel hero in drama, and therefore passive where he should be active, while Wilhelm, actively prosecuting his own story, is a dramatic hero adrift in the novel, which generally tolerates only passive protagonists. This difference occupies Wilhelm's mind, as well as inevitably influencing the reader's understanding of Wilhelm's story, so that the same ironic representation of subjectivity as was remarked upon above (in the context of the David and Goliath play of Wilhelm's childhood) results: both Wilhelm's inner life and his understanding of it are placed before the reader as being of central importance. At the same time Goethe's will to impose a generic stamp upon the novel form is clear. (The function of *Hamlet* in the *Lehrjahre* is so specific and important that a short section is devoted to it below.)

It is also clear that Schiller was sensitive to the precarious genre status of a work he admired so much, yet felt he ought to disapprove of. As he wrote to Goethe on October 20, 1797, although the *Lehrjahre* as a novel is by definition not poetic, it nevertheless contrives to oscillate ('schwanken') between poetry and prose and thus to produce a certain mood for which Schiller could not find a name.[9]

Devices from the popular novel are given a new value by Goethe.[10] This largely accounts for the unnovelistic air of profundity which characterises the novel, especially its later parts. Two of the most prominent, the motif of the secret society and the progress of the plot towards a happy end in which the hero gets married, are indeed used to demonstrate the inner consistency of the individual, which the necessity of error and the inevitability of chance might have caused us to doubt. They thus become part of the symbolic equation with the help of which Goethe distils universality from specific details and circumstances.

As we saw above, in the context of the *Sendung*, Goethe's revision of his early work was really a bracketing of the realism of his early semi-autobiographical and Fieldingesque text within a larger, symbolic, equation which included, but also situated, reality. 'Reality' became the field of error through which every individual must pass ('human error has to happen somewhere'),[11] but which does not necessarily for that reason make it impossible to make a universal statement about individuality.

In genre terms this meant that Goethe was raising the common novel to the rank of serious art, enlisting it in the cause of establishing a neo-classicism. This had its disadvantages, in that his text sacrificed social immediacy ('Gesellschaftsunmittelbarkeit'),[12] which accounts not only for its comparative dullness, but also for a certain magisterial ironic vagueness which tends to obscure its own authority behind the veil of autonomous art – 'the veil of poetry' of Goethe's poem *Zueignung* – which both hides and discloses the truth. On the other hand it is largely to this combination of high and low that the novel owes its extraordinary and maybe unique capacity for mediating between the specific and the general, in a way which is (most appropriately) never entirely free of a certain sense of the mysterious or marvellous.

Again, a desire for symmetry marks out the *Lehrjahre* for us as a point of balance. This time it is a balance between the strict and timeless literary system inherited by the eighteenth century, and the informality of modern literature brought about by the rise of prose and the dominance of the novel: a brilliant balance of randomness and regularity.

Wilhelm Meisters Lehrjahre is a site of convergence in historical as well as literary-historical terms. Its generic affiliation to both the nobility of universal art and the social immediacy of the novel, to both poetry and prose, already indicates how it accommodates impulses from different social groups, court culture and 'Bürgertum'.[13] The *Lesedrama* (reading drama) similarly facilitated a specifically German compromise between the public courtly mould of the theatre and the private reading habits of the educated middle classes.[14]

In theme, too, the *Lehrjahre* is a point of historical convergence. The son of a merchant becomes assimilated to the enlightened nobility. This highlights and simplifies certain trends in contemporary German society.[15] The feudal nobility and the market place were moving closer together.[16] Real social change was occurring amongst the non-noble and not traditionally privileged groups of society, the merchant class and the middle-class intelligentsia, while the nobility sometimes adapted, sometimes remained recalcitrant.[17] Werner, Wilhelm's brother-in-law, represents the merchant class as financially dynamic ('nothing but money! . . . there is nothing more insufferable to me than the burden of old possessions', 'so ein alter Kram von Besitztum', p. 287), but historically inert ('transact your business, make money, be merry with your household, and do not concern yourself with the rest of the world', p. 287). Wilhelm embodies the potential of the new social forces; he is intelligent, adaptable and mobile. His theatrical obsession reflects an historical phenomenon, the 'Theatromanie' of the 1770s.[18] The rococo nobility of Books Three and Four personify the backward-looking and trivial petty nobility of the German lands, while the Society of the Tower and Lothario's family symbolise the potential of the older privileged classes to adapt and develop. In Book Eight Werner and Lothario enter into business with one another; at the end of the book a mesalliance of great symbolic import, between a noble woman and a commoner, Nathalie and Wilhelm, is on the immediate horizon. The book thus blends glimpses of historical authenticity (Werner, the rococo nobility) with idealist representations of contemporary aspirations, such as were influential at the court of Weimar.[19] It is historically conciliatory and utopian in a sense not utterly divorced from contemporary conditions, even if the implication that the ideal of humanity could unite the estates unsurprisingly proved to be illusory, and is characterised by some critics as reactionary.[20]

Finally, the most decisive and most complex form of convergence occurs in the philosophical idea of the aesthetic. The philosophical category of aesthetics originated with the German Alexander Baumgarten's *Aesthetica* (1750), and became a central focus in German idealist thought thenceforth.[21] Goethe and Schiller's Classicism and the debates surrounding it, and Kant's *Kritik der Urteilskraft*, are major moments in its elaboration. The aesthetic as a philosophical category devoted to theories of the beautiful, inevitably combining subjective and objective elements, offers the possibility of reconciliation between mind and body, society and individual, universal and particular, idea and history, desire and law. It functions as a powerful retardant against the atomising tendencies of scientific thought since the Enlightenment.

The idea of the aesthetic thus makes provision in its nature for the convergence of disparate things. For Schiller it was through the medium of the aesthetic that humanity could make the sort of progress it had tried but failed to make in the carnage of the French Revolution, reconciling individual freedom with the need to observe the rule of law. The *Lehrjahre*, with its studied indifference to the events in France which had taken place during its period of gestation, its disparaging view of Republicanism as a foolish fantasy acted out among theatre people, fatally vulnerable to the eruption of anarchic and predatory forces,[22] and its focus upon the developing individual as the master-dimension of the real and possible world, 'narrates how the French Revolution could have been avoided'.[23] It is an aesthetic act with relevance beyond the confines of art. It is an ideological move and an influential contribution to the construction of a view which seeks to overcome the tragedy of bourgeois ideology, in which unprecedented individualism is pitched against socio-economic conditions which inhibit it.[24] In this aesthetically legitimised novel, private and public are kept together in an 'institution of art'.[25] This aesthetically protected space makes it possible to adumbrate a solution to the problem of how autonomous individuals can be bound together in stable community without sacrificing their defining autonomy.[26]

Wilhelm Meisters Lehrjahre is so prominent a moment within the ideology of the aesthetic because it is – to use a phrase of Karl Philipp Moritz – a 'Roman eines Lebens',[27] a novel of a life, with mutually defining emphasis falling upon both components of the term. The novel gives sense to the life and the life gives sense to the novel. These two forms of meaning, that of the aesthetic artefact and that of the human subject, converge. Two processes of authoring come together: that by which Wilhem Meister authors his own life and that by which Goethe composes his novel. By contrast, Faust and the form of *Faust* problematise each other, and the treatment of symbolisation in *Die Wahlverwandtschaften* (*Elective Affinities*) questions the means by which it produces its own meaning, and thus the meaning of the central character, Ottilie. But *Iphigenie auf Tauris* and *Hermann und Dorothea* offer parallel examples of a convergence of genre and personality, in which an aesthetic procedure and a view of the construction of the human subject support each other.

Wilhelm Meisters Lehrjahre, like the Genius, 'the culmination of Kant's critical project',[28] is a certain realisation of the concept of the individual, enhanced by the aura of the aesthetic, as the site of a convergence of the real and the rational. In Goethe's novel the partial subject is centralised within the aesthetic construct, where it enjoys immunity and representative status: representative in its very partialness. This paradox is held in focus by irony. Lukács stressed how essential it is not to confuse the idea of the aesthetic with art itself: 'With very few exceptions, the actual works of art produced at the time of the development of the aesthetic cannot really bear comparison with those of earlier flowerings in the history of European art. What is at issue here is the philosophical meaning attributed to the principle of art in this period.'[29] The aesthetic is not centrally a discourse about art at all, but about what talking about art can do for the concept of the individual. It can posit that part which can speak undistortedly of the whole. It can turn subjectivity into individualism, and make the anarchy of desire available for the purposes of the law.

Wilhelm Meisters Lehrjahre is arranged around a masculine character, and from the point of view of a masculine narrator. The protagonist's name means 'master'. This is ironic, since the novel announces itself as being about years of apprenticeship. But the novel's ironic tone emanates from a magisterial narrative authority which, by means of this very ironic power, places the masculine subject at the centre of interest. Wilhelm knows he is not a master, yet this knowledge commands the field of the novel: 'Wegen der herrschenden Vorurteile will ich meinen Namen verändern, weil ich mich ohnehin schäme, als Meister aufzutreten' ('In compliance with the ruling prejudices, I will change my name, as indeed I am ashamed to appear as a Master', p. 292). It is the activity of the subject that is now at the centre. This activity, to be sure, is figured in the words quoted above as an abnegation of an explicit claim to the authority bestowed by the name of Meister, and as a capitulation before the power of 'ruling prejudices'. This prominent weakness, however, has entered into an alliance with the authority of the author of the text and together they constitute the aesthetic discourse of the *Lehrjahre*. It is the paradoxical power of this discourse of subjectivity that it has a place to speak of its own weakness, which is thereby transformed into strength. The invisible, implicit power of this alliance is not less than that of the explicit forms of traditional authority it replaces. It is the magisterial ironic act of the author of the text to *show* Wilhelm's lack of mastery, but to reinstate him at the same time as the subject of the book, and thus in an important sense, as the author in the text – the author, that is, not of fictions, but of himself.[30]

This form of authority is historically specific. It can be said to have come about in the very transition from the *Theatralische Sendung* to the *Lehrjahre*. Baioni, for instance, argues that the addition of the conversation on fate (Book One, Chapter Seventeen) destroys what, in the earlier version, had been one of the finest narrative passages in German literature. The *Sendung* was still characterised by a vitality before which the ills of contemporary Germany seemed susceptible to correction by cultural intervention (i.e. the founding of a national theatre). But the French Revolution left such hopes for the effectiveness of culture remote.[31] Instead, there is the assumption of a new cultural stance, now at a distance from life. This change is illustrated in the addition of that fateful conversation on fate,

> [with which] Goethe assumed that narrative position proper to the Weimar restoration that transformed the *Theatralische Sendung* into an evidently carefully planned novel. With absolute omniscience and not without a conspiratorial wink at the reader, the narrator now puts himself in the place of providence and guides his hero through the novel. In his hands Wilhelm becomes no more than a faceless compliant doll.[32]

Wilhelm's 'facelessness' ('Gesichtslosigkeit') is, in my view, a function of his new status as a device for the representation of subjectivity, a quality or condition distinguished by a peculiar blindness to its own face. The connotations of his being no more than a compliant puppet are important and we shall return to them. The point here, however, is that Baioni characterises usefully the form of narratorial authority which is at issue. His characterisation confirms that offered by Werner Hahl of the tenor of German bourgeois culture as it became at the end of the eighteenth century. This was a culture which, in its two characteristic manifestations, liberalism and idealism, began by turning away from the relational, causal thinking of the Enlightenment,[33] and produced a corresponding artistic discourse:

> by virtue of its lack of intention (Absichtslosigkeit), the work of art is intended to appear to be more than just a human product about which it would be possible to have differing opinions. It is intended simply to be, and thus to imply a higher order of being beyond the need for explanation or doubt.[34]

The ironic, distant, disinterested narrative voice, which nevertheless speaks from a knowledge of an overall plan, is part and parcel of the construction of a specifically aesthetic form of authority. Goethe as author enjoys another sort of 'facelessness', that of 'the narrator', a disembodied and non-contradictable voice, pervasively present in the organisation of the text, but never immediately manifest in it; always, by definition, as author of the text, outside it. In this respect, Goethe's novel enjoys the autonomy of the aesthetic.

The maxim, the discourse of the unquestioned, codified voice of the fathers, remains an important stylistic resource in the novel, but only in conjunction with this specific sort of irony. Irony and maxim combine to inaugurate a game of assertion and counter-assertion, which assures aesthetic command beyond the merely discursive. This powerful play can best be summed up in a paradox contained in Wilhelm's *Lehrbrief*: 'Words are good but they are not the best. The best is not to be explained by words' (p. 496). The book as a whole, as in the case of Wilhelm's abjuration of his own name, achieves the same effect by relativising its own authority by the voice of its protagonist: '"For heaven's sake, no more of these wise maxims! I feel them to be but a sorry balsam for a wounded heart"' (p. 553).

Wilhelm is formed ('bilden') by three institutions: the theatre, the tower and the novel itself. The theatre is the sphere of Wilhelm's act of self-liberation, the subject's assertion against the restraints of social reality. This assertion evidently takes place in artistic terms, but whilst making the important connection between subjectivity and art, this particular form of artistic response is too simply subjective to be allowed to stand within the more complex regime of the aesthetic. Instead it becomes the 'objectification' of Wilhelm's inner life,[35] a motif at once for the representation and for the distancing of subjective life.

The institution by means of which the next stage of the unfolding situation of Wilhelm's subjectivity is represented is the Society of the Tower. It gives an aesthetically autonomous vantage point from which the objective meaning of Wilhelm's subjectivity can be articulated. But it must pay for its clarity and independence as an expressive device with the very isolation of the aesthetic, 'the specific impotence of art'.[36] Like the theatre, the tower, which is also very theatrical in its procedures, loses its power once Wilhelm has reached the level of consciousness for which it stands. As Wilhelm is initiated into its mysteries, they are dispelled by that very initiation, and its function changes (p. 548).

But, as with the theatre, this does not retrospectively devalue the principles which had once been embodied in the tower. For they are enshrined in the third great masculine and aesthetic institution of the novel, the institution of art. The twin 'institutions' of the theatre and the tower are the most evident devices by which Wilhelm's development is represented. They are the social forms in relation to which his mature self takes shape. But they are of necessity provisional, and they are both ironised within the novel. That is how the discourse of the aesthetic expresses the truth that subjectivity cannot be objectively represented. But if the theatre and the tower can only anticipate the aesthetic consummation of Wilhelm Meister's *Bildung*, the novel itself delivers it. It is the novel as a whole, and specifically as an aesthetic artefact, that provides the final context for the subjectivity of Wilhelm Meister.

This aesthetic novel contains irony, but is not itself ironised (as *Tristram Shandy* for instance, might be said to be). The institution of art transforms the weak subject into the strong subject in these three institutional steps, theatre, tower, novel. In the gesture of placing Wilhelm at the centre, the author of the text displaces himself, both closing his own interiority, partialness and fallibility within the artefact and disclosing it in his privileged emanation (Wilhelm). It is the triumph of art over autobiography.

The style and organisation of the novel therefore convey a sense of subjectivity *aufgehoben*. This is to say that it is both preserved as authentic interiority and incorporated into a larger whole in which its inevitable partialness, its negative aspects, are transcended. A similar thing happens on the level of plot. Here we have on the one hand the story of the erring individual whose excessive subjectivity is corrected by a process of education. The plot is thus linear. But it is also circular, because the hero's goal is related to his starting point, and so his subjectivity is vindicated and transposed onto a higher level.

This circularity is a specifically masculine affair because it is a matter of inheritance.[37] There is a strong patrilinear logic underpinning the adventures of Wilhelm's progress through life. The culminating experience in his years of apprenticeship is, after all, the rediscovery of his own son, Felix:

> The longing of the child for cherries and berries, the season for which was at hand, brought to his mind the days of his own youth and the manifold duties of a father, to prepare, to procure, and to maintain for his family a constant series of enjoyments. . . . He no longer looked upon the world with the eyes of a bird of passage . . . Everything that he proposed commencing was to be completed for his boy; everything he erected was to last for several generations. In this sense his apprenticeship was ended . . . (In diesem Sinne waren seine Lehrjahre geendigt.) (pp. 501–502)

Wilhelm recognises the principle of inheritance and the importance of what he has just inherited from his father. Personal progress is seen as part of a larger circularity. What had appeared as a sowing of wild oats returns as the law of paternal succession. This law does not simply condemn subjectivity as selfishness, but makes sense of it because the responsibility Wilhelm feels in relation to another subjectivity is rooted in the sense that he is himself being repeated in it. The consciousness of another's subjectivity, derived from and thus validating one's own, at the same time as one is consciously distancing oneself from it, is the foundation of socialisation, 'all the virtues of a citizen' ('alle Tugenden eines Bürgers', p. 502).

Wilhelm also repeats his own father. Although he leaves and thoroughly outgrows the sphere of his father's world to accede to another, far broader and greater one, his father's world in several aspects anticipates the one to which Wilhelm does finally come. Although Wilhelm's father appears to be a narrow materialist, whose ethos and influence Meister escapes and leaves behind, he nevertheless displays a certain blending of material and spiritual values: 'But nothing was so much desired by old Meister as to confer upon his son those qualities of which he himself was destitute, and to leave his children advantages (Güter) which he reckoned it of the highest importance to possess' (p. 40). This formulation is a cliché (it is part of a satirical portrait, after all), but in the context of the novel it assumes a resonance beyond cliché. The same applies to the following: 'Withal, he felt a peculiar inclination for magnificence; for whatever catches the eye, but which at the same time possesses inner worth and durability' (pp. 40–41). The function of this detail is poised between satire and symbolism. One can imagine this attitude being typical for one of the elder Meister's social background (and the young Meister finds his father's ostentation distasteful, p.12), but it is also a formulation of one of the fundamental insights of the book, namely that inner and outer should be harmonious in their reflection of what is valuable: indeed, that that which is valuable has no way of manifesting itself, if not in both these areas simultaneously. The original Meister ethos, notwithstanding the empty opulence to which it tends, and to which Werner objects with prosaic self-righteousness (p. 287), is not one simply to be set aside, gone beyond and forgotten; it is one to be repeated but, so the book's message goes, at a heightened and thus intrinsically more valuable level.

Wilhelm's father is also surprisingly associated with the Tower, in a dream in Book Seven (pp. 425–426). In Wilhelm's (second) dream, under the impact of his first contact with Lothario's circle, a parallel between the groupings – Mariane and Meister senior, Natalie and the Tower – emerges. In this dream, Wilhelm sees Mariane walking with his father, thus linking them and rendering them equivalent to the constellation of Natalie and the Tower, for in both instances one is dealing with an alliance between a desirable woman and a source of regulating authority, 'the father and the bride'.[38] In both constellations, that into which Wilhelm is born (his father; a worthy mother of his own child: 'And in her character the mother that is gone was not unworthy of you', p. 497), and that to which he aspires (a new source of authority, a woman worthy in all respects, to whom, in the dream, the child is then transferred), there is a complicity between the elements involved, and together they situate and define where Wilhelm is and what he is becoming. Particularly interesting is the confusion Wilhelm feels in his dream about leaving the first couple in order to join Natalie: this seems both right and wrong to him at the same time, 'nature and inclination called on him to go and help them; but the hand of the Amazon detained him. How gladly did he let himself be held!' (p. 426). In his confusion, Wilhelm cannot yet be aware of the congruence which actually exists between the two constellations, although it is represented in the dream code by the Amazon's rescue of the child. Wilhelm is naturally drawn to both, for they are both limits and contours of his being; but within the natural model which is the book's conceptual reference, there is no contradiction: 'goal and genesis'[39] are in some inscrutable way consubstantial. In psychoanalytical terms the original triad of subject, father and object of desire (symbolised in pre-Oedipal, unresolved form in the painting of the 'kranker Königssohn' ['King's sick son'], who is sick for love of his father's bride), returns now in resolved form in the configuration of the Tower, the father as Super Ego, and Natalie as the object to desire whom no longer implies catastrophe (or, psychoanalytically speaking, castration).[40]

Within the interpretation of the Tower itself, Wilhelm's father sanctions his son's development from beyond the grave, acknowledging in a voice which appears to be, but is not, his own that his son has achieved what he had envisaged for him, but in terms beyond his own limited capacity for imagining: 'I am thy father's spirit (Geist) . . . and I depart content, since my wishes for thee are accomplished, in a higher sense than I myself contemplated' (p. 495). Hence, in a manner of speaking, Wilhelm grows up not as a rebel and overthrower of the narrow world of his father, but in accordance with his father's wishes; 'nothing was so much desired by old Meister as to confer upon his son those qualities of which he himself was destitute . . .'

After his father's death, Wilhelm's inheritance is turned into cash by Werner, and, again surprisingly (especially for Wilhelm), becomes part of the financial reform programme of the Tower. This purely financial motif is enriched by a symbolic inheritance which reaches back before the father's death and links Wilhelm's birthright with Natalie and the Society of the Tower. This is Wilhelm's grandfather's art collection, which, having been sold by his father for cash, turns up again later in the possession of the heirs of its purchaser, the Oheim (uncle). Thus when Wilhelm goes to the house of the Oheim, and discovers there the identity of his future bride and the context towards which he has been developing through all the mistakes of the novel, it is as if he is also coming into his own inheritance: 'so now he found himself too, as it were, in his inheritance' (p. 520). In the psychoanalytical terms to which we shall return, the Oedipal barrier is now overcome in the refinding of the painting of the King's sick son as an item of the art collection. (In the story depicted the son's sickness is diagnosed as lovesickness for his father's bride, and can thus be cured by the union of son and stepmother with the father's blessing.)

The problematic of art is restated in this motif not, as in the theatre, as a problem of personality, but as a matter of ownership and appreciation. The subjective aspect of art, the extent to which it is linked to desire and to which it is a maternal inheritance (the puppet theatre was a gift from Wilhelm's mother), is 'aufgehoben' in its objective aspect. Where the painting of the King's sick son had held a subjective fascination for the young Wilhelm, he later learns to appreciate its aesthetic quality (which is not great), and to relate to paintings for objective reasons rather than subjective ones. Masculine qualities of control, ownership and discrimination thus regularise and socialise the threatening forces of subjectivity, whilst at the same time still validating them.

In these terms one can understand how the *Lehrjahre* is a specific and peculiar variation of the *Künstlerroman* (artist novel). Such a novel would tell the story of how its subject becomes an artist. The *Lehrjahre* tells that of how its subject does not become one. This is a significant negation, and central to the model informing the *Lehrjahre* as a literary representation of subjectivity, simultaneously free and bound. The protagonist is and is not an artist at the same time: associated with art in a way connected to the very secret of his being, but at the same time, prominently not an artist himself, and significantly mistaken in thinking himself so. The novel itself (constructed as aesthetic artefact) is the achievement of the creative artist, arrived at by dint of, but now safely beyond, the anarchic risks of creativity itself. In a sovereign gesture it can fashion art from the dangers of subjectivity. In these terms too, art successfully exceeds and replaces autobiography. If the theatre is art as subjective, and if the pattern of inherited art is art in its objective aspect, the novel constructs itself as art itself, obeying its own laws only, self-authored, thought and deed in one, neither subjective nor objective but in its very ironic prevarication authoritative and beyond interrogation.

Thus both subjectivity and art are projected doubly in the novel.

Wilhelm Meister represents precarious and partial subjectivity, but the narrator's voice bespeaks a full and stable subject; the theatre is a dubious encouragement to the perniciousness of irresponsible individualism, the ownership and appreciation of works of art is a sign of assured control. In encompassing these antinomies in its narrative technique and in its plot, it betrays its kinship with the debate about 'the aesthetic' discussed in the Introduction.

The philosophical suppleness of the *Lehrjahre*, its power to reinstate, as it were, masculine authority without forswearing subjectivity, was best explained by Schiller, using Kantian diction, shortly after he had received and read the final Book of the novel:

> Apprenticeship (Lehrjahre) is a relative term, entailing the idea of mastership, and indeed, the idea of the latter must explain and provide the basis for the former. Now this idea of mastership, which can only be the fruit of mature experience, cannot itself guide the hero of the novel, it can and may not stand before him as his purpose and his goal, since were he to become conscious of it as his goal, he would by the same token have attained it. It must therefore stand behind him and guide him without his being aware of it. In this way the whole work assumes a pleasing purposiveness (Zweckmäßigkeit), without the hero himself having a conscious purpose. The understanding (der Verstand) thus discovers that an affair has been brought to a successful conclusion, while the imagination (die Einbildungskraft) retains complete freedom.[41]

The aesthetic contrives to bring together authority and creativity without the latter undermining the former. The modern subject is both self-authoring and subject to objective laws, just as the aesthetic object is at once unique and regular.[42]

Hamlet is the locus classicus for the problem of modern complex subjectivity. The play stands at the 'intersection of ancient and modern literature',[43] and Hamlet himself is the hero for whom heroism has become problematic.[44] As the example of one who delays incomprehensibly, Hamlet functions as a symbolic representation of subjectivity itself, a partial state, imperfectly engaged with the world. But as the hero of a tragedy he functions within a representation of the implacable world in which subjectivity is only a will o' the wisp in an otherwise austere landscape. Hamlet's hesitation points to interiority as the seat of dramatic motivation, and the space of subjectivity is thus opened up – prominently of course in soliloquies – but only to be closed by a tragic resolution. Perhaps the most famous representation of interiority in European literature also accommodates an older view of the subject, not as endowed with its own unique interiority and thus potentially autonomous, but as the site of various moral qualities which are ultimately rooted in a supra-personal scheme of good and evil.[45] Having foregrounded the subject's potential freedom by thematising the actual lack of it ('the Hamlet of the first four acts of the play is above all not an agent'),[46] the play paradoxically ends by having its protagonist relinquish the struggle 'towards identity and agency',[47] and act at last not as a free agent but as 'the consenting instrument of God'.[48]

If *Hamlet*, whatever individual interpretation of the play as a whole is favoured, is undeniably a focus for complex problematic subjectivity, the predominant German reading of the play has been to concentrate on the character of Hamlet, to blend the two aspects of the play together, and see the drama as the tragedy of subjectivity. Goethe's (or Wilhelm's) interpretations of Shakespeare's drama in Books Four and Five of the *Lehrjahre* are themselves important moments in the formation of this distinctively German image of Hamlet (which includes also the contributions of Blanckenburg, Schlegel, Hegel and Nietzsche). Wilhelm sees Hamlet as an otherwise entirely positive, indeed exemplary, but non-heroic individual in a situation which calls for heroism:

A lovely, pure, noble and most moral nature, without the strength of nerve which forms a hero, sinks beneath a burden which it can neither bear nor cast away. All duties are sacred for him; the present one too hard. Impossibilities have been required of him; not in themselves impossibilities, but such for him. He winds, and turns, and torments himself; he advances and recoils; is ever put in mind, ever puts himself in mind; at last does all but lose his purpose from his thoughts; yet still without recovering his peace of mind. (p. 246)

In these circumstances the twists and turns of Hamlet's inner life, his subjectivity in short, become visible and take centre stage in the tragic impossibility of carrying out the task imposed upon it (namely the 'heroic' task of revenge). The way Wilhelm analyses Hamlet's inner turmoil cannot help but remind the reader of

Wilhelm's own uncertainties, and thus the representation of his own inner life is enriched by his interpretation of the fate of Hamlet's. But of course the whole tendency of the novel is to spare Wilhelm Hamlet's fate. Whereas in the play the arrival of the ghost means the imposition of an impossible task upon Hamlet (a task not absolutely impossible, but impossible for him), the arrival of the ghost in the production of the play signals the intervention of the Tower in Wilhelm's life.[49] *Hamlet* as the tragedy of subjectivity is thus instrumental in the adumbration of the construction of the modern non-tragic subject. If *Hamlet* begins 'to define an interiority as the origin of meaning and action', but 'cannot produce closure in terms of an analysis which in 1601 does not yet fully exist',[50] it is exactly that closure which the *Lehrjahre* seeks in its adaptation of Shakespeare's play.

Setting itself up in a certain sense as the antithesis of *Hamlet* is an important means by which Goethe's novel legitimates itself as literature. This is the effect also of the specific discussion of the genres of drama and novel in Book Five, Chapter Seven. Whatever the differences between the two kinds, they are worthy of being discussed in the same breath ('both are capable of excellence within their kinds, as long as they keep within the limits proper to them', p. 307). This literary play between the novel in hand and the Shakespearean authority also contributes in an important way to the construction of subjectivity offered by Goethe in the *Lehrjahre*. The whole issue of literary authority is implicated. While Shakespeare is effective within the *Lehrjahre* as a powerful literary instance or example, validating the novel's status as itself literature, the effect is not to produce imitation but conscious variation. Influence is replaced by intertextuality.

The production of *Hamlet*, with Wilhelm in the title role, is the transitional point at which the subjective inner life of Wilhelm passes into 'the typical pattern of human existence' proposed by the novel as a whole.[51] It is the culmination of the whole theatrical theme which had been at the centre of the *Sendung*. It is 'the end of illusion'. In what became the first five books of the *Lehrjahre* this theme comes to function as a representation of Wilhelm's psychology or subjective life. The theatre, as a specific conjunction of erotic desire and self-projection, lends itself naturally, not to say brilliantly, to this thematic function. In terms of the *Lehrjahre*'s construction of itself as literature, *Hamlet* forms part of a series of links between life and literature, subjectivity and art. The play itself objectifies the subjectivity of its main character within tragedy. The tragedy is then subjectively refracted in Wilhelm's interpretation of it, which, in turn, is objectified in the production of the play in which Wilhelm plays Hamlet. Literature is thus constructed as a process of self-finding and self-loss, 'experience' and 'poetry', enmeshed with each other and mutually realising. This then lends support to our reading of the *Lehrjahre* itself as the objective aesthetic realisation of real subjectivity, art's triumph over autobiography, or the apotheosis of *Erlebnisdichtung*.

Hamlet is 'the most significant mirror for the *Lehrjahre*', its most important intertextual reference. Like all mirrors it has a subjective and an objective aspect.[52] Hamlet is the subjective projection of Wilhelm (he sees and plays himself in Shakespeare's character), but *Hamlet* is the objective image of Wilhelm's inner life, offered to us as readers.

The most detailed study of the complex relations between *Hamlet* and *Wilhelm Meisters Lehrjahre* is David Roberts's monograph on the subject, *The Indirections of Desire*. In his analysis it becomes clear how the Hamlet motif intersects with the motif of inheritance. The ghost who appears in Shakespeare's play is the ghost of Hamlet's father, and the impossible task laid upon Hamlet is a matter of succession and thus of inheritance. Hamlet succeeds in doing his duty by his father only at the cost of his own life. The transmission from father to son entails tragedy.[53] This is an intensification of the story of Antiochus and Stratonike, the King's sick son, in which the young man is sick for the love of his father's bride. Here too the continuity and renewal of the succession from father to son is fatally blocked. Both references convey how Wilhelm's inner life is blighted by a form of psychological arrestation which prevents him from progressing beyond the block variously represented in the situation of the King's sick son and Hamlet. Law and desire are irreconcilably at odds. It is only by acting out[54] this inner configuration that Wilhelm can be spared the fate of the Danish King's sick son.

Hamlet is not just the nodal point of paternal continuity, it is also enmeshed with problems of desire. The common term for these is 'incest'. In Shakespeare's tragedy, Claudius has, to use Hamlet's word, incestuously married his brother's widow. Psychoanalysis sees in this a displaced Oedipal configuration: the secret unconscious desire to murder the father and marry the mother, which Sophocles' hero had unwittingly carried out himself, is now transferred from the central character onto his antagonist.[55] Hamlet's delay – the central problem of the play, and the space of the representation of subjectivity – can thus be explained by his unconscious identification with Claudius (who has done what Hamlet unconsciously desires to do).[56] It is also the spectre of incest (again at a discreet remove) which constitutes the block between father and son (the block to development) in the case of the King's sick son, whose malady is traceable to his love for his father's bride. Incest is also the secret behind the characters of Mignon and the Harper, as revealed in the later books.

There is thus a good prima facie case for using the Oedipus Complex as a conceptual framework or model for the detailed and differentiated exposition of the 'indirections' of the *Lehrjahre*, as Roberts does. This use can also be defended on the more general grounds that we are dealing here with the complex relation of law and desire in the construction of modern masculine subjectivity, and that Freud's model, which after all emerges from and belongs to the same cultural tradition as Goethe's own work, is the most persuasive available. Otto Rank, as a pupil of Freud's also working within this tradition, goes so far as to associate all poetic creativity with the machinery of the Oedipus Complex and the construction of the masculine – since for him questions of poetry inevitably entail a masculine perspective[57] – which this facilitates.[58] We shall return to this at the end of this chapter, in the context of a much more radically deconstructive reading than that attempted by David Roberts. It is important at this stage, however, to grasp Roberts's Freudian reading, since it adds a further dimension to the sense of the novel as a site of convergence, and deepens our sense of the significance of incest and inheritance within it.

The successful progress from son to father, which is to say from immaturity to maturity, from Mignon to Felix, is achieved by sublimating the incestuous leanings in which Wilhelm's (and everybody's) subjectivity is first manifest. (In Freudian terms the Super Ego is heir to the Oedipus Complex in the sense that the masculine subject internalises and makes his own the paternal law which forbids his original incestuous orientation towards his mother.) Hence in a series of episodes around the production of *Hamlet*, the block experienced by Wilhelm, which can now be explained as his Oedipal sense of the catastrophic nature of engagement with sexuality, is overcome, specifically by the agency of Natalie.[59] (Again, to gloss, the original experience of masculine sexuality is tragic in the sense that it carries with it the threat of destruction: castration in Freud, or blinding in the tragedy Freud used to explain his theory, *Oedipus Rex*.) Thus the 'death' of Hamlet comes to mean the death in Wilhelm of the destructive structure and direction of his inner life.[60] This sublimation is the key to socialisation and development. The dark aspects of subjectivity, for instance the preoccupation with Mignon, are regressive and impede growth. But since they are intrinsic to the very constitution of subjectivity they also (like Hamlet) represent the tragedy of subjectivity, they are 'the tragic mirror to the natural dynamic of development'.[61] And because they are indivisible from subjectivity they remain its inner meaning beyond the sublimation process (or, strictly, preserved within it), and can only be countered in the terms of Goethe's mature ethic by 'Entsagung' (renunciation, forswearing).[62]

If the source of desire is constant (Wilhelm), its objects vary, but in their variety bespeak the complex regularity informing the *Lehrjahre* and its model of humanity. The feminine voice in the novel is the first-person voice. In contrast to the masculine voice of the maxim, the woman's voice speaks on behalf of the particularities of individual subjective experience. What women say is that the secret of the identity between subject and world is not accessible to discursive exposition:

> 'The person to whom the universe does not reveal directly what relation it has to him, whose heart does not tell him what he owes to himself and others, that person will scarcely learn it out of books; which generally do little more than provide names for our errors.' (p. 460)

These words are spoken to Wilhelm by the character Therese, in relation to whom he also receives an object lesson in the importance of relying upon the impulses of the whole person, and not of reason alone (p. 534). The irony is that the *Lehrjahre* is indeed a book which gives a name to errors, calling them the education of life, and so the last word remains with the men.

Wilhelm's attachments to women convey the passionate erotic intensity of his engagement with the world, and the devastation he experiences when the world proves resistant to his subjective appetite for appropriating it. This is established at the beginning of the novel in the climax of the First Book, when Wilhelm is disappointed in Mariane. 'The blow had touched the very roots of his whole existence' (p. 77). As in Goethe's earlier works like *Werther* and *Tasso*, uncorrected subjectivity, for all its authentic first-person spontaneity, is shown to be potentially self-destructive in its very intensity, which can so easily mistake the world (as in this case) and turn with overpowering violence against itself.

The women in the book are thus the means by which Goethe conveys an overwhelming sense of Wilhelm's authentic subjectivity. In their relation to Wilhelm they remain part of a masculine configuration in which the feminine is included as the personal. They indicate the routes that lead from immediate subjective experience towards the ethical and the universal. In his youthful ardour, love for the theatre and love for an actress mingle: 'his passion for the stage combined itself with his first love for a woman' (p. 14). For all the 'cruel determination' of the Society of the Tower, Natalie, related to it yet distinct from it, retains a fascination for Wilhelm which has it roots in his deepest stirrings.

To expand: the *Lehrjahre*, through its deployment of woman figures, proposes a complex schema of the process of socialisation as intimately compounded of self and other. The puppet theatre was a gift from his mother, so that it is presumably she, and not Mariane, who enjoyed Wilhelm's 'first love for a woman'. (In the *Sendung* it had been a gift from his paternal grandmother, while the mother is negatively portrayed, a character rather than an imago.)[63] The connection between the springs of Wilhelm's subjectivity and the mother go even further back in the chronology of the novel itself, because the puppet theatre is offered as compensation for the loss of the painting of the King's sick son, which represents the originary dyadic orientation upon the mother.[64] It is in the experience of 'the love of the mother' that self and other coexist most intimately, and from there self and other must begin the arduous task of splitting from each other.

This process, inevitably full of 'indirections', then continues through the series of women which structures the *Lehrjahre*, one to each book: Mariane, Mignon, The Countess, Aurelie, Philine, The Beautiful Soul, Therese, Natalie. Each embodies a different aspect of Wilhelm's engagement with the world, a phenomenology of his progress. Mariane as naive desire, Mignon as inarticulate longing, The Countess as social ambition, Philine as sexual love, Aurelie as the threat of female desire, Therese as the attempt to subordinate desire to rational considerations, Natalie as the triumphant union of ethical and personal. Natalie is the transformation of the first, simple, desire for the world Wilhelm had felt in his love for Mariane at the start. It is Felix – the fruit of the for so long apparently fruitless union with Mariane – who is Wilhelm's real 'other', and he is no other at all, but the same again. The woman figures are introjections of otherness within the subjective space of *Wilhelm Meisters Lehrjahre*. They are ways of refusing to admit finally that there is an 'other' to masculine subjectivity.

The most sophisticated introjection of otherness in the novel is the inclusion of the 'Bekenntnisse einer schönen Seele', 'Confessions of a Beautiful Soul', which actually *displaces* the male hero. Here the feminine gains ascendancy for the space of a Book, and Wilhelm is present only invisibly as an implied reader. Goethe went some way towards incorporating an authentic female voice into his novel, because he based the 'Confessions' upon his personal acquaintance with Susanna Katharina von Klettenberg, an intensely religious pietist friend of his own mother. This Book is about a woman's religious self-development, and thus about personal development bracketed off from the vicissitudes of interaction with the world of activity. If Philine and Aurelie are progressively more sharply defined as 'other' against Wilhelm, the 'Stiftsdame' is a completely independent representation of the personal. The *schöne Seele* develops with reference only to Christ (the men she finds attractive in the earlier part of her life are attractive because of their suffering, and are thus anticipations of Christ). As a representation of 'the personal', the first-person, confessional mode of discourse, she is the objectification and distancing of Wilhelm's own sense of the personal, the conscious sense of personal development as 'other', just as his theatrical career culminating in Hamlet is the objectification of his unconscious subjective identifications. (*Hamlet* and the 'Confessions of a Beautiful Soul' are thus the two main intertextual references by the addition of which the subjective *Sendung* is translated into the objective *Lehrjahre*.)

By putting personal development in brackets in this way, Goethe can proceed to build it into a model of the social interaction of personalities. This is done by identifying 'specific occasions' – moments of first-person spontaneous authenticity, the personal as represented by the feminine – with the field of chance or *Tyche*, to cite the title of the second stanza of *Urworte. Orphisch.*[65] This is the sphere in which men must labour. In this sense, the tables are turned between masculine and feminine. Whilst on the personal level women guarantee Wilhelm's identity-in-change, because they are the evidence that he is one desiring subject (*Daimon* and *Tyche* join in the third stanza of Goethe's poem under the name of *Eros*), on the supra-personal or ethical level it is men whose lot it is to work this field (the arduousness of which labour is expressed in the fourth stanza of *Urworte. Orphisch*, *Ananke*). It is they who must experience subjectively its interminably intractable nature in the realm of 'activity' ('Tätigkeit'), the insurmountable inconstancy of their own desires, and the implacable need for 'renunciation' thereby entailed. To assume this burden is the lesson of the Tower and the way of successful socialisation. On this ethical level (the level at which maxims operate) a woman embodies for men the unchanging image of the ideal of humanity in the name of which the men strive. Natalie is the secularised, which is to say socialised, completion of The Beautiful Soul.

This contrast is brought out most clearly by Natalie herself, reporting the words of her uncle:

> 'It is not my fault,' said he, 'if I have not brought my inclinations (Triebe) and my reason into perfect harmony.' On such occasions he would joke

with me, and say: 'Natalie may be looked upon as happy for as long as she lives: her nature asks nothing which the world does not wish and for which it does not have a use.' (p. 539)

Perhaps the Oheim's humour was akin to the novel's irony, for in his jocular assessment of Natalie's personality he is enunciating the novel's implied ethical maxim: that there is continuity between the personal and the universal, that masculine subjectivity does have no ultimate other (the final stanza of *Urworte. Orphisch* is about *Elpis*, Hope, a Goethean addition to the more tragic configuration of his ancient sources). While the Oheim cannot, as a man, reconcile law and desire ('reason' and 'my inclinations'), he constructs Natalie as one who can. The novel takes on this construction, offering Wilhelm's desire for Natalie as the masculine experience of desire for the coincidence of law and desire: a subjective experience in the name of which men carry on the struggle of 'activity'. The maxim which expresses objectively the subjective experience represented by the figure of Natalie is again a coincidence of law and desire: 'Der Mensch ist nicht eher glücklich, als bis sein unbedingtes Streben sich selbst seine Begrenzung bestimmt' ('A man is never happy until his unbounded striving has itself marked out its proper limitation', p. 553). Together, they confirm the significant analogy between the individual subject and the aesthetic work: 'like the work of art the human subject introjects the codes which govern it as the source of its free autonomy'.[66] The maxim stresses the codes (the 'law' aspect), Natalie the freedom (the 'desire' aspect), of this ideal elevation of the construction of masculine subjectivity.

This thematic use of gender already suggests that the book, for all its obvious focus on the masculine, is interested, in its overall organisation, in the expressive possibilities of androgyny. (Many critics have observed that Wilhelm Meister's initials are also those of Weib [woman] and Mann [man].) In its representation of the subject, the *Lehrjahre* expresses certain aspects by reference to men and others by reference to women. Thus the theatre and the tower on one hand, and the line of women from Mariane to Natalie on the other, are two dimensions within the structure of one personality, in which masculine and feminine elements are combined.

The novel's interest in androgyny achieves its most concentrated form in the most famous figure of the novel, Mignon. In one sense, Mignon is just another of the women in Wilhelm's life. Yet the point about her is not her femininity but her indeterminateness: '[Wilhelm] returned home, forming many a conjecture about this figure, yet unable to arrive at any distinct conclusion' ('und konnte sich bei ihr nichts Bestimmtes denken', p. 110). She (for want of a less definite pronoun: the *Sendung* uses all three of the possibilities German has at its disposal) never enters fully into the form and identities of this world, because, so the inevitable implication runs, she is of another.

From nearly her first appearance (in Book Two), Mignon is uneasy about the way she appears. She scrubs her face in order to remove her stage make-up, but mistakes the redness in her cheeks caused by the rubbing for even more stubborn make-up (p. 107). In other words, she experiences her real face as a mask, and has a morbid desire to reveal an inner self behind it; to collapse subject and object into an impossible unity.

Finally she gives formal expression to the temporary and compromise nature of her being in this world. This is presented in terms of the superficiality of all identity, even the distinction between the sexes:

So laßt mich scheinen bis ich werde.
Zieht mir das weiße Kleid nicht aus!
Ich eile von der schönen Erde
Hinab in jenes feste Haus.

Dort ruh' ich eine kleine Stille,
Dann öffnet sich der frische Blick,
Ich lasse dann die reine Hülle,
Den Gürtel und den Kranz zurück.

Und jene himmlischen Gestalten,
Sie fragen nicht nach Mann und Weib,
Und keine Kleider, keine Falten
Umgeben den verklärten Leib.

Let me appear, till I become, take not my white dress away. I hasten from the beautiful earth, down to that closed abode. There to rest a little space, and then, fresh eyes open, I leave behind my pure disguise, this garland

and this girdle. And those heavenly figures care not for man or woman, and no robes or garments obscure our transfigured body. (pp. 515–516)

It is no accident that these thoughts are expressed in song. Mignon's 'style', the style for androgyny in the novel, is the lyric. She and the Harper are inarticulate and enigmatic 'alien' beings, who are simply not at home in ordinary language, be it magisterial generalisation or first-person confession.

Neither Natalie nor the Tower is capable of socialising Mignon, but at the same time the text leaves us in no doubt as to the depth of Wilhelm's feelings about or towards her. Her death troubles a thematic economy otherwise notable for its delicate symmetrical poise, and the elaborate exequies arranged for her by the Society of the Tower (Book Eight, Chapter Eight) do not go far towards allaying this sense of unease.

Mignon's androgynous mysteriousness was more pronounced and coloured in the *Theatralische Sendung*. The revelations in Book Eight, Chapter Nine of the *Lehrjahre* about Mignon and the Harper's background dispel the mystery which so effectively envelops these figures in the early fragment. But they also make the thematic connection with incest – Mignon is the product of actual brother–sister incest and the Harper is her father – suggesting that whilst there is something irresistibly attractive about their world of longing and sweet poetic melancholy, it has sprung from an irredeemable transgression.

One could accept this 'package' more easily, as a novelistic variant of what Ernst Robert Curtius calls 'inexpressibility topoi', if insistent traces of androgyny and incest were not also present elsewhere in the book's economy. For instance: the novel opens with Mariane dressed as a 'junger Offizier' ('young officer'), a detail stressed with the entrance of our hero: 'with what rapture he clasped the red uniform to his bosom' (p. 11). Or again, Natalie, referred to insistently as 'die Amazone' ('the Amazon'), first appears wrapped in a man's cloak (p. 227). These details, though slight, are not trivial because they are situated at crucial points in the text. Moreover, Ronald Gray has shown how Wilhelm is in fact led throughout by an ideal of dual sex: 'His imagination, first guided into a definite path by the story of Clorinda (the character from *Jerusalem Delivered* whose "Mannweiblichkeit" had fascinated the youthful puppet enthusiast), seeks the fulfilment of its dreams first in Mariane, then in the Countess, and Therese, and finally beyond all doubt in Natalie, the Amazon herself.'[67]

As we already know, the incestuous connection between Wilhelm and Natalie is the Antiochus and Stratonike motif, the King's sick son. This painting is Wilhelm's favourite as a boy. It represents a young prince, sick for love of his father's bride. Once part of his grandfather's art collection, it is sold by his father, only to be encountered again in Natalie's possession, where it plays a pivotal part in the eventual union of Wilhelm and Natalie. Natalie thus fulfils or corresponds to a yearning Wilhelm has experienced since childhood, a yearning associated with semi-incestuous desires.[68] Evidently, however, the incestuous twist to the tale in this instance is not irredeemably transgressive, but an indication of organic regularity and development on a profound level.

Ronald Gray has reflected upon the meaning of incest and hermaphroditism in Goethe's work. His reflections are helpfully lucid. In alchemy, as in other spiritual, philosophical and mystical systems, hermaphroditism is a quality of perfection.[69] Hence Mignon and Natalie, in some measure, reflect or embody the notion of perfection. The spectre of incest, however, looms across the path to perfection.[70] This is because, in the alchemical system, 'the only road to perfection was through "death", either physical or spiritual',[71] and the horror of incest, as Gray speculates interestingly in a footnote on Kierkegaard, 'is . . . one form of that dread which may lead to fuller knowledge of the divine'.[72]

In Mignon the obscure concatenation of androgyny and incest connotes a oneness unattainable in this world. In Natalie, however, Wilhelm discovers the ideal complement of his being, the feminine to his masculine, the moon to his sun. The block placed by the hint of incest in the painting of the 'kranker Königssohn' is overcome symbolically when the character Friedrich asks with reference to that very painting: '"How call you the beauty who enters, and in her modest roguish eyes at once brings poison and antidote?"' (p. 606). Union with Natalie is thus figured as the death which gives rise to life. 'Natalie, as the ideal of perfection, can only be attained by Wilhelm if he is willing to accept from her the double-sided cure.'[73]

For Gray, Mignon is the expression of Goethe's personal feelings about Italy and ancient Greece, and his own 'longing for redemption from isolation'.[74] The symbolism of Mignon, and its meaning in relation to Goethe's understanding of himself and his art, is treated once more in the *Wanderjahre*.[75] Natalie, on the other hand, represents an early, and in Goethe's eyes unsatisfactory, solution to a problem which he continued to rework in plots of ever greater complexity throughout his later life: 'The course towards perfection led to a symbolical marriage with the soul's bride . . . But at the same time this marriage appeared to involve "incest"'.[76] Ultimately, for Gray, it is part of Goethe's ongoing quest to mediate between ideal and real.

Gray's survey conveys a sober and convincing picture of the ways Goethe strove, consciously and maybe unconsciously too, to talk of ultimate matters within the realistic medium of the novel: 'Goethe goes as close as he dares to introducing purely mystical beliefs into a realistic work.'[77] But his conclusions about the meaning of androgyny, and the closely related incest, within the economy of the novel are too intertwined with biographical considerations and considerations regarding Goethe's oeuvre as a whole to be useful in themselves in our context.

We are left with the paradox that there are two forms of androgyny, two values to incest, two intimations of oneness, in the economy of the novel, which appear to be antagonistic to one another.

The first is the work of combination which we mentioned as characteristic of the meaning of the novel as a whole: the gender-relations employed to articulate a complex but coherent view of subjectivity, and the use of a regular series of women figures to furnish the aesthetic structure of the novel in interrelation with the unifying presence of the protagonist. This is the system in which Natalie plays her part, as Wilhelm's feminine complement. Her implied androgyny is symmetrically balanced in that of Wilhelm himself, evidenced (as well as in his initials) in the role women play throughout in the novel's representation of (masculine) subjectivity, a subjectivity manifest both in the fact and the objects of its desiring. This is the successful resolution of the Oedipus Complex, in which the initial orientation upon the mother is sublimated by the intervention of paternal law into the internalisation of codes referred to as the Super Ego.

The second is the tragic bleak world of Mignon and the Harper, which is not integrated into that meaning, but appears embedded in another semantic system. As Schiller put it, talking of the aesthetic wholeness of the book: 'Like a beautiful planetary system, everything in the book belongs together, apart from the Italian figures who, like comets, and as terrible as these, attach this system to another and greater one far away.'[78]

They are explicable in relation to the Freudian system, as unassimilated Oedipal impulses which, though by definition very deep-seated, are regressive and not socialisable. But it is, in Freud's terms too, less an integration than the discovery of tragedy (*Oedipus Rex*, after all, is a tragedy) which lies at the heart of the formation of the individual human subject. And the specific problem here is that the world of Mignon and the Harper is also the world of poetry, song, and its defeat or marginalisation questions the aesthetic achievement of the work as a whole.

The first type of androgyny relates to the novel's aesthetic autonomy. In an ironic gesture, the novel recommends a view about life from the point of view of art, while remaining at the same time distrustful of art: Wilhelm is dissuaded from a life of theatrical involvement; the Society of the Tower appreciates and possesses art but does not produce it; Natalie has little time for it (p. 526). Yet this process of combination, this play with the sexes, has no other justification than the appeal to art. Indeed, one can argue that artistic activity is itself distinguished by its licence to leave the strict demarcations of ordinary life (for which the division into male and female is the paradigm) and turn towards and affirm the essences which lie beyond. Hence the novel depends upon an inscrutable ironic play between the ethical and the artistic, an oscillation which defines the space of the aesthetic.

The second type of androgyny, that associated with Mignon and the Harper, calls into question this mediation between, on the one hand, the essential realm toward which art points, and, on the other, this life of distinct forms, identities and ethical determination. If, as Goethe once said, the novel was written entirely for the sake of Mignon,[79] this throws a strange light upon the otherwise triumphantly successful aesthetic union between masculine authority and subjectivity in the 'system' of the *Lehrjahre*.

Having sketched out these aspects of the *Lehrjahre* we have, in a sense, said all we need to say about it in order to proceed with our analysis of other texts in relation to it. However, we cannot lightly dismiss a dissonance which in its implications leads beyond the triumphant harmony of the *Lehrjahre* toward the whole historical and artistic context in which the mode of representing subjectivity addressed in this book finds fuller definition. We therefore turn from a treatment of the *Lehrjahre* as a site of all kinds of convergence and harmony to its function as the source of quite divergent evaluations. The place to begin is with some historical explanation of why one might be predisposed to seek synthesis in it in the first place.

The celebration of the *Lehrjahre* as a triumph of harmonious combination is in part at least the product of a specific history in German literature and literary consciousness. This history begins for the *Lehrjahre* with Schiller's profoundly perceptive, but at the same time already programmatically positive, interpretation, from which we have quoted several times. The majority of individual readings ever since, and, perhaps more importantly, the general consensus of opinion on the novel, have assumed this sense of the novel's compendious harmony.

This programmatic affirmation of the *Lehrjahre* was reinforced very influentially by the Romantic generation. Friedrich Schlegel wrote in 1798 that only the French Revolution and the philosophy of Fichte could be compared in importance with the *Lehrjahre* as indicators of their age,[80] thus lending Goethe's text an extraordinary universality and representativeness from a point of view actually quite alien to Goethe's own classical position.

The end of the nineteenth century brought important developments in the reception of Goethe. At this time the aesthetic-cultural authority characteristic of Weimar Classicism became associated with the ideology of the German Empire. Wilhelm Dilthey, whose characterisation of the *Bildungsroman* in *Das Erlebnis und die Dichtung* of 1906 did much to fix the stereotype of the *Lehrjahre* as a novel of unproblematic personal development, can be taken as exemplary in this respect. Dilthey ironed out his sense of the difficulties and contradictions in Goethe's world view, in order to reach a congruence between contemporary German achievements in the political sphere, and those of German Classicism of a hundred years before.[81]

In Dilthey's revisions of 1907 to his Goethe essay of 1878 the pattern for a certain kind of harmonising view of Goethe is set for decades to come. Dilthey holds the view that in Goethe's conception of nature there is no 'separation between an event and its significance, no distinction between nature and spirit (Geist)'.[82] He goes on, with particular relevance to the discrepancy between two sorts of androgyny outlined above: 'the opposition between, on one hand, destruction and death at the hands of fate and, on the other, divinely guided human activity, is now overcome'.[83] As Heinz Schlaffer puts it, the contradictions in Goethe's works have been overlooked by most readers because they confuse their idealised image of Goethe the man with the world of his poetic imagination. 'Unreconciled contradictions are overlooked in the pious hope that everything will make sense in the light of the final ideal resolution.'[84]

Goethe becomes the 'nodal point of centuries of cultural achievement',[85] against the background of which prevailing cultural assumption it is not hard to see why there is a desire for symmetry in operation, when one tries to give an objective account of a major work of Goethe's. There is a tendency to defer all uncertainties in anticipation of their final ideal resolution. We fall victim to the 'Auratisierung' (auratisation) of Goethe and especially of Goethe's life, rather than of his words, which is a central part of Christa Bürger's argument about the establishment of an institution of art in German Classicism, and which she exemplifies by reference not primarily to Dilthey but the related case of Gundolf.[86]

These historical encouragements to read Goethe in general, and the *Lehrjahre* in particular, as the embodiments of an achieved and unchallengeable aesthetic synthesis do not mean that the *Lehrjahre* is not in fact, and is not meant to be, a work of remarkable synthesis. They simply help to explain why the perception that this is so has come to obscure the dissonant moments within the economy of the text – moments which, it must be emphasised, the text itself might be said to dissimulate in the name of its moral, philosophical and specifically aesthetic commitment to wholeness. That these moments are there, however, is attested by the existence of an insistent alternative school of opinion about the *Lehrjahre*, springing largely from the divergence between Natalie and Mignon (to put it in shorthand) which goes back to Goethe and Schiller themselves, and which it is important to have squarely before us.

'The demands made on me by this book are unending and can in the nature of the thing never fully be met, although everything must, in a certain sense, be resolved', wrote Goethe to Schiller on 25 June 1796. For Schiller, however (8 July 1796), the 'idea' of the book was clear, and expressible in abstract vocabulary: '[Wilhelm] tritt von einem leeren und unbestimmten Ideal in ein bestimmtes tätiges Leben, aber ohne die idealisierende Kraft dabei einzubüßen' ('Wilhelm moves from an empty and ill-defined ideal to a definite and active life, but without losing the idealising force'). But he felt that Goethe had failed to make this quite explicit enough. Although he concurs, Goethe intimates resistance to the notion, and reveals, in the reference to dissimulation, the role irony plays in absorbing the implications of this resistance:

> The weakness which you quite rightly identify stems from my innermost nature, from a certain realistic tic (aus einem gewissen realistischen Tic) because of which it suits me best to disguise my existence, my actions, my writings from the eyes of other people. Hence I will always sooner travel incognito, dress more modestly than grandly, and, in conversation with strangers or half-acquaintances, always speak on an unimportant topic or at least employ less important-sounding turns of phrase, and always behave as a less serious person than I really am. Thus, one might say, I interpose myself between who I am and who I appear to be (und mich so, ich möchte sagen, zwischen mich selbst und zwischen meine eigene Erscheinung stellen). (9 July 1796)

There is further evidence that for Goethe himself Wilhelm Meister was a more problematic character than Schiller was keen to see. Witness, for instance, Wilhelm's outburst to Therese in Book Seven, Chapter Six: '"Wie glücklich ist der über alles . . . der, um sich mit dem Schicksal in Einigkeit zu setzen, nicht sein ganzes vorhergehendes Leben wegzuwerfen braucht!"' ('"How fortunate beyond all others [cried he] is the man who, in order to adjust himself to fate, is not required to cast away his whole preceding life!"') (p. 459). And before one hastens to assert that the book's overall wisdom relativises this complaint, it is worth recalling again the famous remark Goethe made to Kanzler von Müller in 1821: 'Wilhelm sei freilich ein "armer Hund", aber nur an solchen lasse sich das Wechselspiel des Lebens und die tausend verschiedenen Lebensaufgaben recht deutlich zeigen, nicht an schon abgeschlossenen festen Charakteren' ('Wilhelm is certainly a "poor dog", but only such types can be used to reveal clearly life's ups and downs, the thousand different tasks imposed by life. Strong, rounded characters can never serve to demonstrate all this with such clarity').[87] Seven years earlier (as we saw), to the same interlocutor, Goethe had also intimated that the entire novel had been written solely on account of the figure of Mignon.

In Goethe's hints and uncertainty, in contrast with Schiller's philosophical decisiveness, this alternative tradition of reading *Wilhelm Meisters Lehrjahre* had its beginnings. It was quickly taken up and extended by the poet Friedrich von Hardenberg (Novalis). Novalis, like the Romantic generation in general, praised the *Lehrjahre* very highly when it appeared. However, in 1799 he turned against it because he said it betrayed poetry: 'Es ist im Grunde ein fatales und albernes Buch – so prätentiös und preziös – undichterisch im höchsten Grade, was den Geist betrifft – so poetisch auch die Darstellung ist.' ('At bottom it is an unfortunate and foolish book – so pretentious and precious – unpoetic in the highest degree in its spirit, however poetic it is in its style and form'.)[88] He deplores the division of poetry against itself.

Novalis appears to have been impelled to a decision for or against the *Lehrjahre*. For him, the compromise reached there was not an authentic one. Julian Schmidt, writing a little later in the century and from a realist point of view, was of the same opinion. He criticised Goethe for making Wilhelm betray his own class. For Schmidt, the novel's neo-classical harmony depended upon an 'Entsagung' (renunciation) which, far from being harmonious, was actually a subordination, an inglorious 'Einordnung' (heartless integration) into the prevailing social structure. It had very little to do with genuine freedom, and a great deal to do with what Schmidt saw, polemically, as the political failure of the German middle class.[89]

This evaluation of Wilhelm's 'Entsagung' as subjugation rather than as the means to fulfilment characterises the alternative readings of the *Lehrjahre.* Heinz and Hannelore Schlaffer call them the 'poetic', as opposed to the 'philosophical', interpretations.[90] Karl Schlechta, in his genuinely original book on the Meister novels, perceives more life in the disorder of Mariane's room than in the immaculate allotment of Therese.[91] He directs his attention towards the details and accidents of the book, and away from the grand lines of development to which it easily becomes reduced in memory and the inevitable simplification of consensus (even if one allows for the ideological considerations we have mentioned). He has an eye for the aesthetic and spiritual advantages of impurity, and quotes with approval a passage from the *Sendung* which did not make it into the *Lehrjahre*:

> Und ich behaupte sogar, daß, je mehr das Theater gereinigt wird, es zwar verständigen und geschmackvollen Menschen angenehmer werden muß, allein von seiner ursprünglichen Wirkung und Bestimmung immer mehr verliert. Es scheint mir, wenn ich ein Gleichnis brauchen darf, wie ein Teich zu sein, der nicht allein klares Wasser, sondern auch eine gewisse Portion von Schlamm, Seegras und Insekten enthalten muß, wenn Fische und Wasservögel sich darin wohl befinden sollen.

> I would even venture to say that the more the theatre is purified the more it will appeal to people of common sense and good taste, but the more, at the same time, will it lose of its original point and effect. If I may use an analogy, it is like a pond which, if it is to be attractive to fish and birds, must contain a certain portion of mud and weeds and insects as well as clean water.[92]

For Schlechta, Wilhelm's development is tantamount to an irreversible and tragic loss of spontaneity. His entry into the Society of the Tower completely changes him, forcing him to an act of will which deprives him of his original life ('seines ursprünglichen Lebens').[93] This is a view of Goethe's hero in accord with that of Baioni which we cited above, who saw him as a 'faceless compliant doll'.

What is new about Schlechta's reading, is that he does not blame Goethe for this brutal curtailment, but the age, which Goethe in his view rightly perceives and represents as soulless. Wilhelm is an anachronistic representative of an age of wholeness which now survives only in poetry and love, amid the grim self-control and bloodless theoretical freedom of the Tower. For Schlechta, Goethe's fiction is written in the face of this bleak prospect.

If Schlechta's reading sometimes appears to be exaggeratedly hostile to the ideal dimension of Goethe's text, it is because he, as a Nietzsche scholar and editor, is particularly sensitive to those aspects of it which anticipate a modernity more bleak than Goethe himself could probably have imagined. But this does not mean that these aspects are not there. Indeed, Schlechta's interpretation enhances precisely those moments in the *Lehrjahre* which are also picked out by the later works whose variations on Goethe's theme are the subject of this book: for instance, the personal diminution of the protagonist at the hands of socialising authorities, anticipating *Der grüne Heinrich*; or the excessive, seemingly inhuman orderliness of the dispositions of the Tower, pointing forward to *Der Nachsommer*.

Schlechta's book was originally published in 1953. It may have been ahead of its time. After many years as an aberrant curiosity it was re-published in paperback in 1985, with an introduction by the German academic Heinz Schlaffer.

In 1980, Hannelore Schlaffer, acknowledging her debt to Schlechta, had extended the argument by proposing a specific semantic and aesthetic relationship between the poetic and the prosaic levels of Goethe's novel. She argues that his use of fragments of myth, especially in the presentation of Mignon and the Harper, and then most importantly in the *Wanderjahre*, sets up a discourse other than that of realistic representation: 'behind the themes of the time there appears the eternal myth of suffering'.[94] She offers a coherent situation of Mignon and the Harper within a view of the changing function of art in modern times, arguing Goethe's underground resistance to the steady progress of prose into the territories of poetry.

Three years later, in 1983, Jochen Hörisch published a book which recast Schlechta's reading in the terms of contemporary theory. Wilhelm's 'subjection' is now interpreted as Goethe's reaction, in the non-philosophical mode of poetry ('Dichtung'), to the then dominant idealist philosophy of transcendental subjectivity: 'Where "the Cartesianism of modern science and transcendental philosophy" inquires from the point of view of the subject after the constitutive accomplishments of reflexivity, poetry tells that and how this constitutive subjectivity, along with others, is "entangled in stories", by which they are subjected, subjugated.'[95]

Hörisch reads the *Lehrjahre* against the background of the dethronement of the German idealist subject which has taken place subsequently in psychoanalysis, linguistics and economics. Wilhelm Meister is subject to the systems of love, language and exchange which are prior to the subject and in which it is constituted, already self-alienated. As Hörisch puts it in Lacanian terms: 'God, Money and Love, however, are the media in which a self realises its own alterity' ('ein Selbst seiner Alterität inne wird').[96] What Hörisch is doing, in other words, is turning round the reading which sees 'alterity' internalized in Wilhelm's subjectivity and somehow 'aufgehoben' (sublated) there, and giving more sophisticated definition to the forces which others before him had also seen as engulfing the spontaneity and authenticity of Goethe's protagonist.

Despite the *Lehrjahre*'s evident anthropocentric optimism, a trend of interpretation has, as we can see, persisted which either rejects that optimism as unpoetic, facile or reactionary (Novalis, Schmidt, Baioni), or else reads the text with a kind of reverent perversity against itself (Schlechta, the Schlaffers, Hörisch). These divergent lines of interpretation correspond to the energies held in synthesis within the novel, which are amplified in the subsequent debate to the point at which they become independent of the novel's formidable ironic powers of synthesis. Here one once more encounters subjectivity as unhoused as ever it was before the aesthetic took it in and accommodated it. In the divergent line of interpretation subjectivity is a problem once more, although affirmed as a value. We turn now, in conclusion, to an interpretation which has no difficulty in establishing a context in which this problem is re-accommodated, but at a very high price. Not simply that of a particular representation of subjectivity, but of subjectivity itself.

In its conceptual range, Friedrich A. Kittler's remarkable study 'Über die Sozialisation Wilhelm Meisters',[97] dating from the height of radical deconstructionism in the 1970s, shifts our attention squarely onto the position of the *Lehrjahre* in relation to the construction of the modern subject.

To the 'histories' with which we began our account, the biographical, the literary, the sociological-cultural and the philosophical, he adds another, into which they dissolve. Goethe's biography is now an effect of the same discourse as the biographistic *Lehrjahre* itself. Literary history and philosophy become hermeneutic practices which conceal the same discursive strategies. And the shortcoming of the sociological model is that it overlooks the slower and quieter revolution which informs and outflanks the crasser shifts in public institutions to which it attends. For Kittler's linguistic neo-materialism, drawing on Lacan, Derrida and Foucault, there are only discourses which produce, delimit and modify the life of bodies. History is a history of writings and rewritings of the codes which determine the rituals and transitions of human life. The *Lehrjahre* is part of a recoding which produces and reproduces the modern individual from the pattern of the nuclear family, with the historical inception of which, he claims, it is coincident.

The key property of the modern individual is continuity. The operation of the recoding according to the pattern of the nuclear family is to constitute an individual with a self-generating past and future: in other words, a continuous identity which governs his choice of marriage partner and vocation, and facilitates these transitions without the trauma of initiation by which other cultures effect the passage from childhood to maturity. Far from brutalising Wilhelm, the Society of the Tower effects the secondary socialisation which is simply the continuation of the primary socialisation enacted between mother and son in which the modern subject is constituted. Without this first moment, in which the wishes giving definition to the individual's choice of partner and vocation are produced and articulated, the second would not be able to function. The transition is effected by the normal progress of the Oedipus Complex, which it remained for Freud to discover, though he was not placed to see the historicity of his discovery. Kittler, in other words, relocates the brutality observed by Schlechta, Hörisch and others in the net of discourse, from which there is no escape (because it has no outside), and aligns himself with it in terms of an anti-humanist or post-humanist theory.

What is important about Kittler's argument is that it powerfully conveys how the *Lehrjahre* model transcends the literary in its very constitution as literature. For it is literature, the 'Aufschreibesystem' of the individual author, as practised by Wilhelm himself, by the Tower, and by the author of the *Lehrjahre*, which opens the space of the new socialisation practices: 'Only the discourse system "literature" can stabilise and disseminate individuals and the new technologies of socialisation, which do without legal enforcement (rechtliche Fixierung)'.[98] When Wilhelm aligns himself with David 'die Seele entsteht' (the soul comes into being),[99] and not just Wilhelm's, but the soul *tout court*. And, by extending his demonstration to Novalis's 'answer' to *Wilhelm Meisters Lehrjahre*, *Heinrich von Ofterdingen*, here and in other publications,[100] he further indicates how the *Lehrjahre* demands to be read beyond itself, as part of a larger cultural discourse.

Thus, in the terms of my own argument Kittler's work makes it possible to formulate a position beyond the evaluative either–or dichotomy to which our survey of the alternative tradition of reading the *Lehrjahre* led us. In these terms, the *Lehrjahre* can be conceived of as a cultural, functioning model for talking about, for producing and reproducing, the modern subject in its relation to the construction of the self, and the gender roles in play in that construction. It is concerned with the successful negotiation of the transition from primary to secondary socialisation.

Kittler's particular interest is in the 'archival' role of the men, who retain the linguistic, symbolic function of registering and ordering the new maternally inspired experiences which define the modern subject. This gives theoretical definition to the specific mixture of masculine and feminine qualities which characterise the *Lehrjahre* as an aesthetic artefact. In his terms, the particular notion of the aesthetic which informs the *Lehrjahre* is part of a specific construction of 'literature' which is intimately involved with the institution of the new socialisation practices. The marginalisation of Mignon is part of this culturally necessary, indeed culturally constitutive, negotiation of the Oedipus Complex.

It is no surprise that it is in the area of the representation of Mignon, and specifically of her last days and death, that the aesthetic model of the *Lehrjahre* appears at its most vulnerable. This is because there is, in this model, no satisfying solution to the problem of the representation of repressed Oedipal desire. As David Roberts, Ronald Gray, and now Kittler explain, there must be *both* a sanction *and* a proscription of incest. A sanction, because the modern subject is constructed in the love of the mother; a proscription because this initial orientation must be translated into the social order by the intervention of the father's law. There is no ironic or magisterial transcending of this originating split. Before it, the alliance between subjectivity and masculine authority under the banner of the aesthetic fails. The masculine and aesthetic authorities of the text – both in the sense of the institution of the Tower and its proponents in the text, and that of the aesthetic operation of the text itself in its overall organisation – cannot redeem Mignon, who represents subjectivity in its most uncorrected, but also most pure and original, form.

The authority of the *Lehrjahre* depends upon a certain kind of prevarication with reference to final questions. It finds means of imbuing the artificial, the 'made', with an aura and a resonance which promotes it to a signifying power which earns the name 'aesthetic'. As Michael Beddow rightly says, the sort of irony we encounter in the novel is not the sort that 'undermines some of the things [the work] ostensibly advocates'. The kind of irony which does inform the text is one which 'seems to be continually intimating more than it is overtly saying, to be making the "realities" it represents transparent to wider meanings'.[101] From a point of view which is favourable to that ironic stance one can say that those wider meanings are that 'the "fabric" of the world [is] woven of the warp and weft of chance and fate, contingency and necessity'.[102] But from the point of view that perceives the irony as a particular historical and cultural construct, it is the very oscillation between artificial and aesthetic, the very evident ability of the discourse to inspire that which is consciously made with the aura of the meaningful, that is the specific power of the text.

At the limit point represented by Mignon, however, this crucial play between the aesthetic and the artificial becomes transparently tawdry and inauthentic. The aesthetic diminishes into the artificial. It is already prominently visible, and thus vulnerable, when Mignon appears dressed as an angel, in the scene to which we have already referred. Asked about the wings which are part of her costume, she replies: '"Sie stellen schönere vor, die noch nicht entfaltet sind"' ('"they represent more beautiful [wings], which have yet to unfold"', p. 515). The text uses the artificial wings in its aesthetic articulation of deeper meaning, signalling all Mignon's answers as 'bedeutend' (significant) (ibid.). Kittler: 'Mignon im Lied ist ein Engel, ohne ein Engel zu sein, und doch ein Engel' ('Mignon in the song is an angel, without being an angel, but yet an angel').[103] The final failure of this ironic play with the aesthetic and artificial comes with the hollowness and pomp of Mignon's exequies, and the inability of the aesthetic construct of the *Lehrjahre*, brilliant though it is, to accommodate the figure of Mignon and the limit she marks. This failure is, of course, confirmed by the persistence of the alternative reading of the *Lehrjahre*.

The *Lehrjahre* model enables the subject of the story and the subject of the irony to speak to each other across 'ein endlos begehbares und beschreibbares Feld' ('an infinitely traversable and writable field'),[104] a space vast enough to accommodate everything except the limitation and curtailment hidden in their invisible dependence upon one another. The cloak of invisibility is 'der Dichtung Schleier' (poetry's veil), the aura of the aesthetic, which becomes transparent where the complicity of the modern subject with the trangression of incest becomes apparent. This is where the crucial separation between the personality of the artist and the work of art becomes cruelly prominent. Subjectivity and art threaten to collapse into each other, bereft of the redeeming interventions of the social: 'aesthetic' ceases to be a threshold quality between interiority and the printing press. Their secret identity can no longer be decorously veiled and must be violently suppressed. The personality of the artist, Mignon, must die if the work of the artist, the *Lehrjahre*, is to achieve the necessary completion. Yet both have the same source and inspiration: the love of the mother.

The real problem is that Mignon is more human than

Humanity: s/he is situated at the point where the *Lehrjahre* model needs to open out onto the metaphysical, but where instead we are left only with an ugly cauterisation mark. If this sounds like a restatement of the traditional positions around the novel, like an echo of Novalis and a rejection of Schiller, that is not surprising. The choice of such positions is fundamentally very limited. Even if Kittler succeeds in historicising desire in his reading of the model, including Mignon, the immediacy of desire will always retain its ability to de-historicise. Desire and history relate to each other like practice and theory (in some ways they are different words for the same thing). Their mutual antagonism is mutually constitutive: systems feed on what it is impossible to systematise. Without Mignon, no *Lehrjahre*, without the *Lehrjahre*, no Kittler.

Although one construction of art (the aesthetic) is an object of Kittler's analysis and of this book, and relativised as such, that does not abolish the reality of the experience which inspired the historical configurations in which it became manifest (and thus lost its immediacy, just as Mignon loses substance by the necessity of appearing). By the same logic that behind every non-theoretical utterance must lie theoretical assumptions, behind every theoretical one must lie non-theoretical ones too. Kittler writes: 'the correspondence of wishes and social roles makes it necessary to narrate a continuity which eradicates all breaks (Einschnitte) between primary and secondary socialisation'.[105] The vertiginous proximity of consoling harmony and bleak facticity discerned by Schlechta, for instance, in the course of his interpretation, which Kittler himself calls 'the most beautiful and the saddest interpretation'[106] of Goethe's novel, might however give us cause to believe, with Hörisch, that far from eradicating such discontinuities, the *Lehrjahre* in the end fulfils itself by making them appear.

CHAPTER TWO

Agathon, Anton Reiser, Hyperion

DIE GESCHICHTE DES AGATHON

If *Wilhelm Meisters Lehrjahre* is a site of convergence, Wieland's *Geschichte des Agathon* is a site of transition. In it there is a much more visible antagonism between, on the one hand, forms of explicit authority of various kinds and, on the other hand, autobiographical and erotic forces which have the effect of disturbing, even subverting them. These latter will eventually in the *Lehrjahre* combine to help form a new kind of authority, the aesthetic, while the old forms disappear, recede or are themselves transformed.

Throughout his long life (1733–1813), from his early productions under the aegis of Bodmer in Zürich to the great dialogue novels of his old age in and near Weimar, Wieland was a massively literary figure. He was deeply involved with and immensely productive in the literary culture of his time, acting as a point of refraction in German for the literature of other times and places. But in an important sense he was, or became, old-fashioned. It is not that, as a writer, he drew from and renewed conventional literary forms. It is hard to imagine a writer who does not do this. It is rather that he was still part of a culture which found it natural to do this and, crucially, to do it visibly. The cult of originality in the 1770s interrupted his long period of influence, turning against the gesture of deference to authority. In 1782 the first volume of Rousseau's *Confessions* was published, in which the author announced the uniqueness not only of his own personality, but of his enterprise in writing about it. So apparent did Wieland's affiliation to the literary ancien régime become that the Romantic generation could dismiss the most famous German author of the late eighteenth century, on the grounds that he was nothing more than the servant of literary precedent, a plagiarist of Greek, French, English and other 'auctoritates'.[1]

The plot of *Die Geschichte des Agathon* is self-consciously elaborate. As a youth the outstandingly handsome hero is forced to flee the attentions of the high priestess at Delphi. He survives a Bacchic orgy only to be captured by pirates. On board ship he finds again the love of his youth, Psyche. They are parted again when Agathon is sold as a slave. His purchaser, a Sophist philosopher called Hippias, seeks to win Agathon over to his own philosophy. He meets with no success since Agathon's platonic idealism is too strong to capitulate before the worldly wisdom of the Sophist. The philosopher's last resort is to organise Agathon's seduction by Danae, the courtesan. This ploy backfires when she falls in love with him. In conversation with her, he recounts the significant moments of his life prior to the beginning of the novel, notably a political career in Athens. As a result of Hippias' duplicity, Agathon quits this idyll for the court of Syracuse, where another political career, as brilliant and short-lived as the first, awaits him. Agathon having been rescued from external adversity and besetting doubts within by the authorities of Tarent, the novel ends with his resolution to live according to the wisdom of Archytas, ruler of Tarent and a friend of his father. Here Agathon once again encounters Psyche, whose identity as his sister is revealed, and Danae, now a reformed character, with whom he embarks upon a platonic friendship.

Agathon derives its charm from the way in which this engagingly ridiculous plot becomes transparent upon serious psychological analysis. Agathon himself is a stylistic curiosity, a blend of classical hero and modern neurotic. This play between a banal exterior and an evocation of complex interiority is urbanely managed by an eloquent and ironic narrator.

Thus no reader could fail to be aware that *Agathon* is the product of a self-consciously literary culture. But at the same time, the novel – as a novel already a literary production of uncertain register within the range of available literary types – is more complex and heterogeneous than its confidently allusive tone might lead one to expect. In order to give a clear picture of this combination of elements, it will be useful to look at two other novels on comparable themes which will have been present to Wieland's mind as he wrote (as well as to those of his readers as they read), which derive their force and focus from different forms of authority, and which both in their way are less problematic in their relation to those forms than Wieland's transitional text.

Fénelon's *Télémaque* (1699) was one of the most widely read books in eighteenth-century European literature.[2] It is a book of instruction intended for Fénelon's pupils, the grandsons of Louis XIV. Behind it stands not only the authority of the ancien régime but also the new authority of the Enlightenment. Fénelon's choice of a narrative for his text of princely instruction identifies it as an Enlightenment work, in contrast to the *Fürstenspiegel* (works of instruction for princes) from the middle ages onwards, which had simply been cast in the form of treatises. The adoption of narrative reflects the 'new critical and utopian dimensions' of the dawning age of reason,[3] and Fénelon's choice of a narrative form, which set the tone for such texts in the century to come and prepared the way for the *Bildungsroman*, is constructed to reconcile the needs of those two authorities. The clarity of Fénelon's solution really resides in the ease with which it is still possible for him to associate public and private spheres. The engagement with narrative and the interest in education mean that the hero must be exposed to changes and cannot be morally perfect from the start, since if he were, it would be impossible to convey principles of education by reference to his example. But this potentially unstable moment in the text is stabilised by the use of the classical setting, the world of the *Odyssey* (with some help from the structure of the *Aeneid*), which provides the author with a plot whose shape is assured in the minds of the readers from the beginning. The basic situation – the son in search of the father – locates the function of education solidly enough within a patriarchal culture. At the same time Odysseus' son, Telemachus, is little characterised in the source and thus leaves the author with substantial freedom in his treatment.[4] If the law of succession is thus firmly embodied in the text, so too is the operation of Reason: Télémaque is accompanied by a teacher, Mentor, who is a divinity in disguise (Minerva). Here Fénelon's discursive solution of conflicting authoritative determinations is especially adept, because by 'sacralizing the prince's tutor', Fénelon 'cleverly reverses the divine right of kings'.[5]

Because the teleology of the text is assured – the return to Ithaca, the duties of kingship – the subjective partialness we experience in the person of the eponymous hero is securely situated: 'Quand tu seras le maître des autres hommes souviens-toi que tu as été faible, pauvre et souffrant comme eux.' ('When you are the master of other men remember that you were once weak, poor and suffering like them'),[6] admonishes Mentor. Otherwise, the topic of moral vulnerability is displaced onto another character, Idoménée, who becomes the representative 'fallible human being', thus allowing Telemachus to retain something of the aura of the elected one.

The question of desire is dealt with economically and unambiguously. Telemachus' persistent desire is not for this or that woman, but to find his father. Desire as problematic is either displaced onto a woman whose sexuality is equated with enchantment – Calypso – or else, also identified as enchantment, onto the hero's Cupid-inspired manic infatuation with the nymph Eucharis, from which he is cured by the admonition of Mentor: 'Fuyez, Télémaque, fuyez: on ne peut vaincre l'amour qu'en fuyant' ('Flee, Telemachus, flee, one cannot conquer love but by fleeing'),[7] words which anticipate the advice Hamlet's ghost will transmit to Wilhelm Meister: to flee the excessively subjective lure of the theatre. Note the absolute moral clarity of Fénelon's message in contrast to the auratic obliqueness of Goethe's. Finally, the appropriate partner for the future king, Antiope, the daughter of Idoménée, appears at the right structural and thematic moment to dissolve the problem of personal desire without residue, into the pattern of succession. In the background, the source holds the image of Penelope as an emblem of the fortitude of conjugal/political constancy against the vagaries of chance and change.

Agathon is displaced from this context, but has an important relation to it. Wieland, given the political reality of his time, was by no means uninterested in the enlightened education of princes, and in the textual elaboration of it. A substantial fraction of *Der goldene Spiegel* (1772) is devoted to the exemplary education of a prince, and the work secured him employment at the court of Weimar as the instructor of the widowed Duchess Anna Amalia von Sachsen-Weimar's sons (one of whom was to become Goethe's patron), a position which sustained him for the rest of his life. But in an important way, in our context it is not this work which demands comparison with *Télémaque. Der goldene Spiegel* was a more unproblematic, somewhat opportunistic, engagement with the authorities of the time, which, in its shrewd espousal of contemporary alignments (and unlike Fénelon's text in its time) won the approval of contemporary authorities. But in 1758, the time at which *Agathon* was probably germinating in his mind,[8] Wieland had written: 'Once I wished to experiment with the education of young children, at times entertaining the wish to instruct a prince. Now experience has taught me much that I did not know five years ago. My own self occupies me enough.' (Ich habe genug mit mir selbst zu thun.)[9]

In other words, although he was concerned, like everyone else at the time, with the theory of politically and ethically effective education, his experience had tended to translate this area of interest into a preoccupation with himself: a slide from education to subjectivity as part of a single context, signalled by Wieland in the juxtaposition he makes in his letter: once I thought of the education of others, but this has now been displaced by self-scrutiny. This is not merely a personal change, but an historical one. The personal itself is becoming historical. The relation between the public and the private has shifted in favour of the private.

Die Geschichte des Agathon reflects this overlap of the literature of deferential precedent with the increase in importance in the sphere of personal experience. Agathon's personal fallibility is not situated within a clear political and ethical teleology, as had been the case with *Télémaque*, but tends toward being an end in itself. The vagueness of Agathon as an ancient model far exceeds that of Telemachus (the historical Agathon is an obscure figure), and although this enriches the possibilities of characterisation, it deprives Wieland of the strong patriarchal determination which keeps Telemachus in his place. The richly differentiated character of Agathon is potentially a contribution to the ideology of humanity, but there are stylistic problems in conveying this. In order to bring his work to the sort of conclusion convention demanded,

Wieland is obliged to devise a Utopia, and a Utopia combining the antinomy of reason and feeling – which is the philosophical yield of Agathon's personal experience – is hard to find. The topos of master and student which helped define and stabilise the system of *Télémaque* becomes a destabilising factor here because Hippias and Agathon engage in so substantial and genuine a debate, psychologically so well represented, that the last word is never spoken. Wieland handles Agathon differently according to whether he is involved in public affairs or a private one. The novel simply reads differently when Wieland is showing Agathon as public figure and as a private individual: in the former case the narrative is much more schematic. True, Wieland avails himself of a stylistic possibility exploited also by Fénelon, and indeed Goethe, of having the protagonist narrate his own story (including public involvements) in an erotically loaded situation; but whereas for Fénelon the situation is well under control, and for Goethe, it is, as we have seen, a shrewdly chosen device for the centralisation of subjectivity, in Wieland the relation with Danae is fundamentally unresolved, producing, as we shall argue later, an increase in erotic content without a corresponding modulation in form. And at all events, it is only the experience at Athens which Wieland handles deftly in this way; the episode at Syracuse reads like a graft of the sort of stable discourse of which Fénelon is an exponent, onto the psychologically richer and more interesting discourse of the Hippias and Danae parts of Wieland's novel.

There is a certain parallel between Fénelon and Wieland in relation to the way in which they seek to position subjective experience at its most intense, profound and valuable. The parallel is this. When Telemachus visits Hades in search of his father, one of the souls in torment he encounters is accused as follows by his tormentors: 'Tu voulais jouir du fruit de ta propre vertu et te renfermer en toi-même: tu as été ta divinité.' ('You wished to enjoy the fruit of your own virtue and enclose yourself within your own self. You were your own divinity.')[10] The punishment for this crime: 'il se voit, et ne peut cesser de se voir' ('he sees himself, he cannot cease seeing himself').[11] In terms of Fénelon's own theology, this is the moment of despair in which the I is confronted with itself. It is the moment of transition into the genuinely spiritual dimension of 'amour pur' which opens up beyond the space of individual personality. This theology is not thematised in the instructional text, but appears here on its margin to suggest the perspective in which the whole process of education finally makes sense.[12] In Wieland the intense subjective moment is the state of 'Schwärmerei' (enthusiasm). In his, the more open, text it is not silently marginalised, but centrally thematised. Nor is it displaced onto a peripheral character, but located upon what is now the only important stage: the life of the individual male mind. Agathon's relation with himself is the acute problem with which the text consciously concerns itself. It is obviously utterly misguided, since it leads from illusion to illusion and from guilt to guilt. At the same time, it is the value against which alone the whole narrative process acquires meaning, since it is the manifestation of Agathon's subjectivity and what makes him worth inventing. In one way, this shows again how efficient and lucid a discourse is that of the Archbishop of Cambrai and how fraught and murky that of the German sometime civil administrator. What is particularly fascinating, however, is how accurately the sin of the unfortunate man in the French novel reflects the difficulties of Agathon's 'Schwärmerei': for it is precisely the uses of virtue which consistently confuse Agathon, leaving him condemned to stare inwards at the abyss of the inner life without connection to anything outside it ('il se voit, et ne peut cesser de se voir'). It might of course be objected that the differences between the two novels can be put down to the fact that one is Christian in inspiration and the other not. The process of secularisation, however, is vastly too complex to allow of crude distinctions of that nature. First: the mystical theology of 'amour pur' is of the same tradition in theology to which belongs the Pietism from which, in writing *Agathon*, Wieland was trying to free himself, to transcend the 'Schwärmerei' of his early years. The word 'Schwärmerei', indeed, had strong religious connotations, referring to an excessively subjective and obscurely intuitional form of worship. Wieland is marginalising his intense subjective moments in order to establish a public discourse, just as Fénelon kept his controversially subjectivist theology on the margin in order to maintain the clarity of his ethical, political, his public, intervention, which was nevertheless conditioned by it. Secondly, the profound ambiguity of the moment of self-scrutiny is common to both. It is both a perilous weakness and the threshold to the deity, whether the deity is conceived as the God of Christianity, or Man, the secular deity of humanism. Wieland spoke of the spiral which led from the 'enthusiasm' of his youth to the 'Mensch' (Man) of his mature convictions.[13] We seem to glimpse here a turn in the spiral of European secularisation, a hidden congruence in two such different texts.

If *Agathon* fits rather awkwardly into the aristocratic mould of *Télémaque*, it fits no more smoothly into the middle-class one, one in this case explicitly evoked as a guiding authority in the text, represented by Fielding's *The History of Tom Jones* (1749). Wieland's alignment with this literary precedent is already indicated by his adoption of the word 'Geschichte' for his own title. In calling his novel the 'History of Tom Jones', Fielding was distinguishing it from other contemporary novels which were either too moral or too fanciful to be able to claim that they reflected nature.[14] Fielding announces his book in the famous 'bill of fare' introduction as being drawn from nature, and criticises the tyranny of unsubstantiated literary authority in the introductory chapter of Book Five, preferring to give reasons for his own innovative kind of writing, which relies upon the 'good authority' of 'the vast authentic doomsday-book of nature' (Book IX, Chapter I) alone.

Fielding's novel is in other words an early example of European literary realism. His representation of an individual male hero is embedded in a socio-economic consciousness historically distinct from that of *Télémaque*, in that it is, as we have seen, explicitly opposed to immemorial authority, individualistic, secular and middle-class. He sets his story in the present, in recognisable social circumstances, involving identified places, identifiable social classes and types. The fallibility of his hero is an indication of realism (Tom Jones is not an unrealistic paragon like the characters of Richardson), and realism is a function of a confident middle-class individualism. The frank treatment of eroticism is also a function of realism, but here the erotic element (after seeming for a while to have transgressively spilled over into incest) is also structurally subsumed in a confirmation of English social expectations with the revelation of Tom's birth. Tom's desire also finally defines and resolves itself as a search for his father. The plot in general is a faultless machine, facilitating mobility and risk, while all the time guaranteeing a fundamental epistemological, psychological, moral and artistic stability.

For Wieland to invoke Fielding is thus paradoxical in something like the way it is paradoxical for the writers of the Sturm und Drang to base their claim to be representing nature by invoking the authority of Shakespeare. But Wieland then prominently has recourse to one of the authority topoi of the novel which Fielding's programme was dedicated to making irrelevant, by claiming that he is publishing the manuscript of a Greek author about the historical figure Agathon. Fielding's position is then asserted within this frame, by saying that the material in the ancient source can lay claim to the public interest only insofar as it is drawn from the inexhaustible resources of nature herself ('aus dem unerschöpflichen Vorrat der Natur selbst hergenommen').[15] For Fielding this conventional manoeuvre was redundant. He embodied a new confidence of the novel to show life as it is, without need of such ironic fictional authentification.[16] For Wieland in Germany the conditions for such a productive relationship between author, literary form and social reality were not present, and this compelled him to construct a literary compromise in which the social and psychological realism of a Fielding could be developed in the absence of historical particularity. Whereas in Fielding psychological motivation is the fuel of the plot, the plot which eventually integrates both Tom into society and the novel into the expectations and pleasure of its readers, in Wieland psychological motivation far exceeds the needs of the plot, tending, again, to become an end in itself.

Fielding's individualism is present in the voice of the narrator. The authority for his text is visibly grounded in the attitudes and reasons of this robust narrative voice, which provides a rationale for what is narrated and how it is narrated from Book to Book. Wieland derives much from this model. Even though his reference to an ancient Greek source is profoundly against the spirit of Fielding, it is ironised, and the irony seeks the same 'nature' as do Fielding's own narrative devices. Wieland's irony in *Agathon* exploits evident artifice in order to refer to a complex reality more mundane but more important than the urbane discourse constructed to illuminate it. It is a rationalist irony. Reason speaks through the arabesque of artificial literariness, and is a centrally important authority behind the text.

Both Fénelon and Fielding have at their disposal literary forms equal to the task of defining and representing a developing individual male without leaving the personal, psychological sphere an insoluble problem. The lack of such a literary possibility leaves Wieland dependent upon the resources of philosophy for a solution. The other two texts we have discussed are doubtless rationalist too, but their rationalism is encoded in one way or another in the literary forms they realise. In this sense, *Agathon* is a philosophical novel. It depends upon an enlightened, rational readership for its efficiency as an act of communication. The ironic rationality of the narrator has the last word on the character of Agathon, and thus effectively of the book itself. His heroic otherness, his earnestness and virtue, even in the end his good looks, are, though various topoi, a reference to the rest of us, author and reader (man or woman), who, whilst not being like him, are nevertheless able to appreciate him, and, more subtly, understand how, why and in what measure we are not like him (I take this to be the point behind the ironic play of Book II, Chapter I). The irony theoretically enables one to engage with a complicated but focused textual juxtaposition of artifice and a complex reality or nature. Unlike *Télémaque* and *Tom Jones*, however, *Agathon* did not meet with popular success: the audience for this complex mix of game and earnest did not exist,[17] and Wieland was left to complain of the incomprehension of the contemporary public.[18]

The philosophical foundation of the text also runs into trouble with the question of how to represent the personal sphere. In one way the text is stabilised around a moral-philosophical move, namely the thematisation of Agathon's 'Schwärmerei'. This is the name under which that subjective partialness, that thematic human fallibility with which we are familiar from the Meister model, had appeared in this novel. It is a name from eighteenth-century moral discourse. The word 'Schwärmer' (originally religious) is a word with specific connotations concerning the problematic privileging of the personal above the institutional and social.[19] What it means can be examined and discussed rationally, the good and bad sides weighed up against one another, a final balance drawn within an overall system of the types or cases of human nature. In Wieland's work, however, one can observe the mutation in the meaning of the word from a moral-philosophical sense to a problematic one.[20] The 'Schwärmer', the stock figure of the subjective enthusiast who risks mistaking the true world in the heat of his personal projections, becomes the focus in modern literature for the complex negotiation between inner and outer life, no longer a figure among figures but the prototype of the modern subject itself. Centralising the 'Schwärmer', as Wieland does, tends to subvert the framework within which the definition arose.

The final problem with a philosophical founding authority for Wieland's text is that it has no resolution for that central contradiction of the Enlightenment itself between empiricism and reason. While on the one hand reason postulates a morally coherent world, psychological empiricism, the study of the minutest motifs of human behaviour under the influence of external circumstances which is Wieland's programme in the work, yields no such coherence. Instead, 'the "moral world" represents a perverted system of cause and effect of its own, in which the causes are insufficient reasons and the effects catastrophes'.[21] These imponderables find their appropriate level of abstraction in the discourse of Kant, not that of Wieland.

Amongst these different models and determinations at work in *Agathon* there is a further one, of a different sort, which we have not yet explicitly mentioned: autobiography. For Friedrich Sengle, the author of the authoritative literary biography of Wieland, it is the autobiographical element that distinguishes the novel from all its models, and which explains Wieland's concern with the individual.[22]

Wolfgang Paulsen has devoted a monograph to the psychological aspects of Wieland's work, and especially *Agathon*. In it, he says that the work is an autobiographical account which has been modified into an analogy or paradigm, even into a sort of parable.[23] In treating the topic of 'Schwärmerei', Wieland is writing the narrative of the overcoming of his own 'seraphic' past. Paradoxically, this is an autobiographical move against a discourse itself intimately involved in the stirrings of modern European autobiography as a genre: Christian mysticism and specifically the Pietism of Wieland's own background, and of his first literary excursions.

The autobiographical impulse is less a justification for Wieland's text (we are not presented with writing which explains and justifies itself as a writing about the self) than a disturbance of the other literary precedents at work in the novel. At its most diffuse but also most basic level, one might say that the autobiographical moment of the text is manifest in the very failure of the other authorities (Reason, classical legend, educational theory, psychology, ethics) to cohere perfectly. The public aspects of Agathon's life do not mesh with the private ones, psychological realism eats away at the rational overview, the representation of the individual male is suspended between that of a prince and that of a neurotic.

In an important way (as in the debate between Agathon and Hippias), these are the tensions of subjective life, projections of unresolved dissonances to do with the subject's feeling of self and his feeling of other. This becomes most apparent in the notorious lack of the 'sense of an ending' for the book. The text both strives for closure and insists upon openness. The private self is unbounded, the public self is self-limiting. Each projects an image of its opposite. The end of the book is psychologically convincing but philosophically not so, says Paulsen. Perhaps we can interpret this as meaning that the private self adumbrates an image of closure (access to the authority of Archytas, a patriarchal haven), the public self one of openness (the explicit theme of unsolved philosophical questions as they are refracted in the mind of Agathon; the resistance to a facile resolution of the sexual theme in union with Danae). The two remain antagonistic within the literary schemata employed here by the author, although philosophically they would be susceptible of reconciliation in the views of the mature Wieland: 'philosophy for him was not bound to systems, but lived life (gelebtes Leben), a permanent process of thought, to be entered at any point that made sense, a free and liberating play with every possible intellectual position'.[24]

In *Agathon*, Wieland thus plays out his relation with the self by means of a series of relations with existing models and determinants. As Sengle intimates, in the refraction of autobiographical material lies the mutation from one sort of literature to another. As we saw, the prominently 'public' tone of the novel, although it seems to appeal to a defined reading public, was historically much less commensurate, in its specific mingling of elements, with contemporary literary expectations in Germany than one might assume;[25] but it did appear ground-breaking to Lessing, the cultural champion of the middle class, and it served as the basis for the first German theory of the novel.[26] The conventional biographical judgement, that in the period of the creation of *Agathon* Wieland the 'Schriftsteller' (author) became Wieland the 'Dichter' (poet), confirms this sense of a shift of type. Similarly Kurt Wölfel: 'Here we see with perfect clarity the new modern manner of creating a world. The world is no longer communicated in its objectivity, but reflected in the medium of subjectivity.'[27] It is precisely this modern complex seeing which, as Lange argued, lifts the figure of the 'Schwärmer' out of the ranks of stock eighteenth-century literary characters – the actor, the nobleman, the endangered innocent – and makes it into the proper focus for the refraction of inner and outer, the commingling of subjective and objective experience.

The particular effects of autobiography within the economy of *Agathon* are different from those of the *Lehrjahre*, in which the autobiographical elements are 'aufgehoben' into a higher discourse. They inevitably bear upon the crucial relation between narrator and protagonist. Whereas the magisterial narrator and the fallible hero in the *Lehrjahre* together constitute a powerful masculine aesthetic authority, the narrator and the protagonist of *Agathon* are not similarly unassailable. Their relationship is touched by structures of authority of an older kind, such that, for instance, the narrator discourses in a tone of assured urbane irony, and the protagonist has all the external qualities of a classical hero. But Agathon's crises in relation to all types of authority, from the realm of 'Virtue' to the contrasting political forms of Athens and Syracuse, threaten to spill over into the assured space of the narrator, and thus of course into that of the author himself.

There are, however, ways in which Wieland's novel approaches the aesthetic solution of Goethe. We have touched upon one of them already: that transition or mutation noted above from one form of literature to another, from 'Schriftsteller' to 'Dichter'.

Paradoxically, the very philosophical and moral irresolution of *Geschichte des Agathon* fits it well for inclusion in the canon of 'literature' in the middle-class sense, for which a certain authentic opacity is an important criterion. With the storm and stress of the 1770s, 'literature' becomes the site of the irreducibly specific and personal. In retrospect, *Agathon* can be read as a precursor to this autobiographical culture.

Readers today will often refer to its unresolved complexity as its strong point. 'Agathon raises many questions. Its fascination lies in its uncertainty of answer', writes Elizabeth Boa in her Biberach Prize Essay on Wieland, in a representative modern evaluation.[28] Michael Beddow incorporates this sort of judgement into an evaluative argument about the *Bildungsroman* as a genre, seeing it as a 'philosophical' novel distinct from the mainstream realism by which the novel is usually recognised, and in relation to which the German novel is judged, but unjustly, to be inferior. In respect of *Agathon*

> Wieland tries to focus upon the central philosophical problem of his age [the nature of Man] and display its resistance to discursive resolution. He then embarks on an attempt, using the ability of prose fiction to unite in a single representation mimesis of empirical reality and rendering of human inwardness, to take the philosophical issue further towards resolution than philosophical discourse proper had been able to manage.[29]

Although Beddow goes on to argue that this attempt is a failure, his characterisation of *Agathon*, and of the whole *Bildungsroman*, as a place where philosophical irresolution can be animated by mimetic representation conveys well the historical construction of literature as distinct from – in some ways more than – philosophy. This is a literature with its own, specific, form of aesthetic authority, rooted solely neither in philosophy nor in literary precedent, but beyond those things in its access to empirical reality. This literature is predominantly a novelistic one, because the novel is the genre most conducive to the mixing of registers. And for all Agathon's evident irresolution, and in a sense because of it, in Wieland's text the representation of masculine subjective partialness ('human inwardness') has found an aesthetic medium, even if it is not yet the fully fledged aesthetic authority of the *Lehrjahre.*

There is one episode in *Geschichte des Agathon* which brings out particularly distinctly a shift in the relationship between the conception of art and that of authority. Although hardly a conspicuous element of the plot, the specific configuration it involves is an extremely fruitful one in this context: it is the recognition and reunion scene between our hero and his father, Stratonicus (Book 7, Chapter 5). The chance encounter, a topos if ever there was one of the 'Abenteuerroman' (novel of adventure), is handled in such a way as to imbue it with extra significance. The recognition comes to gradual fruition in an atmosphere of expectancy. First there has been a sense of empathy. The stranger then takes Agathon to his house ('which by its dimensions, style of architecture, and magnificence, bespoke the wealth and taste of its owner', p. 587), where there is a superb art collection. An (unspecified) reading from the *Odyssey* before the recognition produces in the reader associations of long-distant travellers returning, and, especially if one remembers *Télémaque*, of the significance of the father–son relationship. A cultured conversation between connoisseurs ('im Ton der Kenner', p. 587) further bonds the two characters. In this scene it is hard not to feel an anticipation of that persistent link between father figures and art which (as we saw) is pivotal in the *Lehrjahre*, and (as we shall see) structurally determines in one way or another *Heinrich von Ofterdingen*, *Der grüne Heinrich* and *Der Nachsommer*. The specific mixture which strikes such a deep and echoing chord involves, first, the question of paternal succession, of a continuity which is greater than, yet still includes the 'problematic' individual male; secondly, an authoritative discourse upon, and ownership of, art; and thirdly, a profound sense of great affective moment, a coming to the surface of deep levels of the personality. Thus are combined the courtly construction of art, its visible authority, held both in ownership and appreciation, and the deeply personal in the form of the discovery of one's own origin and place.

This profound interfusion of art and personality is further deepened by the portrait of Agathon's mother, Musarion. It is the most significant work of art in the scene, not merely because it serves as an occasion for Agathon to demonstrate his mastery of 'der Ton der Kenner' – of the public, representative aspect of art – but also because it reveals something intimate and fundamental about the individuals who meet within its aura, namely, of course, their relation as father and son (the family likeness facilitates the recognition), the very identity of the young prodigal. The painting hangs in a room apart, and when Agathon's attention is finally called to it, it inspires a state in him which cannot be articulated 'im Ton der Kenner', but entails the use on Wieland's part of 'inexpressibility topoi' (p. 590). Art at its most potent level thus is more than the sign of a cultivated milieu, and more than a sign that Agathon is heir to the public authority a fine art collection connotes: it is connected with and actualises the expression of the deepest levels of the personality, to the point where it is not even possible to describe the degree of emotional effect it produces.

At the same time, let us not forget that it is the father who owns this painting, and the son who experiences, and is thus equal to, the depth of feeling it gives rise to; and, finally, the painting's significance does not lie in its content, but in its relation to the two men, and more specifically to Agathon himself. This scene anticipates the configuration of the *Lehrjahre*. Art and autobiography join in one authoritative discourse. Its fusion of outward opulence and inner affect combines not only public and private spheres, but public and private cultures as well. The patriarchal succession so clear in *Télémaque*, and discernible too in *Tom Jones*, begins to become an artistic matter, rather than a social or a political one.

It is an aspect of Wieland's novel as a text of transition, however, that this fusion is not characteristic of the novel as a whole, in which, as we saw, art and autobiography tend to get in each other's way, and public and private are ill at ease with one another. Wieland does not convert the configuration into a structuring device for his entire text, as Goethe will do through the motifs of the art collection, the King's sick son, Natalie and the rest. The 'philosophical' plot of the novel is rather explicit about the limitations of art-related matters within the model state: 'the sciences and fine arts were in no very particular estimation among them; neither were they held in contempt. This indifference preserved the Tarentines from the errors and extravagances of the Athenians, among whom every man, down to the tanner and shoemaker, would be a philosopher and an orator, a man of wit and a connoisseur' (p. 833).

There is no room for a universalised and transfigured 'Kennerschaft' of the sort implied by the *Lehrjahre*. Agathon himself only once aspires to be a poet (in respect of Psyche), and although he is a narrator, his discourse is of a frankly autobiographical kind with no pretensions to poetry. Agathon does eventually come into enough of his paternal inheritance to live a virtuous life (p. 808), but this falls short of symbolic significance, possessing rather a pretty clear moral message about materialism, of the sort which would not have been out of place in Fénelon. If there was any historical or cultural pressure on Wieland to elaborate a middle-class artistic ethos, he resisted it consciously. The conscious authorities at work in his text are literary precedent and contemporary rational and empiricist modes of thought.

But there are more similarities with the structure of the *Lehrjahre* than we have yet allowed. The circularity of the novel's structure is striking, and it is a paternal circularity, a return to the father. It is not just that Stratonicus and Archytas of Tarentum are friends, and that this is why Agathon finds his way to his destination at the end of the book. The connection between origin and telos is richer: after the recognition scene between Stratonicus and Agathon, the former explains to Agathon the circumstances of his birth and how he came to be brought up at Delphi. He had been born illegitimate, but as the result of the triumph of natural morality ('enjoyment was never known to be the grave of real affection', p. 592) over a strict adherence to authority and precedent ('Stratonicus' love was too violent to suffer him to obey the command he had received, to think no more of his mistress', p. 592). Further, Stratonicus inherited a farmstead on an island just in time for Musarion to give birth to Agathon there. This is an interesting blend of that which is official, legal, public and that which is unofficial, illegal, private: an inherited estate upon an island under Athenian jurisdiction, but still an island (that is, a place clearly distinct from the mainland); a mistress and not a wife; and an illegitimate child. Agathon's paternal legacy is thus a mixture of passion and morality, which – and here is the significant echo – is formalised in the balance of individual responsibility and state supervision of the Utopia of Tarentum at the end:

[The Tarentines] had a reasonable confidence in those to whom they entrusted the care of the state; but they required that the confidence should be merited. The spirit of industry . . . which inspired this happy and estimable people, made each individual trouble himself less about his neighbour's affairs at Tarentum than is usual in most small cities. Provided they did not incur scandal by any illegal action, or by any behaviour notoriously inconsistent with morality, every man might live as he pleased. (p. 834)

This circularity is not obviously a characteristic of the *Bildungsroman*, although we have seen how it is actually vital within the functioning of the *Lehrjahre* model. We now need to ask how Wieland's particular brand of circularity relates to that of Goethe. Paulsen makes a great deal of the circularity of *Agathon*, although for him this means that it is not really a *Bildungsroman*, whereas for us it rather means it is. Paulsen establishes clearly and repeatedly that Wieland's intention from the very beginning was for Agathon to end where he had begun, and for the father figure Archytas to await him there. He argues persuasively that this circularity, like so much in the novel, derives from prevalent literary models, in this case the baroque novel.[30] His main point, however, is to show how the conventional precedent-inspired topoi are over-determined by psychological (autobiographical) material. He puts it most succinctly thus: '[Wieland's] special achievement consists not in the radical demolition of such schemata, but in bringing them to life from within.'[31]

The animation of empty forms was also Stratonicus' gift, and the virtue of Tarentum. This connection adds a thematic – perhaps one can already say a symbolic – resonance to the brute inherited formal fact of structural circularity. It is as though the autobiographical dilemma of Wieland himself – which could be summarised as the representation of self-education in inherited forms – is being employed as an ornament to bestow form upon a text which, under pressure from that very dilemma, is resisting formal and thematic closure. To put this another way: in the aesthetic space so strongly indicated in the recognition scene between father and son an authoritative aesthetic of control, symmetry and visible beauty is being replaced by one in which these things are animated and transfigured by personal affect.

Wieland's transitional text demonstrates how what – historically – have become purely ornamental structural patterns of the baroque novel are, as it were, invaded by sense. Ornamental pattern now tends towards significant symbolism: formal regularity begins to say, in an inscrutable way, something about the deepest personal truths of author and reader. The same sort of point can be made about the use of the Greek setting: it is at once a fancy-dress game, a mannered rococo courtly discourse, and a symbolic setting for an exposition of human nature. Paulsen is concerned with Wieland's specific individual contribution to a body of writing which looked almost plagiaristic to the Romantics. But the point we are making here is less an individual one about Wieland himself than a general one about the place of *Agathon* in an artistic and literary development which includes the *Lehrjahre*. Paulsen's formula: the baroque (standing for any pre-existing redundant formalism) over-determined by the psychological, is a formula for the new aesthetic practice which is fully realised in the *Lehrjahre*. That it is not fully realised here is evident in the disparity between the dominant circularity of structure and the unresolved *thematic* question of Agathon's inner life. But that very disparity, and the semantic hesitation between formal pattern and compelling symbolism enjoyed by certain motifs, is itself an adumbration of what will become aesthetic fact in the Goethean text.

It is, then, the very fact that the reunion scene between father and son offers a glimpse (but no more than that) of higher coherence in and beyond the vicissitudes of Agathon's experience which gives the moment its special effectiveness – or, to push the point home, its authority. This implication of profundity is characteristic of the new aesthetic authority, such as it will be fully realised in the *Lehrjahre*, forswearing as it does all explicit or visible forms of self-legitimation, of the kinds Wieland is still consciously seeking and upon which he is dependent. The recognition scene is all the more a prefiguration of the *Lehrjahre* because the image of the mother is centrally involved. The presence of Musarion in a painting signals not only the sphere of art but also that of eros. She was the mistress of Stratonicus, but is preserved in the bloom of desirable youth and presented to her son for the first time held in the gaze of a desiring lover. The conscious symbolism of the 'kranker Königssohn' is anticipated. The deep erotic resonance goes beyond the conventional and superficial erotic tone of many of the passages of the book.

This alternation between a conventional and a profound construction of the erotic plays its part in the other major circularity of the book, the return at the end of the two great loves of Agathon's life, Psyche and Danae. These motifs add to the reader's impression that formally, if not philosophically, the book ends in closure. That this circularity should combine the deepest personal stirrings with the motif of incest is interesting in our context, but the figure of Danae seems more immediately accessible to interpretation than that of Psyche, and may thus be better addressed first. Danae is the courtesan who turns into a human being, thereby enacting for her part the transition that is taking place on the stylistic level in the text as a whole, 'die Belebung von innen her' of stereotypes. Her significance for Agathon is immense, since she conducts him from his idealistic world into the real one through the medium of sexuality. Sexuality ceases to be the subject of a series of rococo topoi and becomes the medium in which feelings and reality unite. Importantly too, it is in Danae's company that Agathon becomes an autobiographer.

The thematic and structural circumstance that, although Danae and Agathon meet again at the end, they do not marry, places this weight of significance into a complex context. Although important, sexuality may not be allowed to associate itself so directly with formal perfection as to appear to be a component in the final resolution of the questions raised by the novel. Although not central, sexuality and its benefits (which exceed it, leading Agathon and Danae herself into recognisable development as moral beings) are nevertheless so important as to claim representation in the formal closure of the novel. Danae must return, but Agathon and Danae may not be united.

However, this solution promotes the significance of the erotic in a less obvious but more pervasive way. Neither Fielding nor Goethe suffers the same compunction about ending his novel in marriage. For the former the existing social form of the novel (which conventionally ends in marriage) was strong enough to bear any weight he wished to place upon it. For Goethe, the translation of novelistic devices from the trivial into the symbolic had become (in a precise sense of the term) an art form. Wieland, by not allowing Agathon and Danae to marry at the end, is refusing to devalue the real significance of their relation by permiting it to end in the banal motif of marriage. Whatever Danae and the theme of eroticism imply exceeds what the organisation of the text can contain. There is, one might say, a surplus of 'Erlebnis' (experience) over 'Dichtung' (poetry).

This brings us back to Psyche. Psyche is a more stable formal device than Danae: prominent at the beginning, she functions throughout as the measure of Agathon's 'Schwärmerei', and reappears in a specific role at the end. Through her Wieland is able to modulate his representation of Agathon's intimations, showing their platonic intensity and their proximity to eros (Danae seduces Agathon by impersonating Psyche in a dance), and finally relativising them by revealing Psyche's identity as Agathon's sister. In this thematic/structural pattern the representation of subjectivity and the erotic is controlled. As at the end of Lessing's didactic drama *Nathan der Weise*, sexual desire is transformed into a family relationship symbolising the family of Man. Thus the excess of meaning associated with the unresolved theme of Danae is drained off into a conventional formal pattern, and given a moral meaning. The 'red light' of incest is turned off before the reader has a chance to see it, and the danger is only ever realised from the point at which it has already been avoided.

Wieland's art or artifice thus has two devices by means of which it contains Agathon's erotic subjectivity into a circularity which encloses it within the aesthetic ambit of the baroque and the Enlightenment. The motif of Danae offers a human fulfilment which is denied the formal novelistic consummation of marriage. That of Psyche touches upon the transgressive intimations of incest as well as other related intimations of wholeness and fulfilment associated with androgyny (she first appears disguised as a man), anticipating motifs in the *Lehrjahre*, *Die Epigonen* and *Heinrich von Ofterdingen* only to deny them in the formal resolution of the conventional topos of the revelation of family relatedness. What is given thematically is taken away formally, either by addition or subtraction. This is to say that the subjective sexual content is not really aesthetically mastered by the novel's formal circularity. They are in opposition to each other, but also, by association, enriched by one another, in such a way as to adumbrate a combination of sex and form pointing towards the *Lehrjahre*.

ANTON REISER

Agathon provided a focus for a discussion of what is meant in the present argument by the word 'authority'. Moritz's *Anton Reiser* (first three volumes 1785–1786, final volume 1790) provides a focus for a treatment of what is referred to here as 'subjectivity'. 'Subjectivity' is the central concern of German idealist philosophy from Kant onwards, as well as being, in ordinary usage, a notoriously imprecise term. What we are dealing with here, however, is the literary representation of subjectivity. I argued above that in *Geschichte des Agathon* subjectivity found representation as a disturbance of systems of authority. In Moritz's 'psychologischer Roman' ('psychological novel', as the subtitle has it), it appears unredeemed by the gracious urbanity of classical European literature. It appears here as a radical, existential partialness, indivisible from, and perpetually problematic in, human experience.

The novel is an autobiography written in the third person. It is divided into four parts, each of which is prefaced by a generalising comment. Apart from these comments the work concentrates upon the experiences of the hero/sufferer of the title, and in this concentration achieves a degree of psychological penetration which makes the text deeply compelling to modern readers. The first Book deals with Anton Reiser's family background and early experiences, for instance as child employee of a hatmaker. The second and third Books recount the vicissitudes of his education and the development of his interest in writing and rhetoric. The final Book focuses upon his misguided attempt to become an actor, and includes an essay 'Die Leiden der Poesie' ('The Sufferings of Poetry'), which also appeared independently under the title 'Warnung an junge Dichter' ('Warning to Young Poets'). This essay makes explicit the moral implications of the book's treatment of

Anton Reiser's literary and theatrical aspirations. The work ends quite inconclusively, with the protagonist failing to realise his ambitions as an actor and without any prospect of a career or even a livelihood.

From Moritz's life, and indeed from the text itself, it is not hard to reconstruct the intentions behind the writing of *Anton Reiser*.[32] Moritz was prominently interested in empirical psychological research and edited the first psychological journal in German, the *Magazin für Erfahrungsseelenkunde*, in which excerpts from the novel appeared. It draws on his own life for material and strives, in its constitution as a novel, to make sense of this life experience. The 'assumption that experience contains its own redemptive coherence is the idea on which *Anton Reiser* is based';[33] and this assumption characterises the Berlin Enlightenment ethos within which Moritz worked to redeem his own early experiences. The novel is autobiography for the sake of science, and this results in an unfamiliar effect of realism. This realism confers literary definition upon subjectivity as a partial and anguished state, '[ein Sammelplatz] schwarzer Gedanken . . . die er durch keine Philosophie verdrängen konnte' ('a point at which black thoughts collect, thoughts which no philosophy could help him to drive away').[34]

It is not that what Moritz experienced was remarkable (although maybe it was); what is remarkable is that it became visible as a problem with such force and clarity. An example: the eight-year-old Anton Reiser is about to have an infected foot amputated. In the first sign of sympathy ever shown towards his son, Anton Reiser's father gives the child tuppence (p. 17). Moritz's psychological interest is in the effect of environment and early experience upon the development of the mind, and thus he records this incident because, as an almost unique sign of parental affection, it made a deep impression upon him and has remained with him ever since. What the reader experiences, however, within the discourse opened by the semi-fictional novel, is the self-consciousness of individual 'Zerstückbarkeit' (vulnerability to dismemberment), an experience thematised explicitly later in the novel when Anton Reiser witnesses the beheading and breaking on the wheel of four criminals outside Hanover (p. 262). The derisory and grotesque compensation offered by his father conveys a discontinuity between subjective concerns and the responses the world at large has to offer them. Experiences are wounds in *Anton Reiser*: to experience is to be continuously opened by the world, and Moritz's text contrives to represent this state of affairs.

The effect of this view surpasses that of a scientific demonstration, even if that is what, in a sense, *Anton Reiser* is meant to be. We are dealing with a discourse which depends upon openness, since this experiential openness is what the scientific project is interested in. But scientific discourse on its own, notwithstanding the Enlightenment optimism of Moritz himself, does not supply a justification of the suffering it examines: it does not offer that completeness which could redeem the openness it reveals.

Passing comment upon the literary and philosophical value of *Geschichte des Agathon*, Sengle had spoken of 'die Wahrheit des Fragments' ('the truth of the fragment'). In a more fundamental and thoroughgoing way *Anton Reiser* makes a claim for this sort of truth. It ends most abruptly at a point where the protagonist's plans are (yet again) rudely and completely dashed. It is the concentration upon the unredeemed partialness of psychological reality that produces the representation of subjectivity. It would not have occurred to Wieland, for instance, to describe his own suffering at school in the way Moritz describes his.[35] Realism here has the effect Kafka's writing will later have in breaking with realism. Kafka's father was, presumably, no more atypical for his time than Moritz's. Kafka senior enjoyed absolute patriarchal dominance of his home like all bourgeois fathers; Moritz's was little affectively involved with his children or, presumably, with the whole concept of childhood in the way his society was not and ours has become. Both authors, however, achieve representations of paternal attitudes which in themselves, and specifically in the way they reveal subjectivity as an anguished relation to authority, make the ordinary significant.

Like Wieland's pioneering novel, Moritz's extraordinary text was not without literary precedent. Behind both stands, for instance, the separatist introspection of seventeenth- and eighteenth-century German Protestantism. This is the common source for that subjectivity which finds its representation, in different ways, in the two works. Both texts demonstrate how subjectivity had a developed presence and language in contemporary consciousness because of the religious practices which fostered it, but how it then became a problem in secular contexts.

This common background notwithstanding, the attitude to 'authority' embodied in the two works is different. Within Moritz's narrative, positions of authority are unstable. The text begins with a particularly effective, because deadpan and scientific, attack upon the spiritual claims of Quietism and the 'Schwärmerei' of Madame Guyon. The book thus opens with a destructive move against both religion and paternal authority, since Anton Reiser's father is an adherent of Madame Guyon. 'Schwärmerei' is here used in the orginal, pre-Shaftesbury, religious sense, as it almost always is in the novel. But the importance of the word, and its negative connotation, in Moritz as well as Wieland, is not a coincidence. The genealogy of the word 'Schwärmer' reveals, rather, the religious ancestry of the problem of subjectivity in these two texts.

What emerges for the modern reader from this attack upon positions of authority is not some programme for their replacement, but a sense of the damage they inflict upon Anton's psychological development. A memorable example of this occurs when Anton meets the awful Brunswick hatmaker Lobenstein, to whose care he is to be entrusted in his early teens. Lobenstein is also a 'Schwärmer' and co-religionist of Anton's father, and thus the attack upon religious and paternal authority is taken further in his portrayal. In proto-Proustian manner, Moritz records the effect of words, sounds and names upon the imagination. The actual encounter with the real person whose image has been lovingly constructed in the mind of the twelve-year-old conveys the violent assault of experience upon the space of subjectivity. Where the imagination had projected a friend and benefactor, there is only the naked face of authority, of a 'Herr und Meister', by whose cold and earnest expression all the love Anton Reiser's imagination had conceived is extinguished like a flame upon which water has been poured, as he realises that he is to be nothing more than an apprentice to this cruel man (p. 57).

The simile ('als wenn Wasser auf einen Funken geschüttet

wäre'), involving the destructive combination of different elements, expresses the mis-relation between subject and object, the reality of subjectivity as the experience of reversal and the partialness of its own projections.

In *Anton Reiser* authority is often figured as arbitrary. There is, for instance, the shadowy presence of the prince, who stands at the margin of the action, subsidising Anton's basic education from a point whence complete but arbitrary power emanates, and profoundly affects Anton's life and the reader's perception of the real space in which it is being lived. Instead of the echoes of courtly culture we receive through the shape and tone of Wieland's novel, we are presented here with a real prince, which simply means the real and unquestioned power to fulfil or deny the aspirations of an individual subject – in both meanings of the word.

More pointedly, there is the instability of Anton's relationship with his father. When Anton, asserting himself for once, gives voice to his deeply felt bitterness and dissatisfaction at the conditions in which he is being forced to live, his father places his curse upon him (p. 257). Later, at the same symbolically charged spot before the city gates, his father bestows his blessing upon him (p. 356). This parallel, to which the text draws attention by having Anton note it, seems emblematic of the constitutional homelessness of the subject, as it is represented in *Anton Reiser*. 'How desolate, how sad everything about me is. And I must roam abroad, forlorn and lonely, no comfort, no guide!' (p. 272), as Anton himself puts it (in the sentimental idiom of the day) at one point, lamenting especially his lack of authentic authority. This is, of course, in strong contrast to the homeward-tending and patriarchal structure of *Agathon* and the *Lehrjahre*.

Another point of contrast and comparison with *Agathon*, which adds to our general theme, concerns the figure of the melancholic. It has been pointed out that the hero of the *Bildungsroman* is not as distant from the earlier conception of the melancholic, the torpor-ridden introspective type, as the constitutionally optimistic *Bildungsroman* might like to admit.[36] It is no coincidence that Hamlet is so vital a reference in *Wilhelm Meisters Lehrjahre*: there is a kinship, as we saw, between the two figures, the exemplary individual and the problematic loner, which Goethe's text establishes in order to relativise it. Somewhat like the image of the 'Schwärmer' (to which it is related), the image of the melancholic once provided the literary possibility of exploring subjective aspects of experience, without centralising that sort of experience in such a way as to make it appropriate to speak of a predominantly subjective culture. The figure of Hamlet himself represents a step towards such a culture, and the definition of melancholy given by Diderot in the *Encyclopédie*[37] also suggests how this emblem of human introspection experiences a shift from a negative to a positive, almost a representative, function. For Diderot melancholy, while being 'le sentiment habituel de notre imperfection' ('the habitual sense of our imperfection'), was also a beneficial state of introspection which increased fruitful self-consciousness: subjectivity, recognised as a sense of partialness, is also an important attribute of humanity. This is exactly the double definition of subjectivity offered by the *Lehrjahre*, as we have seen (and it is why Hamlet has his role to play). Now, Anton Reiser's melancholy is a basic theme of the novel. Moritz's case is reminiscent of that of Wieland in relation to 'Schwärmerei', because here melancholy is removed from its place within an established system of authoritative literary meanings (deriving ultimately from the ancient doctrine of the humours) and relocated in a realistic autobiographical space: a relocation which has the effect, as with the 'Schwärmer', of displacing the authoritative system, whilst developing its terms, by a representation of subjectivity.

Insofar as it is a scientifically inspired work, Moritz's psychological study is the child of the Berlin Enlightenment, but it has literary forebears too. These, however, are significantly distinct from those of Wieland. Moritz's novel takes advantage of the contemporary fashion for psychological prose works like *Agathon* and *Werther* for its official definition,[38] but emerges from a socially much humbler tradition than Wieland's work, in which the historical subjective experience of Pietism is mediated through the schools of Zürich, Warthausen and Weimar. Moritz's autobiographical enterprise is dependent upon the manifold religious (and progressively secular) autobiographical and diary forms of the time, which Günter Niggl characterises in his study of eighteenth-century German autobiography;[39] but precisely by virtue of its scientific rationale, it is bound to exceed the traditional forms it employs, since, although they are all certainly autobiographical, they are also embedded either in a religious context or in some other publicly defined role (such as self-justification; this is true even of Rousseau) and not in a radically individualistic position, as is Moritz in his scientific commitment to himself.[40] Subjectivity is here inscribed in an unprecedented generic openness, 'a mode of self-revelation no longer protected by any formal tradition'.[41]

The question of Moritz's choice of a subtitle for his autobiographical work is nevertheless a vexed one. It describes the work as 'Roman' (novel), while in the preface to the second Book it is called a 'Biographie' (biography) but it is never explicitly termed an autobiography. There may have been several reasons for this. Moritz may have simply wished to increase the objectivity of his scientific and moral demonstration;[42] or he may have held back from explicitly associating himself with the intimacy of the revelations he was putting forward (in possibly conscious contrast to Rousseau).[43] The choice of the word 'Roman' is also slightly surprising, since in the pragmatic vocabulary of the eighteenth century 'Roman' signified something unserious, and the word is certainly used in that meaning within the text.[44] The point in this context, however, is not exactly how this representation of subjectivity relates to earlier literary forms, but how literary forms have their part to play in the representation of subjectivity. One of the most striking things about *Anton Reiser* is that it deals critically with the actual effects of literature upon the subjective life ('nun war ihm aber sein Schicksal nicht romanhaft genug', 'but now his fate did not seem novelistic enough to him', p. 431), and we shall have occasion to return to this at some length later. On one level this preoccupation with the theme of literature is a realistic, scientific re-presentation of the Don Quixote theme. In this sense, the use of the term 'Roman' in the subtitle would be meant ironically – Anton lives his life as though it were a novel (or a play), and until he learns not to do so he will remain misguided. As Mark Boulby puts it: 'until Anton becomes mature enough to write his "history", he cannot avoid living out his "novel"'.[45] At another level, however, as Boulby further argues, the figure of the 'Roman', bringing with it connotations of the implacable 'fortuna' of the baroque novel, is a non-ironic indication of the world view embedded in Moritz's own narrative: of a world of chance in which the individual fate is tragic. In the first case, the literary horizon is contained within the subjective-scientific one; in the second, the older literary structure removes the scientific construction of subjectivity from its scientific moorings, while retaining all its anti-literary specificity, thus situating it in a culturally unmarked area. In both cases subjectivity is at the centre of the picture and literary matters are subordinate to it.

Are there any traces, in this picture, of the sort of structures we discerned in the *Lehrjahre* and *Agathon*? If we look, for forms of pattern and closure, to the sources which operate in those texts, we find only incompleteness. This confirms the image of subjectivity as a partial state. With regard to the circularity of inheritance, we have seen how Anton's father is anything but a stable point of reference for Anton, either literally or symbolically. On the other hand, the stirrings of subjective desire, the love of the mother, simply embroil Anton more deeply in a divided state: 'yet it very often seemed to him that his father, whom he simply feared, was more often in the right than his mother, whom he loved' (p. 14). Scientific precision reveals a conflict at the heart of the socialisation process, one not unknown to contemporary political philosophy,[46] which the other texts, with their patterns of circularity, seek to harmonise. It is significant that the circumstances in Anton's unhappy home are much closer, in their realism, to the domestic situation at the beginning of the *Theatralische Sendung* than to those which prevailed in the 'secondary revision' of that material into the form of the *Lehrjahre*, even though those first five books of the later version represent there the 'reality ingredient' in its larger symbolic mixture: the *Lehrjahre* is the aesthetic antidote to the raw partialness of *Anton Reiser*.

With this damming of the working of desire under the sign of scientific realism (that is, a veto on unlikely happy endings), the erotic becomes unavailable as an aesthetic or formal structuring dynamic. If in some ways 'das Romanhafte' characterises Anton's life, as Boulby says, it must also be said that perhaps more importantly, it stands for that which Anton feels his life is not nor ever could be, namely the scene of erotic attraction, attachment, fulfilment. A novel plot, in other words. The reader's attention is attracted to this absence of erotic determination especially by the strange circumstance that the text includes an alter ego for Anton and Moritz, Philipp Reiser, in whose name the fictional hero's and empirical author's names are curiously combined, and onto whom the whole novelistic problematic of erotic experience is displaced: 'In short it seemed to him [Anton] the most nonsensical idea in the world that he could ever be the object of a woman's affection', we read, since that only happens to the heroes of novels and plays, to whom Anton feels himself so inferior, and who highlight his partialness (and the generic partialness of the text) by contrast to the fulness of a novel. At the same time, with an unwelcome persistence, this alter ego does not let Anton forget the presence of such structuring in human affairs, since the accounts of his conquests are themselves very 'romanhaft' in their structure and sequence, and force Anton to confront in real life those aspects which, in novels, he tended to skip (p. 279, see too p. 451).

As befits what I am calling an exemplarily subjective text, the search for a wholeness to counteract the prominently evident partialness of subjectivity is not conducted by means of the kind of circular structures of incest and inheritance which, in the *Lehrjahre* model, knit together psychological and formal dimensions. Here, that search is carried on *within* experience, not as a construction around or upon it. Subjectivity experiences circularity, the figure of the 'Kreis' or 'Zirkel', as a constriction, a clothing of reality which prevents the subject from coming to full consciousness of itself: 'er drehete sich mit seinen Vorstellungen immer in einem engen Zirkel seines Daseins herum' ('his thoughts always turned in a narrow circle of his existence', p. 93); 'Man fühlt sich nach und nach selbst von der Einförmigkeit des Kreises, in welchem man sich umdreht, unwiderstehlich angezogen . . .' ('one feels oneself gradually irresistibly attracted by the uniformity of the circle within which one moves . . .', p. 449). But at the same time there is within the subject a yearning for homecoming, which is part of the reason, for instance, why Anton feels such a strong affection for the *Odyssey* (we are reminded of the reunion scene in *Agathon*): 'for no book suited his condition so well as this very one, which in every line represents the man who has travelled much, seen cities and *mœurs*, and finally returns to his home after many years, to find the same people there whom he had left behind, and had thought never to see again' (p. 388).

The larger circularity of homecoming does not transfigure the smaller one of circumstances on the level of the plot. The resolution of this disparity takes place on the level of the scientific scrutiny of the details of experience, where are found moments at which the partialness of experience, the fragments of his existence – 'das Einzelne, Abgerissene und Zerstückte in seinem Dasein' (p. 449) – gives way to a sense of higher coherence. A special quality of experience is isolated, and in it is located a sense of coherence and meaning otherwise emphatically absent from experience, which is continually decentred and fragmented by incoherent successiveness. The first such incident takes place outside the gates of Brunswick, when Anton grasps the experience of his stay there as a whole (p. 91), and similar experiences recur – often at city gates, at the symbolic meeting point between the two unreconciled circularities of constriction and final homecoming.[47] Towards the end of the book we thus read another instance of a certain type of experience of Anton's while walking upon the city wall of Erfurt, which was responsible for some of 'the happiest moments of his life, at which his own existence began to be of interest to him for the first time, since he saw it now in a certain connection, and not in a series of fragments and moments' (p. 449).

The resolution of subjective partialness thus takes place not on the level of plot, but on that of scientific investigation. There is no actual resolution, only intimations of it. In this, the scientific project and the religious legacy of confessional autobiography converge, but also resist assimilation into each other, since the 'meaning' Anton discovers lacks the definition of religious revelation, and is motivated in the first instance by an interest in different types of subjective experience (wholeness, partialness) and not by what they might correspond to in the objective world (beyond, of course, their objective status as empirical observations). The two forms of motivation hold each other open. On the one hand we have precise scientific observation of the inner life which tends to break down any closed sense of personality, leaving it open to the winds of social and psychological circumstance; on the other, the old Pietistic impulse to re-find the Other in the self: a perpetually laborious task, given the complexity and changeableness of the life of the mind realistically grasped, and made all the more tortuously open-ended by the absence of a spiritual framework.

This battle for coherence in the structure of the text itself can be most clearly grasped in the question of narrative situation. The relation between narrator and protagonist is enigmatic because this is effectively a third-person autobiography. A distance is set up which tends to keep apart the subjective sufferer and the narrating authority, for the scientific Enlightenment reasons I have mentioned before. But it is a precarious authority. Autobiography is always inhabited by a tendency of the narrated 'I' towards the third-person state, a falling away from the immediacy of that self-experience which is the source of autobiography.[48] Although Moritz takes this tendency to its extreme by writing in the third person from the outset, this does not transcend the tension it radicalises. We are still left wondering about the relation between 'I' and 'he', especially in view of the fragmentary breaking off of the narrative at the end. In one sense, the narrator has self-evidently progressed beyond the neurotic self-imprisonment of the unfortunate Anton.[49] This is clear from his overview, and his readiness with moral and scientific perspectives which situate the raw experience of the subject. He seems to be in possession of the sense of wholeness, of a benevolent circularity, which inhabits but also eludes and frustrates Anton. Thus we read in the second preface what sounds almost like Weimar-classical optimism:

Wer auf sein vergangenes Leben aufmerksam wird, der glaubt zuerst oft nichts als Zwecklosigkeit, abgerißne Fäden, Verwirrung, Nacht und Dunkelheit zu sehen; je mehr sich aber sein Blick darauf heftet, desto mehr verschwindet die Dunkelheit, die Zwecklosigkeit verliert sich allmählich, die abgerißnen Fäden knüpfen sich wieder an, das Untereinandergeworfene und Verwirrte ordnet sich – und das Mißtönende löset sich unvermerkt in Harmonie und Wohlklang auf. (p. 122)

He who looks back upon his past life will at first seem to discern nothing but aimlessness, broken threads, confusion, night and darkness; the more the gaze rests upon the past, however, the more the darkness recedes, the aimlessness is dispelled, the broken threads are re-attached, order enters into the confusion and the discordant sounds resolve themselves imperceptibly into harmony and melody.

But the unanswered question of how the character in the book became the character writing it, how the misguided author in the narrative became the guiding one of the narrative, is insistent, even though it is only implicit. The implication of Boulby's treatment, mentioned above, of the two resonances of the word 'Roman' is that the narrator is himself to some extent subject to the vicissitudes of the world in which Anton is entangled.[50] The announcement of eventual harmony just quoted would in this view be the exact equivalent of the moments of clear-sightedness at city gates (but here at the transition point between two books, where experience rounds itself into shape): a single impulse, marked by harmony in itself, but bereft of the privilege or authority to confer that moment of harmony upon the whole. This is certainly the effect of reading the text, in terms of which the expression of harmony seems like a discrete moment of the reality of Enlightenment experience, all but engulfed by the heterogeneity and randomness of the rest of that historical moment and its subjective reality. Empiricism and reason are characteristically in tension.

Another way of defining the precariousness of the equilibrium between narrator and subject would be to see it in the context of other analogous relations within the text which are unstable, and whose instability relates directly to that of subjectivity itself. The text as we have it rests upon the gaze of the narrator, 'the rigorous, diagnostic perspective . . . which prevents any sympathetic collusion with his younger self',[51] 'an effectively controlled division between observer and observed'.[52] The ambiguity of the values of involvement and detachment has, however, been very much a theme of the text itself. They are virtually the terms of the subject's suffering: on the one hand a terrible sense of isolation contrasting with a longing for some sort of collective identity (the recurrent dream of standing in 'Reih und Glied', in the ranks, e.g. pp. 251, 276, 324, 385, 444); on the other an exhilarating sense of detachment (as at the city gates, or in the prefatory remarks at the beginning of books), contrasting with an asphyxiating experience of immersion in facticity. The small circle of ordinary life and the large circle of insight cannot ultimately be squared together. There is a constant pull between belonging and detachment which defines the subject's predicament: social and psychological determinations refuse to coincide (hence belonging socially conflicts with existential immersion in circumstances, while social isolation collides with existential observer status). There is no guidance for us from the text as it is constituted about how this dilemma can be resolved, merely a silence separating narrator and subject too resounding to be obliterated by the accumulation of scientific minutiae.

There is a very clear example of this instability at the end of the book. Anton sets off to join Speich's acting troupe in Leipzig. As he walks he is assailed by the strange thought that he is watching himself and his own destiny, as if that of a stranger, passing in the distance. This is one of those moments of detachment which prefigure that detachment structurally implied by the whole text. If it is an illusion, it is illusion akin to insight and enlightenment. In it, as elsewhere, scientific and religious models of completeness blend together. But it is inevitably displaced by the more vulgar illusion involved in imagining the theatrical roles Anton will perform in Leipzig. Now, clearly, the theatre here, as in the *Lehrjahre*, is a serious mistake. But, as in the *Lehrjahre* (and without that novel's symbolic machinery), it is hard to dismiss the metaphorical force of theatrical roles as the model for all social roles. Anton is repeatedly shown to be acting theatrical roles in his attempts to be effective in the world, indeed he is explicitly shown confusing social and theatrical ones (p. 395).

Although the text relativises this habit in Anton by being explicit about it, it betrays no inkling itself of how else being in society might be figured, indeed it is highly convincing in its representation of social being as intrinsically theatrical. The authorial role implicit in the text's constitution as scientific autobiography is in some respects simply a perfection of the self-realisation in literature it so thoroughly disparages in Anton. On the other hand, any sense of the self as an existential role, a destiny seen from afar and thus whole, must inevitably be curtailed and interrupted by the constricting roles available in reality, which the subject internalises in its negotiation of the circumstances of the world as it finds them. Thus the equilibrium achieved between observation and involvement by the novel's narrative organisation is always potentially precarious.

Anton's desire to play the part of Goethe's tragic hero Clavigo (pp. 356–361) is the dream of an imaginary coincidence of existential and social roles. In this projection the self is both particular, in the sense of detached and 'true to itself', and held in a strong and favourable relation to a collective, in this case the audience, the community of its fame. It is the projection, in other words, of an ideal solution to the suffering of subjective partialness. The pitch of intensity and frustration at which Anton seeks to secure this and other roles is an important gauge of the urgency of the problem of subjectivity to which it appears to be, but is not, a solution. By far the most prominent moves towards a solution of the problem of subjective partialness are in relation to this question of the theatre and the vocation of the artist. The most important point of similarity and contrast is here no longer *Agathon* (for Wieland, as a member of an older generation, art and its attendant variants, forms and institutions were without a semi-religious aura) but the *Lehrjahre*. Clavigo and *Clavigo* in *Anton Reiser* have a structural function similar to that of Hamlet and *Hamlet* in the *Lehrjahre*.

In *Anton Reiser* the relation between subjectivity and art is articulated in two opposed ways. First, as we have just seen, the artistic sphere seems to offer Anton a public dimension, denied him by the other social realities which only constrain him. Second, disapproval of this misguided sense of artistic vocation is the clearest moral reference of the book. We now need to look a little more closely at these two articulations.

Anton's obsession with the theatre grows out of his obsession with reading, which provides an imaginary escape from the world ('Reading suddenly opened up a new world for him', p. 16), and the pulpit, which provides the example of how words can be used to effect in the world. The world of words is at once a world into which the self can be projected with less resistance than is encountered in the world as a whole, and an opportunity to produce the self for the world, to convert this intimate relation into public currency and establish the possibility of exchange. The theatre is preferable to the pulpit because here a monologue becomes a dialogue (pp. 196–197). Writing can transform inner experience into something reciprocal: Anton imagines an exchange of letters with his bosom friend Philipp in which he will record not trivial events, but 'the inner history of his mind' ('die innere Geschichte seines Geistes'), thus establishing authentic dialogue – something so markedly absent from usual social relations – by means of 'a mutual exercise in style' ('eine wechselseitige Übung des Stils', p. 268). When Anton, as quoted above, lamented the lack of a guiding authority, 'no comfort (Stütze), no guide!', he was already, even as he made this complaint, adumbrating a new form of authority – the aesthetic. He overcomes the misery of subjective partialness, of being the butt of jokes and of being the eternal outsider, by representing these things transformed into literature: 'and the pleasure at this lifted him somewhat out of himself and his own woes' ('und die Freude darüber erhob ihn gewissermaßen über sich selbst und seinen eigenen Kummer', p. 272). It is the authority of literary or theatrical discourse which permits the hope that the partial subject will emerge into the public space, and thus become whole in showing 'how deep his feelings were and how powerfully he was able to express, by means of his voice and his gestures, the content of these deep feelings ('wie tief er empfand, was er sagte, und wie mächtig er wieder das durch Stimme und Ausdruck zu sagen imstande wäre, was er so tief empfand', p. 357). It is no wonder that the part of Clavigo represents such a burning ambition for Anton, virtually the meaning of his life ('gleichsam Zweck seines Lebens', p. 359) – and the fact that he is denied it, so profound a disappointment.

This is the point at which Anton's personal predicament and his hopes for overcoming it become historical. His piece for his friend Philipp about his humiliation, referred to in the previous paragraph, ends with a quotation from Klopstock – 'und um uns ward's Elysium' – so that Anton's private despair is transcribed into a public discourse. Anton's great need for an 'outside', for a social persona which does not hopelessly distort his inner experience, unites passionately (with all the passion of narcissism) with the clamorous stirrings of German national culture. It is as though they were made for one another. Not only Klopstock is involved here, but also Mendelssohn and Lessing, whose works on theatre Anton excerpts with enthusiasm (p. 196), and also Shakespeare, specifically *Hamlet*, the reading of which particularly gives Anton a sense of wholeness, and of his place, as a weak and partial subject, within it (p. 267).

Most significant of all is perhaps *Werther*, the text par excellence in which a fractured subjectivity becomes a strong literary text with power and influence in the world. It is interesting that Moritz describes in a letter to Goethe about *Tasso* (similarly a projection of a fractured subjectivity) how that play 'ins Leben eingreift' (meaning that it will be effective as a text in the world), because this offers evidence of how Moritz saw texts as a form of real intervention.[53] So often does Anton read *Werther* that he comes to think that words and ideas in it are his own (p. 295): his own subjectivity literally fuses with the public literary culture of his time.[54]

Moritz relates to Goethe as part to whole. This moment of historical endangerment is the one negotiated with such culturally seminal authority by Goethe. This is a view endorsed by Goethe himself, who, during their time together in Rome, learned about Moritz's fate while the latter lay – with somehow symbolic appropriateness – with a broken arm, and Goethe attended his bedside. Goethe felt that Moritz's fate had many similarities with his own (a perception perhaps more historically determined than objective), and that he was like a younger brother to Goethe, 'damaged and neglected by fate where I have been favoured and preferred'.[55] Moritz was, apparently, notorious for referring to Goethe as 'God',[56] and, again with an inscrutable irony, he has Anton reflect, among a host of other 'romanhafte Ideen' ('novelistic ideas'), whether he might not go to Weimar with the intention of going into service 'with the author of Werther's sufferings' (p. 479). While both writers are profoundly marked by the subjective revolution of the 1770s, one is constructed as its victim, the other as its favoured child. Similarly, their textual reckonings with the historical issue of subjectivity show the marks, respectively, of subjugation and mastery, and are mutually perceived as such. Presumably what Goethe heard at Moritz's bedside bore some relation to what we read in *Anton Reiser*,[57] giving rise to Goethe's characterisation of Moritz as a casualty of the generation, while for Moritz *Werther* was a genuinely artistic representation of the problem and state of subjective partialness. It is, therefore, not a perverse distortion to want to see in the *Lehrjahre* a text with a peculiarly intimate and real relation to *Anton Reiser*: a positive to its negative.

Anton's 'misunderstood inclination towards poetry and acting' (p. 382) is clearly not only the novel's most important single psychological preoccupation, but also its main moral reference point. Although this emphasis is persistent throughout the novel, it is in the Fourth Book, published after Moritz's stay in Rome and his acquaintanceship with Goethe there, that it becomes dominant and conclusive. This Book culminates in a piece entitled 'Die Leiden der Poesie' ('The Sufferings of Poetry') (pp. 474–491), published independently by Moritz in 1792 under the title 'Warnung an junge Dichter' ('Warning to Young Poets'). Here, clarity is achieved about what was wrong with the subject of the case study: scientific, moral and aesthetic criteria find consonance. For empirical reasons with which the text has provided us in detail, Anton has been confronted with a feeling of his own worthlessness. He has compensated for this by recourse to the lures of the poetic and the theatrical. His mistake can be measured, made sense of, by explaining how far his own subjective efforts have deviated from the nature and quality of creative activity of a sort to provide him with a claim to the status of a real artist. He has wanted to be an artist, rather than actually been one: it is the role of the artist which has attracted him – a role which, as we saw, encourages the mistaken hope that the subject can externalise its intensity and passions, thus translating them into social coin, recognised and exchangeable in the world of real social relations. But the real artist is unconcerned with effect; his creation both arises spontaneously within himself and is in accord with the objective world. These are ideas which are explored elsewhere in Moritz's aesthetic theory, as we shall see presently. What Anton has done is to functionalise the artistic in his genuine and pardonable need for an 'outside', for a role in society. Significantly, the last role he yearns to play is that of a poet – Reimreich – in the (now forgotten) play *Die Poeten nach der Mode*. Equally significantly his appearance, his 'outside', suffers a terrible blow at precisely the same juncture: he begins to lose his hair (pp. 485, 487). Anton's neglected appearance has been an indication throughout the book of his all-too-visible otherness, his naked subjectivity in a world indifferent to the contours of inwardness. The loss of his hair seems to be a concentrated expression of this distance and a symbolic confirmation of the misguidedness of his attempts to gain control of his position and possibilities in the world. The section 'Die Leiden der Poesie' thus recapitulates the empirical exposition of an unhappy individual development, brings out its major pathological symptom, situates this whole case morally by offering itself as a warning, and simultaneously contains an aesthetic corrective to the misguided ideas about art which form the central part of the pathological profile.

This double articulation of the relation between subjectivity and art is one of the major reasons why the text appears incomplete. Like the *Lehrjahre*, but in a much more jagged way, it is about somebody whose main characteristic is that he thinks he is an artist but is not. Instead of the symbolic finale of the *Lehrjahre* and the whole aesthetic construction which regulates the relation between art and subjectivity in that novel, we leave Anton as unaccommodated as before: the troupe he has hopefully trailed to Leipzig has disbanded and dispersed, and this brutal reversal, one of a series of such reversals which have characterised his dealings with the world throughout, is the dominant note upon which the novel, as we have it, ends.

Although the novel's major forms of self-legitimation are scientific and moral, both these forms are concerned with the discernment of pattern in apparently random material, and the fact that the results of these efforts are incorporated in a novel makes this investment in significant form, whatever else it may be, an artistic matter.[58] There is a divergence between what Moritz was willing to accord the status of art, and what our contemporary taste and sensibility will want to talk about in those terms. Hence Boulby, for instance, reminds us that Moritz would have denied that his novel was a work of art,[59] but then goes on to argue for the skill and artistry with which *Anton Reiser*, 'a great work of art', is actually composed.[60] Moritz's poetic practice is more modern than his aesthetic theory.[61] There is the curious contrast between the predominantly negative representation of art and associated matters within *Anton Reiser*, and its undoubted status as a distinguished precursor to the realistic novel, the major literary art form of the following century. Indeed, it is on this point of realism that the novel tends to define itself in contradistinction to Anton's own efforts, the main failing of which is that they take no account of the details of real life, of 'der Reiz des Wirklichen' (p. 483; see too e.g. 299, 475, 477–478). Notwithstanding that realism in the 1780s was a scientific rather than a literary value,[62] the implication of this repeated emphasis is that Moritz might have been being somewhat coy, or might himself have been uncertain, about the artistic status or otherwise of his own production. Indeed one enters precisely this area of ambivalence when Moritz, at the end of his essay on *Werther* (for him a touchstone of genuine art), says, at the time when he was composing Book Four of his own work, that to write such a work without first having experienced the circumstances depicted therein would be as inauthentic as trying to make a novel about an unremarkable life. ('Wer eine solche Darstellung versucht, ohne daß ein solcher Zustand vorhergegangen ist, der muß eben so unwahr werden, wie einer, der bey ganz gemeinen und gewöhnlichen Schicksalen, dennoch einen Roman von seinem Leben erzählen wollte.')[63]

Anton Reiser, half cautionary tale, half confession, seems to be the product of an historical moment of hesitation. Forces are at work within it which will achieve reconciliation in the *Lehrjahre*, but which cannot be reconciled in terms of the categories upon which Moritz is depending. As modern readers we are not willing to let go of Anton's subjective artistic passion simply because a moralising voice 'warns' us about the dangers, and anyway the moral corrective pales before the intensity of the representation of subjective partialness. The Fourth Book gives us the sense that Moritz is putting up powerful resistance, with the historically available moral and scientific categories, to something unresolved. Freud has taught us to suspect that the emphasis and control employed to correct an urge or direction may derive its energy from that urge or direction. Moritz's investment in correcting his own unhappy experiences of the poetic and the theatrical must surely carry within it some of the ardour which informed his fascination with them in the first place.

In 'Die Leiden der Poesie', Anton wrestles with his creation epic. The text documents the expectation that pattern and form will emerge from the chaos of subjective experience (p. 482). This expectation is common to the immersed subject and the detached observer, as we see from this passage, already quoted once:

> He who looks back upon his past life will at first seem to discern nothing but aimlessness, broken threads, confusion, night and darkness; the more the gaze rests upon the past, however, the more the darkness recedes, the aimlessness is dispelled, the broken threads are re-attached, order enters into the confusion and the discordant sounds resolve themselves imperceptibly into harmony and melody. (p. 122)

This expectation is what unites them. But it is not fulfilled within or by the text. As a psychological condition it is a past state of unfulfilment; as a theoretical project its fulfilment lies beyond the text. It animates the text, however, as the promise of unified autobiography, that is to say that state in which detached observer and immersed subject can be held together within one stable discourse, and of aesthetic completeness in which the various incompatible categories of explanation find a common home and harmonious legitimation. It is the hope, in short, of 'Der Roman eines Lebens' (novel of a life), to use the phrase Moritz himself employed in his *Werther* essay. What is gestating in this text is the concept of the individual life in its self-consciousness as a work of art: that union between the particular and the universal, between subject and object, which finds its historical deposit in the discourse of the aesthetic.

Moritz himself had much to say about the aesthetic. *Über die bildende Nachahmung des Schönen* (On the Creative Imitation of the Beautiful, 1788), his major work of aesthetic theory, posits the artist and the work of art as an autonomous unit within nature, a 'Werden', or process of becoming which, while discrete, nevertheless carries in itself something of the autotelic totality of creation itself.[64] The relation between artist and work of art is one of mutual self-fulfilment: the highest aesthetic pleasure is that necessarily involved in a creation in and of creation as a whole. This is the manifestation of an active principle of re-presentation in which nature, as it were, indulges in a secondary process of self-realisation through the hands, eyes and mind of the artist. The aesthetic is a closed circuit of creative energy which non-artists can appreciate only from outside.[65]

The distinction between artists and non-artists is crucial to the argument of Moritz's essay, and regularises his autobiographical perception of 'the dangers of poetry' as they are represented in *Anton Reiser*. The artist is informed by a principle of activity and creativity (Tatkraft, Bildungskraft), whereas the non-artist may gain access to artistic phenomena by virtue of a certain faculty of receptiveness (Empfindungsvermögen). The autobiographical element of the treatise emerges most clearly in the emphasis Moritz places upon the dangers that can arise for the non-artist from exposure to and involvement with art. The faculty of receptiveness can occasion the ambition on the part of the non-artist to emulate the activity of the artist, to share the unique pleasure of creation. This is to copy a copy, rather than to copy creatively ('bildende Nachahmung') according to and within nature's plan, and thus it is doomed to inauthenticity. The form of 'authority' problematicised in Wieland's text is thus here simply invalidated: imitation of a model is never artistic because it introduces an heterogeneous element into the closed, the autonomous circuit of the work of art and its originator. (Greek art is the exception, where one eternal 'style' obviates the need for originality. Michelangelo and Shakespeare are modern artists in whom idiosyncrasy aspires to eternal value, thus defining the creative artist of modern times.)[66] But there is a whole new problem now, because the greater one's capacity for receptiveness, the greater the danger – here is the autobiographical pathos – that one will mistake oneself for an artist.[67]

Finally, the essay turns to a conclusive reconciliation between subjective partialness and the fulness of creation, in a language which recalls the mystical influences of Moritz's youth. Art becomes the medium through which such existential partialness – the lot of everyone – can become transparent upon the great circle in which individual experience takes on universal significance, and can become conscious of this affiliation.[68] In beauty, the partial subject catches a glimpse of itself *sub specie aeternitatis*.[69]

Moritz's main aesthetic argument, then, is particularly concerned with formulating, in relation to the concept of beauty, notions of wholeness and self-identity which offer an obvious counterpart to the overpoweringly convincing representation of subjective partialness in his great autobiography. If that work documents the failure of a whole range of forms of authority, the essay seeks to establish beyond any doubt a new form – that of the aesthetic. Of course, as Martin L. Davies says, 'the aesthetic dimension fails [Anton Reiser] badly'[70] too, and we have looked at this failure in detail. But, as we have also argued, the very prominence of the artistic fiasco of the young Moritz signals the urgency of the question of art, an urgency which manifests itself again in Moritz's aesthetic theorising. It may well be an over-simplification to see the aesthetic theory as merely a 'compensatory edifice' for its author's own shortcomings,[71] but it is generally agreed that the aesthetic theory does indeed develop the autobiographical issues on another plane.[72]

Moritz's theory is at all events most certainly not only of personal interest. Largely through his close contact with Goethe in Rome, and to an extent afterwards, Moritz played a real part in the formulation of Goethe's and Schiller's aesthetic ideas. His distinction between the artist and the non-artist, for all its painful, self-punishing origins, was seminal in what was to become the important debate about dilettantism.[73] Furthermore, Moritz's essay, in its particular modulation of the tradition of aesthetic thought from Shaftesbury to Kant, was a decisive contribution to the idea of the autonomy of art.[74] He was thus crucially instrumental in the formation of the form of aesthetic authority upon which the *Lehrjahre* rests.

The difference between Moritz's work and the *Lehrjahre* is that for him, the novel and an ideal of beauty, an aesthetic discourse, are yet distinct, while in Goethe's novel they are superimposed. Goethe's aesthetic revision of the *Theatralische Sendung* (a revision upon which Moritz's ideas and personal fate will not have been without influence)[75] is the dialectical synthesis of the antithesis between art and subjectivity embodied in Moritz's work. There the 'armer Hund' of the novel confronts the true artist of the theory, by whose standard Schiller said that Goethe himself would be found wanting.[76] In the *Lehrjahre*, the partial subject is aesthetically redeemed by the symbolic form of the work as a whole, whose secret is that it disposes of the voice, the voice of aesthetic authority, which places partialness at its very centre. The redeeming aesthetic form of circularity, enriched by the erotic dynamic (lacking or displaced in Moritz's text), is set into the structure of the text itself, while in Moritz the 'circle' appears only in glimpses at the quasi-mystical limits of both psychological and aesthetic speculation.

However, it is worth ending this discussion of *Anton Reiser* by stressing that the divide between it and the *Lehrjahre* is not as clear as might at first appear. *Werther* was for Moritz unambiguously a work of art,[77] because it represented so appropriately, and thus transcended, the subjective partialness which he, Moritz, could only figure in scientific and moral categories, or in a negation of the aesthetic category. Yet *Anton Reiser* is constantly pushing towards a symbolic resolution of the fragmentary and serial nature of empirical experience, and thus tending to resolve itself into a *Werther*-like artistic transcendence of partialness of the sort theorised in the aesthetic essay. While not claiming symbolic status itself, it claims awareness of the symbolic – that is to say that moment in representation when the particular becomes transparent upon the universal, when meaning becomes sensually manifest, and by extension when the individual human life, potentiated by art, becomes representative. This awareness is clearest in the case of the evocatively named (and historically authenticated) Dr Sauer.[78] Sauer is the type of the gifted man whose gifts find no outlet in, or else are overcome by the resistance of, the uncomprehending world (pp. 461–462). In this sense he is an objectification of Anton himself, as 'partial subject' par excellence, rather than as an example of a misunderstood poetic drive. Moritz/Reiser's (they overlap here) memory holds an image of Sauer which is symbolic in the terms of the aesthetic:

> Das Bild wie Sauer mit blassen Wangen, und untergeschlagenen Augen, bedeutungsvoll in diesen stygischen Fluß herunterblickte, kam Reisern lebhaft wieder vor die Seele, als er einige Jahre nachher die Nachricht von seinem Tode vernahm. – Denn wenn irgendein bedeutendes Bild sich formte, wo Zeichen und Sache eines wurden, so war es hier. (p. 465)

The image of the way Sauer, pallid and with downcast eyes, cast a glance full of meaning into this Stygian river, returned vividly to Reiser's mind's eye when he received the news of his death some years later. If ever there was a significant image in which sign and meaning were one, this was it.

What makes this symbol exemplary, however, is not only that it seeks out a moment at which meaning becomes sensually accessible, in the terms of contemporary aesthetic theory, but also that what is being thus symbolised is subjective partialness: a state of melancholic unknowing is being transfigured into meaning and thereby overcome. This is, *in nuce*, the strategy of the *Lehrjahre* and the culture it represents. It is a culture in which failure can be redeemed in the form of symbolic structure.

HYPERION

Schweigen müssen wir oft; es fehlen heilige Nahmen,
Herzen schlagen und doch bleibet die Rede zurück.

Hölderlin's *Hyperion* (Volume One 1797, Volume Two 1799) is a text of much higher earnestness and singleness of poetic purpose than the others previously discussed. As novels, these other texts are in some sense constitutionally impure. Hölderlin was primarily a lyric poet. Apart from repeated drafts of a tragedy, *Empedokles*, which was never finished, *Hyperion* was his only other major non-lyrical work. It is the attempt to speak in a pure voice. To read it is to become aware of the urgency with which the author is striving to produce an authentic and undivided discourse. It is informed by the asymptotic project of finding a single writing 'I' in whose unimpeded utterance all the differences and divisions that enter the world with self-consciousness and language will disappear.

The text is composed of a series of letters in which a young Greek idealist recounts his formative experiences to a correspondent in Germany. We learn about the teacher who inspired Hyperion's idealism, the friend and warrior with whom he strove to put it into practice by joining the Greeks' struggle against the Turks, and the lover who is an embodiment of the ideal itself. All of these experiences have ended in disillusionment or loss, and they are recounted in a philosophically resigned but poetically transformative retrospect.

Not a great deal is known about Hölderlin's views on the novel as a genre. Certainly in taking it up he will have been seeking to enhance its status as art. In this respect he does resemble the Goethe of the *Lehrjahre*, ennobling the novel form, although there is a crucial distinction to which we shall return at the end of this chapter. Hölderlin read the early Books of the *Lehrjahre* as they appeared, and approved of them, and this coincided with the composition of *Hyperion*. It is not known whether he read the later books, and it is unlikely that they would have appealed to him.[79] It seems likely he disapproved of Wieland's thinking man's Greek novel, *Agathon*.[80] His own Greek setting, he wrote, would provide the framework in which to offer the public a more substantial hero than the 'wort- und abenteuerreichen Ritter' ('knights rich in both words and adventures') of contemporary taste.[81] He referred to the novel genre as 'terra incognita' which held enormous promise (p. 299). It must have seemed to him that it was a genre which, despite its 'immeasurable' potential, was disappointing in its actual achievements.

The novel form Hölderlin finally chose, after some experimentation with other modes, was the epistolary. This was the dominant form of the serious novel in the eighteenth century and had contributed significantly to the development of a voice in literature for secular subjectivism, notably in the works of Richardson and Rousseau. The epistolary form was orginally characterised by a diversity of subjective voices, since the letters of two or more correspondents were included. In *Die Leiden des jungen Werther* Goethe increased the subjectivism of the genre by including only the letters of Werther himself (not the replies), and the voice of an editor. Hölderlin took this purification one step further. His single correspondent is his *own* editor. He writes to a correspondent about himself in the past, and is thus both subject and object of his own discourse in a way Werther, always writing out of an immediate situation, is not. In writing about himself, Hyperion presents a poetic realisation of himself, occasionally including other documentation (letters from others) when it contributes to his self-production in writing.

There is little, then, on the surface that encourages us to seek connections between this intensively subjective and poetic text and the novels of the school of *Wilhelm Meister*. Whereas they are conventionally regarded as narratives of development and integration, *Hyperion* is an elegiac evocation of failure and loss. Yet, as Wilhelm Dilthey said, in a passage famous because it offers the classical definition of the *Bildungsroman*, Hölderlin's novel 'grew in the same soil' as the *Lehrjahre* and similar novels.[82] Like them it springs, as Dilthey explains, from the individualism of the age, and the specific German interest in combining the representation of an individual life story with general truths about human beings. Moreover, Hölderlin's novel in its original conception would have been the archetypal *Bildungsroman*, germinating as it did in the fertile soil of Schillerian idealism. The first results of Hölderlin's work on the Hyperion theme in fact appeared in Schiller's journal *Thalia* in 1794. They announced the representation of an individual development from a state of naive totality to a state of reflective wholeness (from a 'Zustand höchster Einfalt' to one of 'höchster Bildung', p.163). Dilthey puts the difference between the final version of *Hyperion* and the classical *Bildungsroman* down to the unprecedented preoccupation of the modern age with the darker side of human existence, and to Hölderlin's own artistic personality and direction.[83] From our point of view what distinguishes Hölderlin's novel from the culture which nevertheless gives birth to it is precisely its uncompromising commitment to the production of an unsullied voice, to poetry.

Just as the concept of 'authority' provided an entry into our discussion of *Die Geschichte des Agathon*, and that of 'subjectivity' a way into our discussion of *Anton Reiser*, so the concept of 'art' (as in 'poetry') guides us in our discussion of *Hyperion*. These three terms are the decisive ones in the aesthetic configuration of the *Lehrjahre*.

The way to approach the subject of art in the context of *Hyperion* is however not directly but *ex negativo*, as it were, through the notions familiar from our other two discussions in this chapter, of the partialness of subjectivity and of problems with authority within the new subjectivist literary culture.

In Hölderlin's text subjective partialness can no longer be mistakenly identified as a personality defect. Hölderlin-Hyperion is proud and glad to be a 'Schwärmer'[84] in spite of all the suffering it entails, indeed because of it. Subjective experience, especially the terms of its intense suffering, are contiguous with intimations of totality. In earlier versions of the novel (the metrical version and *Hyperions Jugend* of 1794/5) written under the influence of the philosopher Fichte,[85] whose system can be said to be a legitimation and potentiation of subjective partialness, the sense of lack was precisely the clue to man's true infinite potential: 'Wohl dem, der das Gefühl seines Mangels versteht! Wer in ihm den Beruf zu unendlichem Fortschritt erkennt' (p. 214). ('Happy the man who understands his own feeling of lack! The man who recognises in it the calling to endless progress.')[86]

In the final version subjective partialness moves into a significant and dynamic relationship with its opposite. The novel's opening pages document the juxtaposition or succession of two states: an overwhelming sense of deprivation, and elation at union with the universe. The twin moments of partialness and wholeness which coexist sporadically and irresolutely in the pages of *Anton Reiser* are here harnessed to each other in one rhetorical system as the powerful driving force of the text: 'O ein Gott ist der Mensch, wenn er träumt, ein Bettler, wenn er nachdenkt, und wenn die Begeisterung hin ist, steht er da, wie ein misrathener Sohn, den der Vater aus dem Hause stieß, und betrachtet die ärmlichen Pfennige, die ihm das Mitleid auf den Weg gab' (p. 9). ('Oh, man is a god when he dreams, a beggar when he thinks; and when inspiration is gone, he stands, like a worthless son whom his father has driven out of his house, and stares at the miserable pennies that pity has given him for the road.')

And at the novel's point of greatest insight, Hyperion can explain to his correspondent Bellarmin: 'Ja! ja! werth ist der Schmerz, am Herzen der Menschen zu liegen, und dein Vertrauter zu seyn, o Natur! Denn er nur führt von einer Wonne zur andern, und es ist kein andrer Gefährte, denn er' (p. 150). ('Yes! yes! sorrow is worthy to lie at man's heart and to be your intimate, O Nature! For it but leads from one bliss to another, and there is no other companion on the way.')

This thematically crucial concentration upon subjective partialness brings with it a corresponding consciousness of the absence of systems or structures of authority to which the subject might traditionally have looked for healing: 'O ihr Genossen meiner Zeit!

fragt eure Ärzte nicht und nicht die Priester, wenn ihr innerlich vergeht!' (p. 42). ('O you who live in this age with me! Seek not counsel of your doctors nor of your priests when your hearts wither away!') The available discourses of contemporary wisdom, for their part, actually create the very conditions for subjective isolation: 'Ach! wär' ich nie in eure Schulen gegangen . . . Ich . . . habe gründlich mich unterscheiden gelernt von dem, was mich umgiebt, bin nun vereinzelt in der schönen Welt, bin so ausgeworfen aus dem Garten der Natur, wo ich wuchs und blühte, und vertrokne an der Mittagssonne' (p. 9). ('O! had I never gone to your schools! . . . I . . . learned so thoroughly to distinguish myself from what surrounds me, that now I am solitary in the beautiful world, an outcast from the garden of Nature in which I grew and flowered, and am drying up under the noonday sun.')

The image of an atrophy or arrestation in the rich processes of nature is used elsewhere to convey the subject falling away from its function and fulfilment in the world: 'Was ist der Mensch? . . . wie kommt es, daß so etwas in der Welt ist, das, wie ein Chaos, gährt, oder modert, wie ein fauler Baum, und nie zu einer Reife gedeiht?' (p. 45). ('What is man? How does it happen that the world contains such a thing, which ferments like a chaos or moulders like a rotten tree, and never grows to ripeness?') Again it can lead to its opposite value, as in these lines, addressing nature, from near the end of the book: '"Es fallen die Menschen, wie faule Früchte von dir, o laß sie untergehn, so kehren sie zu deiner Wurzel wieder"' (p. 159). ('"Men fall from you like rotten fruits, o let them perish, for thus they return to your root."')

The novel represents subjective partialness via the absence of father, fatherland, patriarchal gods. The emphasis upon subjective experience is associated with the destruction of masculine systems of reference. It is noticeable, for instance, that the figure of disinheritance is employed in the passage quoted above – 'ein misrathener Sohn, den der Vater aus dem Hause stieß' – to express the state of partialness. Later in the novel Hyperion is actually disinherited by his father for involvement in the unsuccessful Greek uprising against the Turks in 1770 (p. 119). Nor are possibilities of integration and effectiveness offered by the fatherland: 'Wohl dem Manne, dem ein blühend Vaterland das Herz erfreut und stärkt!

Mir ist, als würd' ich in den Sumpf geworfen . . . wenn einer an das meinige mich mahnt' (p. 7). ('Fortunate the man whose native country flourishes to rejoice and strengthen his heart! For me, it is as if I were cast into a swamp . . . if anyone reminds me of mine.') When Hyperion intervenes actively in a bid to restore the heroic culture of Athens, not only is this the occasion for his own disinheritance, but it also serves to reveal just how distant such an order – touched by transcendence – actually is: 'wie bist du so herabgekommen, väterlich Geschlecht, vom dem das Götterbild des Jupiter und des Apoll einst nur die Kopie war?' (p. 107). ('How have you so declined, ancestral race of which the divine images of Jupiter and Apollo were once only the copy?') And at the moment at which the novel's greatest positive insight is spoken (from which we quoted above), we can also read, juxtaposed with it, the following terms of despair felt by Hyperion at the nadir of his fortunes: 'und wär' ich auch auf meiner heimatlichen Insel, in den Gärten meiner Jugend, die mein Vater mir verschließt, ach! dennoch, dennoch, wär' ich auf der Erd' ein Fremdling und kein Gott knüpft ans Vergangne mich mehr' (p. 150). ('And if I were on my native island, in the gardens of my youth, which my father bars to me, ah! even then, even then I should be a stranger on earth, and no god would join me to the past again.') The sense of paternal disinheritance gives way to one of separation from the gods themselves.

The underlying lyric-elegiac situation of the text might be called a stand-off between subject and object, between an – in relation to our other texts – enhanced, but agonised, subjectivity, and ruined authority. But this is a novel as well as an elegy. The preface to the final version of *Hyperion*, although it has abandoned the Schillerian development from naivety to reflective totality originally promised, nevertheless promises a progression, a narrative: 'die Auflösung der Dissonanzen in einem gewissen Karakter' ('the resolution of dissonances in a particular character', p. 5). A state is articulated in terms of a process. If we now look for the masculine and feminine determinations we derived from the *Lehrjahre*, the following picture emerges. The narrative is bereft of those masculine determinations – the Society of the Tower, the utopian State of Tarentum, the symbolic circularity of inheritance – vital to the structure of the Goethean model, because such forms are already ruined in the basic lyric modality from which the narrative originates. Individual male progress must seek its logic from within the subject, which means in terms of the *Lehrjahre* model, must seek it under the sign of the feminine, the first-person voice, the figures of desire. It is an attempt to speak without a third person – that purity of voice to which Hyperion and Hölderlin aspire, and to which we shall return. This project is bodied forth in a series of individual human relationships each of which, in different ways, answers Hyperion's subjective need in the form of validating reciprocity, and each of which is then, according to the underlying logic of the book, painfully taken away. The encounters are with Adamas, the teacher, Alabanda, the warrior and Diotima, the woman.

It will be objected that the first two encounters are not with women. They nevertheless take place under the sign of the woman. Marlies Janz, in a feminist treatment of the novel, notes ingeniously that to both Adamas and Alabanda, in their relationships with Hyperion, are attributed qualities which within the phenomenology of masculine and feminine of the time are feminine: their company facilitates that access to nature denied to Hyperion in his periods of subjective abandonment.[87] Hyperion's relation to them as individual male figures is strongly contrasted with his rejection of masculine collectives; the degenerate men of Smyrna and the 'Bund der Nemesis', the secret society of which Alabanda is a member, and which is as negative a term in the economy of Hölderlin's novel as the secret Society of the Tower is a positive one in Goethe's. Moreover, the episodes with Adamas and Alabanda are clearly part of a series, the culmination of which is the encounter with Diotima, through whom the series retrospectively assumes a prevailing feminine value. Diotima's unchallenged feminine presence was brought out in the final version by reducing the importance of her father (or the father of her predecessor, Melite) which had been distinct in the *Thalia* fragment. (Unlike Novalis's Mathilde, with whom she otherwise has much in common, Diotima has no equivalent to Klingsohr.) What these three encounters offer is a subjective, feminine re-imagination of the three levels of masculine authority whose ruin is otherwise so prominent in the work: the father (Adamas, the sage); the socio-political formation (Alabanda, the activist); and the gods (Diotima – 'himmlisches Wesen!', 'heavenly being').

These episodes provide the occasions on the level of the narrative for formulations of that plenitude to which otherwise lack and loss are the only reliable witnesses. They are the moments in Hyperion's story at which he feels at one with the world, as opposed to the periods at which he feels detached from and agonisingly at odds with it. This is thus a projection, on the level of the plot, of the incessant oscillation on the level of the dense poetic text itself between despair and euphoria. Adamas as Hyperion's teacher, rather than imposing a sense of separateness upon him in the manner of the official wisdom of the day, fills him with 'ungetheilte[n] Begeisterung' ('pure inspiration', p. 14). This education in the culture of the Greeks, which revolutionises Hyperion's consciousness of the world and its possibilities, is an education which speaks directly to the subject, producing it out of itself, without alienation, for effectiveness in the world: 'Es ist ein köstlich Wohlgefühl in uns, wenn so das Innere an seinem Stoffe sich stärkt, sich unterscheidet und getreuer anknüpft und unser Geist allmählig waffenfähig wird' (p. 14). ('There is a precious sense of well-being in us when our inner life thus draws strength from what is its material, differentiates itself, and establishes truer inner relationships, and our mind gradually comes of age to bear arms.')

This notion of arming the subject – so often described as 'angefochten' (beleaguered, embattled) in this time of adversity (e.g. pp. 8, 9, 48, 119) – of training up one's own interior resources for agency in the real world, is the vital component in Hyperion's friendship with Alabanda. This friendship nourishes itself on the projection of pure subjectivity effective in the world: 'so drangen unsre Seelen in kolossalischen Entwürfen hinaus; nicht, als hätten wir, unmännlich, unsre Welt, wie durch ein Zauberwort, geschaffen, und kindlich unerfahren keinen Widerstand berechnet, dazu war Alabanda zu verständig und tapfer' (p. 27). ('So our souls drove ever forward in colossal projects – not that we effeminately created our world as if by a magic spell and, childishly inexperienced, expected no resistance; Alabanda was too intelligent and too brave for that.')

This aspect of the dream of wholeness is significantly that of a subjectivity which is not 'unmanly', which is not denied access to effectiveness in reality simply because it rejects all existing masculine orders of authority. It is the revolutionary dream of Rousseau's subjective ideals triumphant on earth. The immediate love and understanding between the two men, fusing in each other's arms, is already an armed fusion: 'Waffenbruder! rief er, lieber Waffenbruder! o nun hab' ich hundert Arme!' ('Brother at arms, he cried, brother at arms, o now I have the strength of a hundred [men]', p. 28). In this re-imagination of the masculine under the sign of the feminine, inwardness is turned outward without loss.

But it is Diotima who is the major occasion for the formulation of a fullness, in Alabanda's words, a 'göttlich ungetheiltes Leben' ('divinely undivided life', p. 136), from which reciprocity, redeeming subjective partialness, can spring. She transforms Hyperion's own subjectivity into a mirror: 'in welchem Spiegel sammelten sich, so wie in mir, die Stralen dieses Lichts?' ('in what mirror, as in me, were all the rays of that light concentrated?', p. 61), and in their understanding of each other 'Göttliches spielt mit Göttlichem' ('divine plays with divine', p. 73). Here, what language without a third person might be like is made clearer. It is the ideal of pure relationship in which heart would speak to heart without the detour around what is ordinarily understood as language, with its freight of other people's meanings and the inevitable separateness of the speaker: 'Immer mußt' ein Dritter uns stören, trennen, und die Welt lag zwischen ihr und mir, wie eine unendliche Leere' (p. 70). ('There was always some third person to intrude on us, separate us, and the world lay between her and me like an unbounded emptiness.')

Like Mignon's, Diotima's medium is song. Her song is the only medium which could express the joy of their relationship: 'Worte sind hier umsonst, und wer nach einem Gleichniß von ihr [der Freude] fragt, der hat sie nie erfahren. Das Einzige, was eine solche Freude auszudrüken vermochte, war Diotima's Gesang, wenn er, in goldner Mitte, zwischen Höhe und Tiefe schwebte' (p. 68). ('Words avail not here, and he who would seek the like of such joy has never known it. The one thing that could express such a joy was Diotima's own singing when it floated between height and depth, in the golden mean.')

Subjectivity is on the verge of transforming itself into pure (musical) relationship: 'Zum Tone möchte man werden und sich vereinen in Einen Himmelsgesang' ('one would like to become all music and united with each other in *one* celestial melody', p. 53). (Compare the words from the final panegyric of the book: 'Lebendige Töne sind wir, stimmen zusammen in deinem Wohllaut, Natur!', 'Living tones are we, we sound together in thy harmony, Nature!', p. 159.) This in contrast to a related image of partial subjectivity: 'Wie war denn ich? war ich nicht wie ein zerrissen Saitenspiel? Ein wenig tönt' ich noch, aber es waren Todestöne' (p. 52). ('How was it with me, then? Was I not like a shattered lyre? I sounded a little still, but they were the tones of death.')

Diotima is presented with such intensity that the reader will experience her, in the second book of the first volume, as Hyperion's 'telos', the goal towards which he has been tending, which, when reached, abolishes time and place: 'Was sind Jahrhunderte gegen den Augenblick, wo zwei Wesen so sich ahnen und nahn?' ('What are centuries compared to the moment when two beings thus divine and approach each other?', p. 53). (The near-anagram collapses the subjective 'ahnen', 'to divine, sense', into the objective 'nahn', 'to approach', suggesting the removal of the subject–object divide itself.) As such she is the distillation of all the women figures in this sort of fiction of individual male development, from Danae to Clawdia Chauchat: 'das Ewig Weibliche' made novel character. 'There is a direct route from Goethe's experience and evaluation of love to Hollywood – but not from Hölderlin's', writes Eudo C. Mason.[88] But one can legitimately ask: what other route toward the metaphysical is there within a secular patriarchal culture, arranged and organised around the perceptions and subjective disposition of the individual heterosexual male, than The Woman? In the 'Eros' stanza of Goethe's *Urworte Orphisch* the erotic and the metaphysical are intentionally dissolved together, as they are, in a way, in his *Selige Sehnsucht*. It is no accident that Nathalie is so closely related to the *Stiftsdame*. Diotima is anything but *sui generis*. What is special about her is, again, the supreme urgent earnestness with which this particular imaginative direction is pressed.

What *Anton Reiser* and Anton Reiser lacked was love. Without love there is no form in this sort of context, for it is love which supplies direction and completion, uniting desire and pattern, spinning plot from the deepest places of interiority. This function of love is brought out with full radiance by the example of Diotima. And yet, of course, Diotima does not have that aesthetic-structural function. Diotima is the 'telos' of Hyperion, not *Hyperion*. Union with her does not inform and guarantee the formal closure of the novel for a reason diametrically opposed to the reason why Danae fails to do so in *Agathon*. For Wieland, the erotic is too trivial to bear such structural-thematic weight. For Hölderlin, it is too important.

For the novel's development – Adamas, Alabanda, Diotima – does not, of course, remain untroubled in any simple sense. The story Hyperion is retelling in his letters to Bellarmin involves not only the finding of these moments of fulfilment, but their irrecoverable loss too. (One needs to stress, of course, that on the local level of the text's poetic language, through the retrospective filter, absence and presence alternate all the time: no formulation of fullness without its concomitant lament.) The narrative level has its own opposition of possession (Book One) and then loss (Book Two). The meetings with Alabanda and Diotima in the first Book correspond to the catastrophic failure of the brotherhood of Hyperion and Alabanda to be effective in history, and with the death of Diotima, in the second. Given the ruin of the masculine structures of authority – father, fatherland, patriarchal gods – the novel imagines a new order, re-born within the feminine. At the end of the book it seems as though this too has failed.

But this is not the whole story. Finally, our detour round the partial subject has brought us, as promised, to the idea of art. Beyond Diotima, in the narrative progression, stands Hyperion as poet. Diotima has to die in order that Hyperion's development may reach its goal.[89] (Without apparently demurring, Ryan explains that, having planted an ideal in Hyperion, Diotima really has to die, otherwise she might hold him back in his development.)[90] Diotima's major function is to die; the text might just as well be called 'Der Tod der Diotima'.[91] Heroines often die in this sort of text, as a major contribution to the 'Subjektwerdung' ('becoming a subject') of the male protagonist. One thinks of Marianne, Aurelie, Mignon in the *Lehrjahre*, Anna in *Der grüne*

Heinrich or, perhaps the closest parallel to Diotima, Novalis's Mathilde. Hölderlin tried to explain to Susette Gontard, the autobiographical Diotima who came to inhabit his fictional elaboration of Hyperion's quasi-divine beloved, that this death was structurally inevitable.[92] Diotima must die so that Hyperion can make a poem of her death, and as he does so the significance of his life, namely that he is a poet, becomes manifest. Bellarmin is sent a copy of the letter of farewell Diotima sent Hyperion before her death. In her death she becomes articulate: 'Stille war mein Leben; mein Tod ist beredt' ('My life was silent; my death is eloquent', p. 147). And what she says (after many other things in a series of memorably beautiful passages) is that she foresees Hyperion's future as a poet: 'die dichterischen Tage keimen dir schon' ('your days of poetry are already germinating', p. 149). Only the masculine poet, however, can represent the spiritual purity of Diotima (which, in a rather circular manner, consists in her ability to see this).

Nowhere in the story is Hyperion a poet: his poetic time lies in the future. In response to Diotima's perception of his potential, he says: 'Ich bin ein Künstler, aber ich bin nicht geschikt. Ich bilde im Geiste, aber ich weiß noch die Hand nicht zu führen' (p. 89). ('I am an artist, and I am unskilled. I fashion in thought, but I do not yet know how to direct my hand.') The reader is unsure about whether this is metaphorical ('you are quite right; I am like an artist, who . . .'), or to be taken literally. It matters little, since the estate of poet imperceptibly becomes that of human subject, made aware of his inalienable rights by the agency of the desire of the woman: 'da übte das Herz sein Recht, zu dichten, aus' ('Then my heart indulged its poetic right', p. 70), we read, of times when Hyperion reflects upon the 'eiserne, unerbittliche Gesez . . . nicht Eine Seele zu seyn mit seiner liebenswürdigen Hälfte' ('the iron, inexorable law . . . that would not let it be one soul with its adorable other half', p. 70).

It is something of a topos in the texts with which we are concerned that the male hero tells his story to a female lover. It happens in *Agathon*; it was one of the main changes Goethe made to the *Theatralische Sendung* that Wilhelm's youth was told by him to Marianne, and not by a third person. Rather similarly, Judith and Dortchen Schönfund read Heinrich Lee's *Jugendgeschichte* (while the topos is farcically, but nevertheless significantly repeated in Keller's Novelle *Pankraz der Schmoller*). The same configuration arises in the present text (p. 66).

Although we are not presented with the story as it is being told to Diotima (since we already know it), what we have already read as written to Bellarmin is, as it were, retrospectively animated with Diotima's consciousness of it. Diotima not only knows Hyperion's story, she understands it better than he does himself. She places it in context, situating his subjective suffering and thus making him whole, in a manner of speaking, by virtue of her consciousness of his lack of wholeness. 'Scherze über dein Schicksal . . . nicht, denn ich versteh'es besser, als du. . . . Es ist eine bessere Zeit, die suchst du, eine schönere Welt . . .' (pp. 66–67). ('Do not mock your destiny . . . for I understand it better than you do . . . It is a better time that you seek, a more beautiful world.') She at once recognises and validates his subjectivity. Here once more, the uncompromising intensity with which she is imagined by Hölderlin brings out the function incipient to varying degrees in the other comparable narrative situations. The ear of the desired woman closes the self-alienation brought about by language. You are reunited with your own story, you make sense, in the element of the desired woman's consciousness. To close back upon this fullness by representing it, is to approach what we referred to at the outset as the 'pure' poetic voice.

It is significant that in her final letters Diotima unites all three kinds of voice we isolated in the *Lehrjahre*: song, as her proper form of expression; first-person speech, in her account, at last 'eloquent', of her own ultimately fatal experience of Hyperion; and apodictic utterance, in her setting forth of the spiritual affirmation of the alternation of absence and presence as the authentic terms of human fulfilment: 'Wir stellen im Wechsel das Vollendete dar' ('We represent perfection in change', p. 148). In representing this uniquely unified mode of utterance, Hölderlin-Hyperion becomes the poet he is always about to be in the text. The culmination of the feminine progression of the narrative is the transformation of the 'masculine masculine', the hero (whose irrelevance in times like these is clear from the fate of Alabanda and Hyperion's abortive intervention in the Greek uprising), into the 'feminine masculine', the poet. Diotima's feminine agency transforms subjectivity into art, and the partial subject into the poet.

Lawrence Ryan was the first to draw attention to the fact that this progression towards the vocation of the poet is actually continued in the narrative arrangement of the text.[93] He argued that far from being a 'lyrical novel', in the sense of an artless compilation of lyrical utterances, it is actually highly organised as a novel. He shows how Hyperion progresses through a series of stages along what Hölderlin had called in prefaces to earlier drafts of the novel an 'exzentrische Bahn' (an 'eccentric path' – the 'Dissonanzen' of the final version, and what I mean by 'partial subjectivity'). Each stage is a movement away from, and a pull back towards, the mysterious centre of life from which we are separated by the fact of individuation. Ryan's major point is that the act of narration itself is a further stage in Hyperion's progress. Not only does he recount to Bellarmin the stages of his earlier life, but the reader actually witnesses Hyperion's development as he narrates his own life, and comes to discern in it a pattern and coherence he had not been able to grasp at the time of experiencing. As the subtitle implies, what the eccentric path is leading towards is the vocation of poet. The poet's activity is not eccentric in the arbitrary and endangered sense of all the earlier stages, because it is not purely subjective, but in accord with the mysterious centre of life. This kind of consonance is what Diotima explained in her farewell letter, and this represents the highest stage of consciousnes of the novel, to which Hyperion unwittingly aspires in his narration of his own life: 'Wie Harfenspieler um die Thronen der Ältesten, leben wir, selbst göttlich, um die stillen Götter der Welt, mit dem flüchtigen Lebensliede mildern wir den seeligen Ernst des Sonnengotts und der andern' (p. 148). ('Like harp players about the thrones of the most ancient, we live, ourselves divine, among the quiet Gods of the world; with our fleeting lovesong we temper the blissful seriousness of the Sun God and the rest.')

Interestingly, Ryan's reading of the text constructs it as an ideal counterpart to the fragmentation of *Anton Reiser*. Whereas there we had notions of wholeness and experiences of separateness, failing to find a single perspective capable of embracing them both within a single discourse, and whereas we had there a third-person voice in the present and unredeemed subjective experience in the past, tending towards a unity they could not enact textually, here those absences become presences. An 'I' in the present re-reads the 'I' of the past, transforming it in the process. Discrete subjective experiences of ecstasy and separateness become poetic discourse, coexisting as the very mark of the divinity of human experience, of which the text before us is an enactment. Hölderlin's poetic programme, and his achievement as it is expounded by Ryan, are very close to Moritz's theoretical definition of the true poet, in whose work nature continues to reproduce itself and through whom the voice and operation of creation itself can be perceived, forming itself in ever higher manifestations of its own developing nature.[94]

Hyperion is thus the figure of autobiography redeemed by art. The 'I' of the narrative present reading the 'I' of the past unites with it in a poetic transfiguration of self-consciousness. Whereas the young Hyperion's projections of himself and the reality of the situations in which he found himself failed to coincide, the final 'Entwurf', the poetic text before us, takes him up into itself as into one identity, in which the diachrony of a life history and its changes is resolved into one synchronic image. A process is transformed back into a state, or becomes transparent upon the state which conditions it. Dilthey wrote: 'Hyperion is Hölderlin himself.'[95] Ryan concludes: 'at the end of the novel Hyperion is beginning to be the poet Hölderlin himself now becomes.'[96] This is the very myth of the 'pure voice' of poetry. As Hyperion puts it in a moment of high enthusiasm: 'In [der Kunst] verjüngt und wiederholt der göttliche Mensch sich selbst' ('In art divine man rejuvenates and repeats himself', p. 79).

Ryan thus teaches us to locate Hyperion's secret in its formal arrangement, and that this formal arrangement is circular. Hyperion comes to himself, just as Wilhelm re-finds himself in his discovery of his inheritance in the possession of Natalie. Although the story is one of failure and loss, the narrative itself is despite all a fulfilment. Autobiography becomes art. The *Lehrjahre* also grounds its legitimation in its aesthetic status, transforming partialness into significant meaning. It too relies upon patterns of circularity for the aesthetic structure in which it invests meaning, and it too took up the autobiographical realistic material of the *Theatralische Sendung* into a larger aesthetic system. Both texts, as we have said, are novels which seek to increase the dignity of the genre so that it may bear this authoritative role. Both thematise the feminine as the objectivisation of the subjectivity of their male protagonists, and enlist the qualities they associate with the feminine in support of the aesthetic authority they propose. And yet in spite of these important apparent parallels at a deep level of structural organisation, the two works differ profoundly.

In the terms of our argument the decisive difference between Goethe and Hölderlin with regard to the aesthetic organisation and import of their respective novels is that the artificiality of Goethe's work is explicit. It is part of the aesthetic effect of his novel to be obviously artificial. On the other hand, it is perhaps not surprising that it took critics over 150 years to discover the structure of *Hyperion*, since it is folded into the thematic and philosophical texture of the book. What this prominent artificiality means is that Goethe appears in his own text twice, in two distinct disguises. First, he appears as 'realism', autobiography, as the partial subject, Wilhelm. Second, he reappears as the authoritative voice which speaks the discourse within which this partialness may be represented, taking responsibility for the visible imaginative choices which have gone into the composition of this specific text. Without, now, the torment and fragmentariness of a Moritz, or the fading forms of authority of an ancien régime literariness as in *Agathon*, the individual human first person is matched by the third person in which it can speak of itself and for itself authentically, but also with authority. The authenticity of the subjective source – itself, of course, an effect of the construction of the text, and perhaps Goethe's most memorable rhetorical achievement – is alloyed with the effect of artificiality to give the feeling that the artefact is at once arbitrary and significant. This particular combination might be said to be the secret of the 'aesthetic' itself.

Whereas the *Lehrjahre* achieves its stability by concentrating upon this one complex artistic strategy, which we identify as the aesthetic, Hölderlin's novel displays what might be termed a double artistic determination. We have referred to these two determinations variously as lyric and narrative or state and process. *Hyperion* is both 'open' and 'closed' at the same time. Ryan stressed the structural narrative principle which makes of it a closed work. But at the same time, at the end of his book, he has to address the fundamental openness of the text, which it has in common with all Hölderlin's work in the nature of his conception and practice of poetry: 'the poetic utterance is both "open" and "closed". It is turned towards the universal precisely in its own closure (gerade indem sie sich zur eignen Gestalt sich abrundet).'[97] David Constantine, in his monograph on Hölderlin, tries to make this gnomic utterance more comprehensible: 'closure is not the end of any work by Hölderlin, and the process of *Hyperion* breaches its apparent and pleasing circularity. The process itself is a continuous engendering.'[98] It would thus appear that the developmental model which was so much part of Hölderlin's time, which informed Hölderlin's first drafts, and which has been uncovered by Ryan even in the final one, is, however productively, at odds with the basic lyric alternation of absence and presence of which we spoke at the outset.

This can be amplified by a look at the conclusion of the novel, about which, since Ryan, there has been considerable critical debate. Ryan's developmental model was in some embarrassment about the hymn with which the book concludes, followed only by the words 'So dacht' ich. Nächstens mehr' ('So I thought. More soon'). For him, this cannot be the climax of the development he discerns, since it is the record of an epiphany enjoyed by Hyperion before he started on the narrative progression which transforms him from 'eccentric' partial subject into poet. He turns, therefore, to other moments in the text around the death of Diotima (notably, p. 150, the passage beginning, 'Bester, ich bin ruhig. . .'), at which the 'hermit' can persuasively be argued to have assimilated in the narrative present his most grievous loss, and with it the other shortcomings of his life, grasped them as a pattern, and in doing so, acceded to the condition of poet, to whom is vouchsafed the vision of a higher harmony in which the apparent lack and fragmentation of ordinary life is transfigured. But as critics since have been bound to stress, this downgrading of the final hymn is untenable.[99] The passage is too persuasive – in its language, in its placing, and in its very close association with the spirit of Diotima herself – for us to believe that it has been superseded by the chronologically latest realisation gained after the narration of Diotima's death.[100]

There have been critical resolutions of this problem. It has been argued that the hymn should be read at two levels: first, as it was experienced in the past, still a moment of ecstasy with its transitoriness inscribed within it, and second, as mediated through the raised consciousness of the Hyperion who has now completed his narrative to Bellarmin, and who thus understands the office of poet, indeed executes it in the quotation of his own earlier ecstasy in the now coherent textual context.[101] Or else the hymn can be interpreted, as by Constantine, as the entry into language of an experience which was originally non-linguistic, whence, the inevitable loss of immediacy notwithstanding, it can feed back productively into the process of the poet's life.[102] From our point of view, these critical resolutions, however satisfying and right in their way, are not necessary, since the hesitation about endings bears out the sense that a double artistic determination is at work. The moments of highest consciousness represent the end of the developmental model, the narrative dimension; and in those terms, the novel itself is a closed work, the production of one who, now assured as poet, can produce such works. The closedness of the work buttresses the assuredness of the poet. Ryan: 'the entire work is but a proof of the legitimacy of the narrator'.[103] The final hymn, on the other hand, undercuts this certainty (as does, of course, the marvellous last line), and reinstates the endless alternation of presence and absence as the condition of a text which is not finished, since in these terms, no text ever can be.

The same double determination can be demonstrated if we return briefly to Marlies Janz's feminist reading. She is addressing the first artistic determination, the aesthetic one, in terms of which, as Ryan showed, the novel is the construction of the male poet. And there is certainly something unsatisfactory (not to say repellent) about the notion of Diotima having to die, as Hölderlin after all said she must, in order for the poet to become a poet by transforming her into poetry. But, from the point of view of the second artistic determination, that of poetry as an unending alternation of absence and presence, the point that the novel might just as well be called 'Der Tod der Diotima' ('The Death of

Diotima') appears trivial. If Diotima had to die for the poetry to come about, the logic also requires that the male poet-subject himself must similarly be sacrificed, since the succession of absence and presence is unending, inevitably enveloping him too. 'Der Tod der Diotima', after all, was not yet finished when Hölderlin began to plan and work on *Der Tod des Empedokles*, in which it is not just the Jungian 'anima' but the male poet-subject himself whose absence is adumbrated in successive drafts. This is the same poetic trajectory and the same poetic integrity: absence and presence mercilessly entail each other and there is no end to the dialectic.

I can formulate what, from my point of view, is happening in *Hyperion* as follows. Hölderlin is attempting to write a text of significant individual development, an artistic transformation of autobiography, somewhat in the manner of Goethe. Yet given Hölderlin's personal poetic disposition, he is unwilling or unable to relinquish the first person in favour of a third person who would give it the steady social voice. It is noticeable, for instance, how Hölderlin disdains the construction of thematic-structural circularities out of the available material of personal experience. Where Goethe elaborates a system of inheritance, which brings out a continuity underlying the change as well as a structure to his novel, Hölderlin's hero is metaphorically and literally disinherited. Where Goethe offers Natalie as both the fulfilment of Wilhelm's deepest stirrings and the end of the book, Hölderlin's text turns upon the sublimation of the death, in the narrative, of the feminine ideal. Diotima, as we saw, does not have to bear this demeaning structural function. And where Goethe is at pains to separate the 'artist' Wilhelm from the artist who wrote *Wilhelm Meisters Lehrjahre*, Hölderlin is equally at pains to fuse the Hyperion who suffered partialness and loss with the one who transfigures these in poetry. Starting out from the partial subject, as did Goethe, Hölderlin seeks to find salvation from within that individual subject: by the sheer heat of poetic intensity, to forge the subject into object. That this leads into insoluble difficulties is evidenced, in the case of *Hyperion*, by the double determination of the text as achieved aesthetic form and site of never-ending process.

Hölderlin was, and became ever more, obsessed with formal

perfection as means of expressing his farthest-reaching and most abstract poetic impulses. His revisions of the later poems in the period leading up to his madness are legendary; Constantine says that he revised them to a 'frightening degree'.[104] The motto he chose for the final version of *Hyperion*, 'non coerceri maximo, contineri minimo, divinum est', from Loyola's epitaph, suggests equally his fatal fascination with a state in which the utmost precision becomes congruent with the largest vistas of experience: 'to be not constrained by the greatest, nor captive of the smallest, is divine'. Predictably, it is Diotima, in words we have already cited, who exemplifies the ideal in her song, 'when it floated between height and depth, in the golden mean'. No mediating language, no third-person, may complacently be allowed to interfere with the effort to achieve this, the only genuine mediation. Poetry occupies this ground, between high and low, in a constant and impossible struggle to keep it clear of interference. Hyperion is being extraordinarily, but, for Hölderlin, programmatically optimistic when he says 'es muß so schwer nicht seyn, was außer mir ist, zu vereinen mit dem Göttlichen in mir' ('It cannot be so hard to unite what is outside of me and the divine within me', p. 89). The poetry turns this round by cleaving to this 'negligible difficulty' as an indication of the authenticity of its own struggle.

This particular attitude to poetry is certainly peculiar to Hölderlin and germane to the specific greatness of his work and the tragedy of his life. The French psychoanalyst Jean Laplanche has given a remarkably clear account of the relationship between Hölderlin's art and his schizophrenia, of the nature, that is, of his poetic attempt to speak without a 'third person'.[105] In Laplanche's psychoanalytic estimation of the poet's predisposition toward schizophrenia, it is the lack of paternal authority which exposes the subject to psychosis by leaving him undefended against the pull of re-incorporation by the mother. In Lacanian terms, the father sign is missing in the 'linguistic' structure of the unconscious so that there are drastic limits upon the effectiveness of the psyche in the world, in the sense that any stable or regulated subject–object relationship is continually threatened. There is the spectre of unlimited subjectivity with no outside short of extinction, and thus no entry into the 'symbolic' order, in Lacan's term, meaning socialisation and the system of language. Hölderlin is thus perpetually held in a system of 'two persons' (self and mother), and engaged in a – uniquely resilient – attempt to transcend this dualism. His poetic project is directed against this lack (or 'lack of lack', since the father's role is that of denial). 'It is the only path remaining to the poet towards the independence of his desires.'[106] Poetry, in other words, must assume the function of the missing father.

Schiller, to whom Hölderlin turned for a source of authority, offered exactly what he needed, since Schiller was perceived as having performed, on the historical level, the very task with which Hölderlin was struggling unconsciously on the personal one. As Laplanche explains, 'Schiller is recognised by those of his generation as the undisputed master, whose standing derives from his achievement in disciplining the storms of inspiration blowing from the *Sturm und Drang* by integrating them in a religion or rather a philosophy of the beautiful.'[107]

That Schiller could not actually supply this source in Hölderlin's own case lay, as Laplanche argues, in the basic lack, in Hölderlin's *unconscious* system of a father-position for Schiller to occupy. The attempt to place him there simply confronted Hölderlin with this sanity-threatening lack, which made all stable relationships impossible for want of a boundary. Hölderlin articulated this difficulty in a letter to Schiller, written shortly after the poet's precipitate departure from Jena and the master's presence: 'While I was before you, my heart was almost too small, and when I was away from you, I could no longer hold it together.'[108] In his relation to Schiller, as in that to all forms of binding authority, he is suspended between debilitating subservience and a boundlessness which spells certain self-loss.[109] It is the literary problem of Wieland taken to its absolute extreme.

Hölderlin's poetry remains, thus, a project situated on the margins of viable personality. This psychological limit-situation is not unrelated to the condition of literature as it was defined at the end of the previous chapter. Hölderlin's work is a struggle against re-incorporation into the mother: in other words, it is both inspired by and directed against incest. It is an attempt at socialisation. Indeed, Michel Foucault, from whose notion of 'literature'

Friedrich Kittler's (as defined at the end of my previous chapter) derives, suggests a general cultural relevance for Hölderlin's individual case. In a review article on Laplanche's book[110] and in his own major works, notably *The Order of Things*, he argues that Hölderlin is one of a group of writers (Nietzsche is another) who push 'literature' so far that they reveal its unstable and precarious state in the 'Age of Man': that is, the age of modernity in which man occupies a paradoxical position at the centre of the cosmos, both subject and object of his own knowledge. This age dates from about 1790, and it is an age which *Wilhelm Meisters Lehrjahre* (1795), with its double projection of the subject as partial and central at the same time, epitomises. 'Literature' belongs to this secular and anthropocentric order, where, in the absence (in the face of Reason) of discourses of arbitrary but binding authority, it is a function of language losing its transparency onto power and turning back upon itself. All four of the texts we have discussed wrestle, at different levels of consciousness and pitches of intensity, and with varying degrees of success, with the problem of reconciling openness and closure, desire and law, the private and the public, primary and secondary socialisation. In this they betray their common identity as part of a literature the limits of which are discerned in Hölderlin. 'Every work is an attempt to exhaust language.'[111] In the epoch in which man is both the positive given of the world and the organ through which the world is constituted, literature is an – impossible – search for 'the enigma of its own origin': an impossibility Hölderlin's poetry uncovered before his insanity made it manifest.

In Foucault's long perspective Hölderlin's work and fate are situated at the very border of a kind of literature which we see constituting itself in *Agathon* and *Anton Reiser*, and which the *Lehrjahre* exemplifies in ways explored at the end of the previous chapter. It is the literature of humanity. The central image of the human being holds the world in place, mediating between subjective partialness and distant gods by means of the aesthetic. The aesthetic is essentially a belief in the possibility and significance of formation, 'Bildung', which applies equally to the individual human life and to the individual work of art. The affinity between these two terms, as I argued, is itself vital as a model for an harmoniously unified construction of the world. It is the dream of the 'Roman eines Lebens' ('novel of a life') of which Moritz spoke. *Hyperion*, in which the late Enlightenment ideal of formation in this global sense is pursued with all the unrelenting passion of 'literature', produces an image of the individual which is transparent upon psychological fragmentation and upon the far distance of the gods. It is an image of the paradoxically divine aura of human exposedness which the *Lehrjahre* is constructed to veil, not just in the flimsy artifice of the 'Saal der Vergangenheit', but in its whole immensely sophisticated aesthetic composition, 'der Dichtung Schleier' ('the veil of poetry'). This is precisely the effort to replace the missing father, in the sense of explicit discourses of authority, be they religious, social or more probably an amalgam of both, by poetry. Small wonder, then, that the *Lehrjahre* bears the marks of what it is holding at bay. The veil hides in order to disclose. These marks are apparent least satisfactorily, perhaps, in its irony. One senses in Goethe's irony in the *Lehrjahre* a trace of the unremitting alternation of absence and presence which I have talked about in the case of *Hyperion*, and which lies at the heart of 'literature' in Foucault's and Kittler's use of the word. But whereas in Hölderlin this alternation undercuts the humanist construction, never permitting one construction of the world to remain in place without being negated, in Goethe it becomes ironic prevarication, and as such is integrated into the play of the aesthetic. This is related to the use of irony which official Romanticism promoted into a sort of tatty substitute religion, unsurprisingly abhorred by Goethe. Most earnestly these traces appear in the recalcitrance of Mignon and the Harper to aesthetic assimilation, and in their importance to Wilhelm, and in the alternative tradition of criticism to which the *Lehrjahre* gave rise.

CHAPTER THREE

Der grüne Heinrich

In what remains of this book the 'literary authority', the guiding intertext of a given text, is always *Wilhelm Meisters Lehrjahre* itself. Keller's semi-autobiographical novel *Der grüne Heinrich* dwells upon the partialness of subjectivity, while at the same time never quite detaching itself from the structure and circularities of the aesthetic order of the *Lehrjahre.*

Gottfried Keller (1819–1890) is one of Switzerland's foremost writers, and his life was deeply bound up with that of his country. In the early 1840s he was much involved in radical liberal politics, and his first writing took the form of political verse in support of the liberal cause in the context of the civil war of the mid 1840s. He spent fifteen years (from 1861) in a top administrative post in cantonal government. Against the background of the early death of his father and a childhood spent in reduced circumstances with his mother and younger sister in their native Zürich, his artistic vocation was uncertain. He began by aspiring to be a painter, then a dramatist, only then coming to the literature which established his reputation. His long spell as a civil servant was an obstruction to his creativity. As well as lyric poetry he wrote a play, two novels, and four collections of *Novellen.* He is most remembered for the latter, where he establishes an idiom in which his artistic temperament and his pragmatism reach a compromise, in a style at once moralistic and humorous.

Keller's great novel, *Der grüne Heinrich* (first version 1854–1855), is autobiographical in inspiration. Its core is an account of his youth in Zürich, in which the experiences of a developing consciousness in a concretely realised social and historical setting are memorably represented. The circumstances of his upbringing (minus the sister) are there, as are episodes in his parents' home village where many relatives of the young protagonist still live, and which provides a contrast to the idiosyncracies and deprivations of city life. Heinrich, like Keller, is expelled from state school for taking part in an unfortunate demonstration against one of the teachers. Like Keller, Heinrich embarks upon the career of a landscape painter, which involves his mother in substantial financial sacrifice. Heinrich's vocation, like Keller's own, takes him to Munich (which, unlike Zürich, was a centre of German artistic activity at that time), only to discover that either his talent or prevailing circumstances, or possibly a mixture of both, are not favourable to him making a living from his painting. Descent into real and abject poverty precedes the return home to Switzerland and the renunciation of the ambition to become a professional painter, as also happened in Gottfried Keller's own case.

Keller invented some love affairs to add to the plot of his own biography (he was himself sadly unsuccessful in his romantic attachments and died a confirmed bachelor). He constructed an episode at the mansion of a German nobleman, sympathetic to the Republicanism of Switzerland. In this setting, Heinrich is at last cured of his conventional liberal religious convictions (he is thus a descendant of the *Schwärmer* we have already met). Here he is also introduced to the philosophy of Feuerbach, which taught the affirmation of the sensuous world, and discouraged belief in a deity (according to the philosopher, a projection of the human subject alone). Keller had adopted Feuerbach's views during a period of study in Heidelberg in 1848. Keller finished the novel by inventing his mother's death, which in reality did not occur until much later. Heinrich himself then dies, a sort of literary suicide, unable to support the shame of having occasioned his mother's death by unjustified ambition, and having failed to attend her last hours through dalliance at the noble household.

According to his own testimony, both within and beyond the novel itself, Keller drew upon Rousseau and Jean Paul for guidance in his autobiographical fiction, which undeniably also reflects something of the afterglow of German Romanticism. Goethe, and especially his main autobiographical work *Dichtung und Wahrheit*, were important in this regard too. The deeply literary mentality of both Heinrich and his author has been documented in an article which draws attention to important allusions to *Don Quixote* and *Faust* among others,[1] and further parallels to Cervantes, as well as to the *Odyssey* and *Robinson Crusoe*, have been elaborated more recently.[2] The relation to the *Lehrjahre* is nowhere explicit on Keller's part, but was noted by contemporaries even before the novel was finished.[3]

Composing this novel was a great struggle for Keller, who suffered from indolence and apathy. The fourth volume of the work, already late, was finished under pressure from his publisher, and Keller was never happy with it. In 1879–1880 he published a completely revised version. The eponymous hero now no longer dies at the end, but becomes a civil servant somewhat like his creator. Since he survives, it is now possible for him to tell his own story throughout, whereas before the story of his youth had had to be complemented by a third-person narrative of the Munich years, the episode at the count's mansion, and the melancholic return to Zürich. The revision removes a prominent reference to Jean Paul, thereby increasing the standing of Goethe within the novel, and, in accordance with contemporary aesthetic taste, intensifies the function of symbolism and reduces the topicality of the narrative.

The relations between *Wilhelm Meisters Lehrjahre* and *Der grüne Heinrich* are exceptionally complex. This is partly because Keller's novel is more like Goethe's than any of the others we have to deal with. In it, subject and object, person and world, real and ideal, modify, reflect, amplify and curtail each other with all the suppleness of Goethe's text. And Goethe's already complex model of the relation between real and ideal is itself only one of the moments in Keller's historically later, but thematically cognate, work of mediation. Another source of complexity is the existence of two complete versions of the novel, differing not only in broad outline, but often in subtle elements of emphasis too. It is as though the thematic complexity of the novel needed two entire formulations to work itself out, and even then, just as in the *Lehrjahre*, the fundamental questions are not resolved once and for all.

Keller's novel plays upon the the relation between the theme of the artist and the representation of subjectivity, within a realist context. Heinrich Lee's subjective difficulties are intertwined with problematic artistic aspirations. This already complex engagement with the issue of the aesthetic is further complicated by the world of industrial manufacture and market relations in the second half of the nineteenth century. Heinrich embodies a culture for which 'The ethos of the artist was a secret synonym for the autonomy of the individual.'[4] These are the terms of the ideology of the aesthetic. But this value conferred upon subjectivity by its association with the sphere of art, namely the autonomy of the individual, is under constant threat, and subjectivity threatens to appear unhoused once more as it had been in the pages of *Anton Reiser*. The question of the validity of the link between the artist theme and subjectivity as a quality and a potential is never closed in the successive episodes, or the successive versions, of Keller's novel. It is the doubt itself about this link which is the animating moment of these texts, keeping alive the ever-elusive moment of subjectivity in the face of his sense – a sense he shared with many contemporaries – of the threatening weight of historical contingency. This view now requires justification, since it contradicts the received view that Keller disassociates subjectivity from the sphere of art, corrects the idealism of the *Lehrjahre* and its Romantic derivatives, and relocates the co-ordinates of subjectivity in the sphere of what he called 'konkretes Menschentum' ('concrete humanity'), by which he meant contemporary Switzerland.[5] This will take us to the heart of the complex relations between Keller's novel and the *Lehrjahre*.

The link in the younger Keller's mind between the artist theme and subjectivity is clear in a passage from a letter to Ferdinand Freiligrath of 1847, which bears the imprint of the Romantic image of the artist:

> I also feel alien amongst people. Since poets are nothing other than authentic people (eigentliche Menschen), and the latter thus themselves all poets, they look askance and distrustfully upon a so-called 'poet' (Dichter), as if he were a traitor, telling tales out of school, and letting out the little secrets of mankind and humanity (Menschheit und Menschlichkeit).[6]

The poet is seen as somebody who partakes of the same interiority which everybody possesses, but is also visible as the possessor of that interiority because he betrays it, in both senses, in his capacity as a poet. Poetry is a synonym for subjectivity, since what other quality is simultaneously common to all individuals, and makes them different from everybody else?

This conflation of subjectivity with a quality variously defined as 'das Dichterische'[7] and 'das Poetische' survives into the first version of *Der grüne Heinrich* (XVIII, p. 7) and indeed into the second (V, pp. 6–7). But on the surface, the trend in the development of the work appears the reverse: towards the dissociation of the qualities.

Keller's novel began (according to an autobiographical note of some thirty years later), as a poignant reflection upon the profundity and pointlessness of the author's own experience of failure in relation to his vocation as a landscape painter.[8] The story which was about to be told was characterised in an early fragment as the unlikely *Roman* of a life, gaining brief definition against on the one hand, the mass of objective ordinariness of Swiss life,[9] and on the other the shadow proliferation of stories and motifs which pass before the mind without ever being elaborated and fixed in form.[10] The narrative of an artist was thus to guarantee that significant fusion of experience and form, that 'Roman', which in reality recedes before the divergent instances of circumstance and imagination. The focus of this early conception was the premature death of the artist.

This impulse, or so it soon came to seem to Keller, was excessively subjective, and in a letter of 1849 he claimed that he was tired of carping and that the novel would be his last subjective work.[11] He also felt it to be excessively bound up with the question of art. Writing to his friend, the literary historian Hermann Hettner, during the composition of the first *Grüner Heinrich*, Keller stressed how his failed landscape artist does not become a poet '(in order to avoid the production of yet another novel about an artist)', but develops instead into a rounded human being in the service of his fatherland.[12]

What becomes important is not individual subjectivity, displayed in the post-Romantic manner, but what in Feuerbachian diction is called 'species being', the life of the whole community of human beings. The extremely influential Feuerbach offered an answer to the problem of subjective partialness by legitimating subjectivity, not in its own right, but as the guarantee of human embeddedness in the totality of nature: 'Feuerbach . . . sought the implicit concrete basis for the actualisation of Reason in a post-Christian culture in the existential reality of the individual's absorption (in love and death) in the dynamic totality of the natural cosmos.'[13]

However, the specific death with which the first *Grüner Heinrich* concluded was too intimately bound up with the original artistic–autobiographical conception to lend itself easily to the meaning Keller now wished to attach to his novel. Hettner can be forgiven for assuming, presumably encouraged by the letter just quoted (which had nevertheless talked about a 'tragic' outcome), that the novel in progress was going to have a positive resolution.[14] Keller's own feeling for his autobiographical novel, however, still required the closure of early death. Indeed, such closure was the surest means of securing precisely the effect he had mentioned to Hettner, namely of preventing his hero from becoming a poet (i.e. the author of the *Roman* of his own life).

The second version of the novel is in effect written to correct this only partial dissociation of the universal human theme from the excessively subjective one of the problematic artist. The second version very plainly assents to the interest of the 'species being' in preference to that of the problematic individual subject, by housing the early subjective narrative within the mature perspective of the thoughtful and sober civil servant the young artist has become.

The truth is that Keller's novel at once presupposes and denies a certain link between subjectivity as a universal irreducible human value, and the function of the poet. The subjective stake in this work is both its *raison d'être* and an embarrassment. 'There is not a page in it that has not been lived and felt', wrote Keller in 1850,[15] and in 1871 he could still write that his book was worth revising, 'since I feel strongly that in its matter and even, on a couple of pages, in the form, there is something in it that is yours to give only once in your life'[16] (presumably: the unique specificity of one's own subjective story). Yet his considered view remained to the last that the book was flawed precisely because of its subjective origin and the artist theme which the autobiographical matter naturally implied.[17]

This indecision is certainly specific to the circumstances of

Keller's own life and to the circumstances of the composition of the novel, but it is also specific to Keller's historical moment. Its broader context is the complex reception accorded by 'the age of prose', as Hegel called the post-classical nineteenth century, to the cultural inheritance of Goethe and Schiller. This was the peculiar double-think also characteristic of that other historically inflected version of the *Lehrjahre*, Karl Immermann's *Die Epigonen* (1836). Indeed, the younger Keller at least twice referred to himself by the term 'epigone' which Immermann had popularised,[18] implying a recognition of, but intimidation by, the aesthetic achievements of the recent German masters.

In a letter to Hettner written in 1851 during the composition of *Der grüne Heinrich*, Keller expounded a view of Goethe and Schiller. They are dead, he says, and had no suspicion of how rapidly their world would collapse. The writers of Keller's generation have not really begun to emulate the classical model of the recent past successfully, but they must already look towards the future for their inspiration, and this encounter with an unknown future occasions terrible birth pangs.[19]

Der grüne Heinrich, in its rich indecision, bears the mark of this ambivalence with respect to the great inheritance of Weimar Classicism. But it is too simple to reduce the terms which battle it out in the episodes and versions of Keller's novel to, on the one hand, an idealist *Lehrjahre*, and on the other, a relativist, realistic sense of history. Keller was too aware of the ambiguity in the *Lehrjahre* to see it as simply idealistic. The later Keller resisted the facile contemporary public constructions of Goethe as, on one hand, a latter-day Olympian, and on the other, a subjective idealist.[20] In the context of the opinion expressed by a contemporary cultural pundit, that Goethe could not serve as a model for novelists because of his excessive idealism, Keller remarked (possibly with the *Wanderjahre* in mind too): 'as if "Wilhelm Meister" were not the most reality-hungry (realitätssüchtig) book in the world'.[21]

In fact, the relation between these two canonical *Bildungsromane* is more intricate than my survey has so far been able to show. We have seen how Keller's autobiographical conception did not spring from a desire to emulate or answer *Wilhelm Meister*, but from personal preoccupations coloured by autobiographical writers like

Jean Paul and Rousseau, and tinged with late Romanticism. Yet the fact that both works in the process of composition take up and transform autobiographical moments and motifs suggests an analogous relation to the question of subjectivity and the transformation or *Aufhebung* of autobiography in art.

One major aspect of Keller's novel is that it has a core commitment to first-person narrative, which distinguishes it sharply from the *Lehrjahre*. Goethe's novel is unthinkable in the first person, since it depends upon a co-operation between Wilhelm's mistakes and the voice of the authoritative narrator. To the central question of aesthetic authority we shall return, but we can note how the proximity of Keller's problematic and difficult theme to that of Goethe in the *Lehrjahre* is reflected in the fact that there is an important first-person component in Goethe's narrative too. Whereas Wilhelm's youthful enthusiasm for the puppet theatre had been related in the third person in the *Theatralische Sendung*, in the *Lehrjahre* itself Wilhelm tells it in his own words to Marianne. Since the roots of his subjective-artistic erring lie in that experience, there is an important structural parallel between that first-person account and Heinrich's narrative of his boyhood, which also reveals in partial self-consciousness the roots of his own subjective-artistic deviation. When Keller composed an objectivised and distanced version of his own inner life-story in the form of the Novelle *Pankraz der Schmoller*, he adopted the Goethean device denied him in his own novel. Pankraz narrates his formative experiences to his mother and sister, who nod off, just as Marianne had done in the *Lehrjahre*.

The crucial influence of Feuerbach upon Keller's ambition to universalise his autobiographical text also brought the enterprise closer to the Goethean project in the *Lehrjahre*. The *Lehrjahre*'s ironical and delicate balance between the artist and the subject attracted the first generation of German Romantics, but was also upset by them in favour of the artist. Feuerbach, by famously insisting that God is simply a misunderstanding of subjectivism taken to its extreme, opposed the subjective idealism of the philosophical tradition which arose out of Romanticism and restored to subjective partialness both its value and its position in relation to a totality of nature which it could never aspire to know, but of which it was to celebrate and affirm being part. Hence he could articulate the archetypal definition of literature as the discourse of the partial subject: 'Der Schmerz ist die Quelle der Poesie' ('pain is the source of poetry').[22] This affirmation is more compatible with Goethe's views than the apotheosis of the artist which characterised Romanticism, and which was echoed in the earliest conception of what was to become *Der grüne Heinrich*. In resolutely turning against the artist-centred view of the previous generation under the influence of Feuerbach, Keller was in effect turning towards Goethe.

By the time the original project had become the first version of *Der grüne Heinrich*, it is at all events quite clear that the work had taken on a conscious relation to the Goethean paradigm. To the original *telos* of the work, namely the death of the eponymous hero, is added another structural determinant in the form of the episode in the count's mansion which presents an evident parallel with Goethe's Society of the Tower. The parallel was even more evident in the first version than in the second. In the earlier version not only does Heinrich find a certain identity through education at the end of the novel in the count's circle, but also this has been anticipated at the beginning of the novel (Book One, Chapter Three) when the young Heinrich meets the count on his first night in German lands, and has a conversation with him about matters of overarching thematic import (artistic vocation and Republicanism). Thus a circularity is established, obviously analogous with that set up by the emissaries of the Tower in the *Lehrjahre*. The count, as a nobleman (an 'überbürgerliches Wesen', in the delightful, but regrettably untranslatable, phrase of the first version, XVI, p. 45) with progressive liberal ideas, is an obvious counterpart to Lothario.

The convergence of the Goethean model and the influence of Feuerbach is confirmed by the fact that it is at the 'court' of the count that Heinrich becomes acquainted with the doctrine of Feuerbach. Dortchen Schönfund has embraced an affirmative atheism spontaneously, while the count has reached the same position via the route of reflection, and is a convinced Feuerbachianer (XIX, pp. 258–259; VI, pp. 293–294). In what is presumably an appropriate interfusion of reason and feeling, Heinrich's love for Dortchen intensifies his receptiveness to these new ideas to which he becomes converted (for instance, VI, p. 214). At the court, in other words, Heinrich learns a substantial and life-changing lesson. Furthermore, the count, as well as being a Feuerbachianer, is also a proponent of classical *Bildung*: 'The bourgeois ideal of human personality as a self-developing entelechy, the idea of the individual process of development, has in him a convinced representative and advocate.'[23] The Goethean and the Feuerbachian messages are entrusted to the same messenger.

So far, so Goethean. The novel was immediately received as such: 'Its kinship with "Wilhelm Meister" is clear', wrote Hettner before he had had sight of the fourth volume of the first version of *Der grüne Heinrich*.[24] There is thus an evident tension between this aspect of the work and the original ending in death. Even the commuted second ending seemingly undermines the gains of the episode in the count's mansion. But does that mean that Keller's novel is a revocation of Goethe's? Kaiser concludes that 'the historical project of the novel of development and education (Entwicklungs- und Bildungsroman) is revoked. Instead, there is the great disillusionment – the model is not that of *Wilhelm Meister* but that of *Anton Reiser*.'[25] The mention of *Anton Reiser* is welcome confirmation of our contention that here subjectivity once again assumes something of the unredeemed partialness it had in Moritz's work. And it may well be that within the narrow thematic of *Bildung*, Keller puts a powerful objection to the Goethean vision. Yet in terms of the aesthetic representation of subjectivity, that is not the case.

What distinguishes Keller's novel above all from the *Anton Reiser* 'model' is its form. It does not lack an ending. On the contrary, it has two of them. We now turn, therefore, to the formation of Keller's theme, and in particular to the manipulation of the themes of inheritance and incest, the relations of law and desire, by which *Der grüne Heinrich* achieves a formal definition quite unlike Moritz's novel, and much more like the *Lehrjahre*.

Like Keller himself, Heinrich Lee is left without a father at the age of five. The lack of paternal guidance is why his subjective self-definition is visible as a problem. There are difficulties in composing a public persona. The adolescent's preoccupation with his appearance can go wrong without a fatherly hand in guidance: 'But it is often just this attention to externals that hinders the inner soul from developing quickly, if there is not a man, and he a father, at hand to prune and restrain it by wholesome ridicule, and at the same time firmly to point out to his aspiring son the things that are of true value' (III, p. 236).

Keller's sense of the father's role seems to anticipate Freud in the threat of castration (the original German 'beschneiden' has stronger connotations in this direction than 'prune'), and the scenario of sexual rivalry ('der aufstrebende Sohn', 'the aspiring son'). If this lack of a binding father is reminiscent of Moritz, it is also like the *Lehrjahre*, because Wilhelm too lacks a father at the outset, in the sense of a sustaining guide and a secure social identity. An element of the 'Vaterlosigkeit' (lack of a father) of Anton Reiser is necessary for any literary construction of the modern subject.

The father who can shape subjectivity into social form is a symbolic, not an empirical necessity. The moment of fatherlessness of Wilhelm Meister or Heinrich Lee must not be confused with that of Hyperion. Hölderlin's text was poetically so radical because it was defined by the lack of a symbolic father, an impossible lack in the end for the poet (indeed, for anyone other than a psychotic), since language itself as a symbolic system cannot ultimately exist without such authority. In Heinrich's case, on the other hand, while the empirical father is missing, the symbolic one is not. He is within:

> As my memory of his bodily appearance becomes more clouded, a conception of his inner being has formed itself more and more clearly and distinctly in my mind, and this noble image has become part of the vast Infinite, to which my ultimate thoughts lead me, and under whose protection I believe I make my pilgrimage. (III, p. 23)

The problem facing Heinrich is how to externalise these internalised paternal values. His answer is to pursue an artistic vocation. There is a significant link between Heinrich's experience of anarchic subjective intervention in the objective moral world and the poetic function. When, in one famous episode, he persists with a complete fabrication to the point that schoolmates are punished and he is not, he becomes a presence for the first time: 'Never before had they known me in school to be so eloquent as I was in this narrative' (III, p. 92). Heinrich suddenly discovers his creative capacity, and elaborates a narrative which elevates his otherwise retiring self to the stature of a hero of myth. Furthermore:

> So far as I can dimly remember, the mischief I had caused was to me not only a matter of indifference, but I even felt within myself a sense of gratification that poetic justice had rounded off my invention so beautifully that something striking had occurred, been dealt with, and endured, and this in consequence of my creative word. (III, p. 92)

This intervention is discovery not just of the potential of the subject in the world, but also of the potential of poetic invention. Thus Heinrich's commitment to an artistic vocation is an attempt to adapt the poetic power of his subjective life to the demands of social adulthood, demands implanted within him by paternal inheritance.

Nor is this simply an arbitrary choice of path. As well as having an extremely well-defined and effective social persona, his father had been both a craftsman and creative (III, p. 12). Hence Heinrich's ambition to succeed as a landscape artist is an elaboration of his father's accomplishments, albeit divested of their concrete dimension (his father having been a builder).[26] This specific paternal connection is brilliantly concentrated in the novel's title. Heinrich is known by the colour green which had also coloured his father's social persona, the image of a handsome, slender man 'who wore a fine green coat in the most modern fashion' (III, p. 22). Heinrich's imperfect but authentic succession of his father is thus encapsulated in the circumstance that he wears the same colour (indeed, the same cloth) as his father, but no longer in the latest fashion, and only in the – quite literally – reduced form into which his mother has cut it down for him. The connotations of 'green' also include on one hand spontaneous and healthy growth, and on the other unripeness and immaturity. These properties which express the positive and negative aspects of subjectivity, its potential and its partialness, are thus also present within the colour green, which therefore presents in one word the hopeful union of a public persona and a flourishing inner life.

Heinrich's attempt to express his paternal inheritance in the terms of a successful career as a painter are made into a thematic and structural turning point in the second version of Keller's novel.

At the very stage at which the mature narrator resumes the story after the end of the *Jugendgeschichte*, in the chapter 'Das Pergamentlein' ('The Title Deed', Book Three, Chapter Nine), he recounts his appearance before the village elders at which he has to justify the unprecedented step of encashing his patrimony in order to study painting in Munich. The handling of the episode serves to convey the sense of subjective liberation from principles of succession, without either value-system prevailing conclusively over the other. In a splendid detail, the village elders' complete incomprehension of this modern subjective departure is contained in a glance from the chairman, who has donned spectacles to read the relevant document: 'He immediately directed a serious look at me, though I must have been just fog to him through his spectacles, which were good for reading only' (V, p. 107). The patriarchal consciousness of Swiss rural tradition cannot read the figure of Heinrich at this moment. He becomes blurred. As for himself, he feels at once 'leidend und verantwortlich' ('passive and responsible', V, p. 108), and is conscious of the gravity of this moment at which his subjectivity manifests itself as a blur in the otherwise distinct world view of the community. He can no more read the situation than the bespectacled elder, because his own attempt to achieve social identity seems to trangress, although only in an unspoken way, the very laws of society.

The novel continues to explore this complex theme. On one hand it develops a narrative in which the vocation of painter becomes progressively distinguished from the 'poetic' which inheres in all human subjects. This theme is announced at the beginning of the first version, in a passage in which the hero is still being established as the central subject of the novel to come, and is described at the point of his departure for Munich as having gone beyond mere painterly understanding to reach back to that general poetic quality ('das allgemeine Dichterische') which lies in every person from the beginning (XVI, pp. 44–45). 'The poetic' signifies creativity and potential for understanding, and living according to, one's place in the totality of nature. On the other hand, the novel sustains an awareness of the refraction of this inner illumination in the recalcitrant circumstances of the world, which circumscribes and threatens to nullify it.

This contradiction between inner and outer dimensions of inheritance can best be exemplified by a sequence of events at the geometric centre of the book. In the first place, we have the crucial encounter with the works of Goethe. On his return from a Wilhelm Tell festival in the country, Heinrich finds Goethe's complete works at home and spends thirty (in the second version, with added biblical overtones, forty), days, utterly immersed in them. This intense personal absorption in the works of Goethe signifies the internalisation of a further set of authoritative paternal values. Like his father, Goethe is a deceased personal authority, both living and dead ('eine lebendigtote Gestalt')[27] – Heinrich's first experience of the name is the announcement by a workman that 'der große Goethe ist gestorben' ('the great Goethe is dead') – whose legacy is guidance in the matter of how to conduct oneself in the world, of how subject and object properly relate:

> he who marches in a splendid procession cannot describe it so well as the man who stands at the roadside. The latter is not superfluous or idle; and what is seen is not complete without him who sees (und der Seher ist erst das ganze Leben des Gesehenen) and if he is a true seer, the moment comes when he joins the procession with his golden mirror, like the eighth king in *Macbeth* who showed in his mirror many more kings. Nor can the calm, passive spectator look on without some active effort and trouble on his part, just as the spectator of a holiday procession has enough trouble in getting and keeping a good place. These efforts maintain the freedom and integrity of our eyes. (v, p. 6)

This discursive and thoughtful passage defines the activity of the artist so as to make it compatible with, or a special case of, the universal condition of subjectivity. Immediately before the passage just quoted, the revealing phrase 'der künstlerische Mensch' ('the artistic person') has occurred, a formulation which conflates the artistic faculty and the universal implications of 'Mensch'. A few paragraphs later we find the distinction 'therefore artists differ from other people only in this . . .' (v, p. 7), in other words a distinction the main purpose of which is to express a similarity. The phrase 'Der Seher ist erst das ganze Leben des Gesehenen' sounds like a definition of the role of subjectivity in the world, and the overall emphasis upon passivity, and upon the faculty of seeing, rather collapses the artistic function into the condition of subjectivity. Here too 'the poetic' is being defined, this time as a quality of the things of the world, as much as of their representation ('for it is the same law which makes things poetical, or makes the reflection of their being worth while', v, p. 7).

The momentous encounter with Goethe, then, is an integration point, at which Heinrich is vouchsafed an insight into the proper relation between subject and object, and thus provided with authoritative guidance in his own work of fulfilling the paternal imperative to become a social adult. In his case it is as an artist, but this is in no substantial way different from all the other subjectivities who are both in the procession (of life, society, history) and observers of it.

The difficult refraction of this inner light into the outer world is at first manifested in the fact that Heinrich tries to apply his insights in his practical work as a landscape artist, and fails. The subjective incorporation of the law ('it is the same law . . .') does not lead to its external realisation. All he can do is disturb the forms he had mastered before: 'I produced a miserable scrawl, trying to get out of my old style which I despised; while in doing so I ruined even that' (v, pp. 8–9). As was the case with Wieland's *Agathon*, subjectivity appears only negatively, in the disturbances wrought upon existing forms.

But now there is a curious parallelism. The shade of Goethe is echoed by the shadow which falls over one of Heinrich's hapless attempts at a formally valid realism. It is the shadow of Römer, the established landscape artist, who enters Heinrich's life as the authority who will aid him in the development of his active skills as a landscape painter, just as Goethe had given him a passive understanding of the totality in which each 'künstlerischer Mensch' works. In the first version, this parallel was actually verbally given (xviii, 3 and 9); in the revision we are left only with the 'Then suddenly a shadow fell upon the white sheet of paper . . .' (v, p. 10) with which Römer makes his dramatic entrance. Keller may very well have removed the verbal parallel because the second version has a closer identification with Goethe than the first, and thus he does not want to stress a parallel which puts the function of Goethe into an ambiguous light. But the parallel between Goethe and Römer remains nevertheless, not only because the two influences on

Heinrich's development follow each other immediately at the mid-point of the book, but because the name Keller has chosen to give this character cannot fail to evoke Goethe's own Italian connection (see too v, p. 23).

Although Römer is a 'wirklicher Meister' ('genuine master'), as the chapter title has it, he is also a megalomaniac and a lunatic. This is a strong contrast to the sensitive way in which the Goethe episode balanced the role of artist and the condition of subjectivity against one another. Here the principle is almost reversed, and this violation of harmony is the unfailing effect of reading the two episodes one after the other. Römer, though a gifted artist, is a paranoid psychotic: his feeling for natural totality in his art is ludicrously subverted by his absolute lack of grasp of reality. The configuration of Goethe and Römer is an exemplary vicissitude of authority in the novel. The political delusions which plague Römer trouble the philosophical clarity of the Goethean insight. Heinrich's confusion at this lack of stable authority is expressed in the disastrous act of self-assertion which seals Römer's fate. A public act travesties a subjective truth.

Another pair of experiences can be cited which define the place of the subject in the world as it is seen in this novel. At the end of Book Three, after discouraging experiences trying to make his way in Munich, Heinrich reaches a low point, which is graphically expressed in an enormous doodle, a 'Kritzelei' (iii, p. 299), with which he fills his time in a trough of melancholy. This recalls the 'trübseliges Gekritzel' mentioned above, and generally represents the extreme example of the dangers of Heinrich's chosen genre of landscape painting, which are the dangers of abstraction and of narcissism.[28] Earlier we had read: 'I invented my own landscapes, in which I lavishly heaped together all the poetical motifs, and from these I passed on to such as were dominated by a single characteristic, always introducing into them the same wanderer, in whose person I half-consciously expressed my own individuality' (iii, p. 196).

Representation becomes invention, and the only human link is to the self. The huge abstraction described in the chapter 'The Whimsy' is the nadir of Heinrich's real involvement with the world.

It too is followed by a reversal: vicissitudes characterise the novel's handling of its complex theme. This lapse into a subjectivity disconnected from the world is then corrected by Heinrich's work on the plaster copy of Agasias' Borghese Warrior which by chance adorns his room. This is a development away from landscape and towards the human form, and thus escapes the twin traps of abstraction and narcissism. It is also a development towards a re-assertion of masculine authority within the trajectory of artistic education. Not only is the figure, of course, that of a man, but its attitude has the balance between subject and object perfectly right: an equipoise between 'defence and attack' (VI, p. 1).[29]

Within the artist theme, the subject–object problem is worked through, towards the point where the artist theme is transcended, and its place taken by a personal autonomy from where the vocation of the artist looks like just another profession. Heinrich goes on to general studies which correct his subjectivism, and anticipate the self-education of Hans Castorp on the magic mountain.

This development is confirmed when Heinrich makes his decision to give up his career as a painter, but not without having learned, exactly as Wilhelm Meister does, to appreciate the formal value of appearing what you are. Lessons from art, transferred onto life. The final version describes the moment thus: 'Satisfied with the clear and completed form which my destiny had now assumed, I went on step by step, without haste and without delay, having in view one single aim, to enter under my mother's roof, whether I were rich or poor' (VI, p. 143).

The first version illustrates the point even more forcefully:

> For now it seemed to him that his destiny had taken on the necessary clear and completed form for his return home, and since he was not in a position to return with hopes fulfilled, he could still return in the serious and sacred garb of the mendicant, homeless and in need of charity, and thus display at least a certain shape and appearance to his contemporaries amongst whom it vouchsafed him a recognisable rank and position. (XIX, p. 183)

Here the *Roman* of a life appears to be drawing towards a conclusion, in a momentary grasp of wholeness amid partialness which combines the discernment of wholeness within subjective experience of Anton Reiser (see p. 126 above) with the patterned formation of Goethe's aesthetic treatment of subjectivity as personality. The first version also recalls Anton Reiser's desire for a public persona at all costs, a place in the 'Reih' und Glied' (the ranks) of society. Keller himself, from his dissatisfaction with the intrinsically imperfect work in progress on his novel, dreamed of producing a work in which formal perfection would encompass a whole life.[30]

In a further reversal, Heinrich's artistic endeavours, having just been written off, are restored to him in the episode in the count's mansion. Here they are indications not of his potential as a landscape artist, but of his coherence as a personality. Heinrich now encounters a truly benevolent masculine authority in the form of the count. In close parallel to the operations of the Society of the Tower, it turns out that the count has been monitoring Heinrich's apparently fragmented life and imperfect art, collecting his works, and thereby acting as the steward of a unity where there had appeared to be none.[31]

The count thus exhibits that configuration consisting of the ownership and appreciation of art, and sensitivity to the singular subjectivity of his 'son', which characterises the father-collector figures from Agathon senior to Drendorf senior and the Freiherr von Risach in Stifter's *Der Nachsommer*.

Not only does Heinrich receive a sense of his personal wholeness through the count's activity as a collector, he also inherits the estate of Schmalhöfer, the junk-shop dealer who had effectively saved Heinrich's life during his bleakest days in Munich. This confers a sense of paternal continuity and coherence upon the last in a line of imperfect empirical father figures (starting with his mother in her capacity as a representative of the absent father, whose responsibilities as educator now fall upon her, and including Römer), and suggests a convergence between the lines of empirical and ideal father figures, to a point at which life's vicissitudes are deprived of their power to dislocate personality.

Furthermore, in these wholly favourable surroundings, Heinrich now discovers he can paint again, at least within the limitations of his natural gifts (VI, p. 211). Art here modulates from a problematic creativity, an 'irresponsibility of the imagination',[32] into an entirely commensurate creativity, an authoring of the self. Similarly, Wilhelm Meister, having learnt to act *himself*, leaves the professional acting to the professional actors.

Within the paternal line of development, the 'inheritance' or 'law' dimension, the place of the artist theme in the representation of subjectivity is finely modulated, in the sense of Goethe and in prominent reference to him. But the balance, of course, is upset whichever of the two versions of *Der grüne Heinrich* one takes. But this is not another 'vicissitude' within the elaboration of problematic inheritance, since in both versions the death of Heinrich's *mother* is the decisive event. That is the culmination of the *other* determination, of desire, and incest, of the feminine rather than the masculine. And it is to this that we now turn.

As in the *Lehrjahre*, there are in *Der grüne Heinrich* two levels of the theme of desire, two variants of the circularity of incest. One is expressed in the female characters to whom Heinrich is erotically attracted. The other concerns his relationship with his mother. One produces and guarantees form, the other threatens it.

The female characters ensure form by giving definition to Heinrich's desire. If he is the subject, they are the objects of desire, which is the first component of subjectivity. In Keller's novel, as in Goethe's, women figures bear a great weight of meaning. As Keller revealingly put it, 'the two women figures (Anna und Judith) [are] poetic images of the opposing forces which confront each other within the awakening life of men (des Menschen)'.[33] By vanishing or dying at structurally important moments they convey the need for (masculine) subjective desire to be acknowledged but relativised. Furthermore, by dying or vanishing or otherwise being deferred they make it possible to fashion, from the 'schlechte Unendlichkeit' ('bad infinity')[34] of masculine desire (poetic inspiration), the stern assurance of masculine control.

The contrast with *Anton Reiser* is instructive. Just as Moritz must do without forms of masculine authority in producing his representation of unredeemed subjectivity, so must he do without women figures to shape his plot. As we have seen (above, pp. 88–89), for Anton Reiser love belongs in literature, not life, for life defines itself by being unlike literature. Goethe's aesthetic ennoblement of the novel in the *Lehrjahre* made it possible to charge the figures of romantic fiction with the weight and significance of subjective desire without the appearance of triviality. While Keller benefits from this formal possibility, rounding out (he uses the term 'Abrundung') autobiographical material by inventing women figures,[35] his affinity with Moritz, with whom he probably had more in common than he did with Goethe, is betrayed in the fact that all these erotic connections are unconsummated or otherwise imperfect. It is a constitutive paradox of Keller's autobiographical fiction that the women figures who embody his authorial control (i.e. by occupying load-bearing positions in the structure of the plot) are simultaneously figures of the autobiographical subject's inadequacy.

Keller did not give his autobiographical counterpart a counterpart to his own sister (much to her chagrin), thus avoiding the danger of an incestuous brother–sister attraction. Nevertheless, Anna and Judith are both relatives of the fictional Heinrich: the former, with her palindromic name and tenuous hold on reality, as a figure of narcissism,[36] the latter as an older, once-married woman, a mother figure of sorts, who also, in a rather obvious way, embodies a mother-earth natural vitality in contrast to the ideal non-sensual projection of Anna. They thus repeat, at this level of the woman dimension, the vicissitudinous coexistence of ideal and real we have just examined in the dimension of inheritance.

Dortchen Schönfund appears in a part of the novel characterised by a self-conscious Goethean artificiality, and is thus virtually a self-confessed Kellerian projection. Her name betrays this conscious artificiality ('Schönfund' points towards 'beautiful invention'), and her thematic function is like that of Natalie in the *Lehrjahre*, in that she embodies intuitively the (Feuerbachian) doctrine her masculine equivalent in the thematic economy (the count) has to work hard to acquire (VI, pp. 203–204). She thus stands at the end of a development in Heinrich, offering a way of representing the masculine protagonist in relation to an ideal. In her and the count, and specifically in their relation to each other, law and desire unite to reveal the secret of Heinrich's personality. In some ways, the fact that Heinrich and she are never united (although attracted towards each other) is simply a version of the deferral of the union of Wilhelm and Nathalie at the end of the *Lehrjahre*. It is in the logic of the ideal, expressed with depressing inevitability in the 'unreal' woman figure, that it cannot be ultimately attained.

The second level of the incest theme concerns what Kaiser calls 'die Mutterbindung' (the mother-bond).[37] This is the other side of 'fatherlessness'. Pure subjectivity, what is called in a memorable phrase 'die Verschwendung an sich' ('squandering for its own sake', II, p. 158), the pure profligacy of imagining the subjective life as imaginable without its objective correlate, is linked to the maternal ground of subjectivity. Without the strong guidance of the father to socialise the affective potential of the mother's son, there is always the threat for him of formlessness, of a blurring of social identity. Ultimately the threat is of re-absorption into the maternal element, of the loss of any individual definition whatever.

There is also the empirical mother who, in the absence of the father, has to fulfil his socialising role. Frau Lee presents her son, on the point of his departure from the maternal home, with a dozen shirts she has made herself. Frau Lee's whole social practice of thrift is absolutely opposed to anything not commensurate with the modest circumstances in which she and her son find themselves. Yet these shirts are finer than they need to be. 'But they are all as white as snow and if you can acquire finer clothes before these shirts are worn out, you need not be ashamed of them, because they are made of decent and honest linen' (XVI, p. 16). She has spun him a second skin, yet this intimate private maternal gift is not, she hopes, incompatible with the assumption of a public role. This is a particularly tender representation of the dual function she is called upon to fulfil in relation to her son, a beautiful metaphor for the concepts which in cold jargon are called primary and secondary socialisation. Of course, and more prominently, her cutting down of his father's cloth to make Heinrich's green clothes conveys the same configuration, and it is only at this point, taking in both masculine and feminine determinations, that one can appreciate the full richness and resonance of the title Keller coined for his autobiographical novel.

She negotiates the same precarious path in her attempts to establish a solid basis for Heinrich's art studies. Keller's writing is especially poignant, for instance, in this paragraph, which stands in isolation in the text:

On receiving this letter, my mother dressed herself in her best clothes, which were plain and uniform in colour, and with a clean neatly folded handkerchief in her hand, she began solemnly to make the round of the authorities accessible to her. (IV, p. 2)

This path is precarious because Heinrich's ambitions as a painter are maternally inspired in two ways at least. First, there is the idea of making a living from the exercise of the imagination as an artist: we recall Goethe's attribution of his own 'Lust zu fabulieren' ('pleasure in inventing tales'), quoted as a motto to the Introduction above, to his mother. Second, Heinrich's desire to be a landscape artist, although historically an effect of the Romantic fashion, is also linked to the mother dimension, since, as we saw, it is close to dangers of abstraction and narcissism, both manifestations of a failure of, or distance from, adult socialisation. The appeal of the Romantic fashion to the young Heinrich is not an accident. Whereas Moritz was not seduced by the Romantic attitude, since it did not yet exist (except in embryo in his favourite prose work, *Werther*, and in his own aesthetic theory), it is an historical reality and thus a subjective possibility for Heinrich Lee. Indeed, as he will discover, he has come to it at a time when it is already rather out of date.

Heinrich's particular circumstances strengthen the link between the mother dimension and painting, since he is inspired to want to become a landscape painter by the 'flight to mother nature', a return to his origins in the country. By doing this he reverses his own father's move from the country to the city. Once embarked upon his journey in what Kaiser calls 'the mother-land of painting' ('das Mutterland der Malerei'),[38] Heinrich precariously skirts the undifferentiated continuum of the dyadic mother–child relationship. He very nearly lapses back into it completely at the moment when he elaborates his vast doodle, at the low point of his development in Munich. This is metaphorically a spider's web, 'a monstrous gray spider's web' (V, p. 300). The spider, according to Freud, represents the mother as danger of entrapment and incorporation, and in Keller's imaginative universe the sphere of spinning is the space of the undifferentiated primary unity of mother and child.[39] We recall the shirts which Frau Lee had spun for her son, and indeed her association with spinning elsewhere in the novel.

Heinrich's decision to abandon painting is also a decision to head back to the 'only goal' of 'his mother's roof' (VI, p. 143). The play of masculine and feminine determinants is kaleidoscopically intricate now (and thus perhaps exemplarily realistic), since to give up this ambition is both to fail and to follow his father, both to let down *and* to return to his mother. Insofar as this return to the maternal roof is a dangerous lapse back into the primary continuum, it is at the first instance prevented by paternal intervention in the form of the count and his entourage and properties. The masculine dimension includes within itself acceptable forms of the feminine: Heinrich's creativity is vindicated, and there is a real woman, an adult object choice, rather than an incestuous-narcissistic lapse back into the primary desire for the mother. But of course, the maternal dimension asserts its power. Heinrich misses his mother's last days by spending time in the count's company formulating his personality.

The prevailing incestuous determination of the first version of the novel is clear. The death of Heinrich, which Lukács called 'zufällig-subjektiv' ('accidental-subjective'),[40] has a certain subjective necessity as Heinrich returns to 'mother earth', relinquishing his individual definition in favour of a quiescent return to the cycles of nature: the grass grows fresh and, of course, green on his grave.

The Romantic-literary preoccupation with incest was moreover present by a peculiar allusion. Heinrich is involuntarily reminded of Byron's *Manfred* after the death of his mother. He is inwardly shattered by the full realisation 'that [his mother] must finally have believed that she had perceived (durchschauen) him to be not a good son, and he recalled involuntarily those dreadful words which Manfred speaks about a female blood relation of his, who has been destroyed through him:

> Nicht meine Hand, mein Herz das brach das ihre,
> Es welkte, mich durchschauend.' (XIX, p. 323)

This allusion quite unambiguously, although euphemistically, makes a comparison between Heinrich's guilt vis-à-vis his mother and Manfred's incestuous love for his sister. Keller seems to have altered the wording of the German version of Byron's text to insist on the word 'durchschauen', which is not the word used by the translation he apparently consulted (see XIX, p. 386).[41] The original reads 'it gazed on mine, and wither'd' while the translation read 'an meinem hing's, und welkte'. By using the word 'durchschauen', Keller creates common verbal ground which makes a comparison possible. Astarte saw into her brother's heart and discerned the incestuous longing there; Heinrich's mother, in his melancholy imagination, saw through her son's pretensions, and recognised him as a ne'er-do-well.

But the incestuous implication is unavoidable. Heinrich's failure is associated unambiguously with his artistic vocation. In discerning this, the prominent allusion to *Manfred* implies, his mother discerns in this vocation the equivalent of incestuous desire. This signifies that the vocation was subjective to the point of being unsocialisable. We find ourselves in the realm of Mignon and the Harper, both embroiled in the fatal effects of incestuous desire. Mignon was unable to assume or identify permanently with any appearance, choosing instead to 'scheinen bis ich werde'. The word 'durchschauen', upon which Keller has chosen to play at this point, conveys insubstantiality. Heinrich imagines himself becoming transparent to his mother, and as he imagines this she becomes transparent to him, a pure instance of his own negation. This is more than just a social failure. It is the dissolving of the social self, the dispersal of that personality which had gained definition in the count's circle.

We now come to the end, or, better, endings of *Der grüne Heinrich*. The conclusion we have just described, to put it into *Lehrjahre* terms, represents the triumph of Mignon over the Society of the Tower. Aesthetic resolution is engulfed by a translinguistic extra-social totality. The second ending reverses this. Heinrich now survives, and the masculine determination reasserts itself in the reappearance of Judith, one of the aesthetic form-giving female figures of the book. She too repeats the function of Natalie in the *Lehrjahre*, by being both the *telos* of Heinrich's development and a deferred ideal, since, in agreeing not to marry, the two characters agree not to write a novelistic ending to their real lives. As if to clinch the reassertion of the masculine determination, in which feminine and masculine are combined in the aesthetic, at the very end, after Judith's (structurally convenient) death, Heinrich inherits back from her his own *Jugendgeschichte*, to which the later narrative can be wedded, to produce the consummation of the text we have just finished reading.

It is indeed time now to focus upon this question of the status of the text we have just been reading, and on the kind of authority by which it legitimates itself. In our context the whole question must hinge on the authority of 'the great Goethe', which, as we have seen, is invoked within the text. Is it authoritative for the text, as well as in it? For Hartmut Laufhütte, the author of a full-length study of the novel, this authority does become effective in the final, first-person version of the work. This narrative arrangement, as he seeks to demonstrate, suggests how the later Heinrich has assimilated and applied to literature the insights derived from reading Goethe which the younger Heinrich had tried in vain to apply to painting. Hence the entire text acquires a certain artistic and moral legitimation; the vicissitudes described are overcome by virtue of the fact that they are being represented poetically.[42]

Laufhütte's interpretation can be objected to on the grounds that Keller did not wish his novel to be about a poet (he explicitly wished to avoid 'das ewige Literaturdichten'). Thus in the first version the story of the failed artist is told by a detached narrative voice, and decisions about whether or not the novel is the work of a poet are referred to the aesthetic judgement of the reader. In the second version the narrative organisation is entrusted to a rather sad civil administrator who is the very antithesis of a poet or artist of any description. Again, one is invited to base one's judgement of the achievement of the book upon Keller's achievement, not that of the narrator. Gerhard Kaiser's study of Keller seemingly contradicts Laufhütte's view. It is based upon a specific personal dynamic which informs Keller's life in its relation with his literary production:

> An author invents his life, but he may smuggle this invented life and the circumstances of its invention into poetry, and declare it to be a novel, only by keeping silent about the novelist and his authorship in the novel itself. Were he to tell of it, Green Henry would be revealed as the author Gottfried Keller who would also be revealed as a private individual. The blind spot around which the novel is written would have disappeared, the enigma surrounding Keller resolved: that failure in life is the precondition of writing.[43]

In these terms it is clear why the relation between the author in the text and the author of the text must be distinct for Keller's construct to work. It is because the authority of the text must not be contaminated by the failure it recounts.

Far from constituting an important difference between *Der grüne Heinrich* and *Wilhelm Meisters Lehrjahre*, however, this configuration establishes a compelling parallel. For, as we have argued above, the failure of the hero in the *Lehrjahre* is the single most important textual signal of subjectivity. It is the trope by means of which subjectivity is represented in a work of art. Keller's novel, like Goethe's, depends in order to function, upon a separation between protagonist and author. Only thus can the partialness of the protagonist who is the exemplary bearer of subjectivity be prevented from undermining the aesthetic completeness of the text. Only thus can the de-centred subject be reinstated at the centre: it is the paradoxical power of this discourse of subjectivity that it has the space to speak of its own limitations.

Furthermore, the key similarity here is not just that two failures speak, thanks to an unacknowledged alliance with an aesthetic authority which ensures them the place to do so, but that this figure of failure is associated with art. In other words, these are both stories about failed artists. This specific subject construction entails the figuring of subjectivity as both partial (fatherless failures) and creative (artistic), but somehow redeemed by the very creativity denied it on the level of plot. It is not hard to see why the identity of protagonist and author must be hidden, although in both cases we are dealing in some sense with autobiographical texts. This is the triumph of art over autobiography, its translation into the realm of the aesthetic. Hence Keller wrote: 'It was not my intention to include this account of my youth out of subjective vanity (eitle Subjektivität), because it is my own story; but although it *is* my own story, I set myself the task of seeing myself objectively, and providing others with a warning (mich selbst mir objektiv zu machen und ein Exempel zu statuieren).'[44]

In this sense, the authority Goethe has provided in the development of the novel does come to legitimate the novel itself. For the function of that paternal authority has been, as we have argued, to articulate in relation to each other the artist theme and the representation of subjectivity. Goethe can provide the necessary authority for Keller because Goethe represents the perfect synthesis between the world of the artist and that of the ordinary citizen.[45] In the terms of the Oedipal model, he confers form upon the 'Verschwendung an sich' of subjective desire. As with Meister, the unbound subjectivity associated both with the mother and with the springs of poetry has to be suppressed if it is to fulfil itself: 'this first Heinrich is that part of the ego that must be sacrificed if the ego is to survive'.[46] Goethe's authority is psychological as well as artistic: he regulates Heinrich's development away from the vocation of an artist towards a full personality, and then, on the level of the text, guarantees that this subjective narrative attains compelling aesthetic form.

The *Lehrjahre* employs self-conscious artificiality as a central aesthetic strategy. If the self-conscious Goethean artificiality of the count's court is now relativised by what succeeds it in the story, its significant – Goethean – artificiality has the last word in the achieved form of the novel. In the first place, the death of Heinrich's mother, even in the first version, obviously does not signify the triumph of formlessness over form. Quite the opposite. Although this is its thematic connotation, its formal role is the reverse. A motif of dissolution is employed to achieve aesthetic closure. Heinrich and his mother disappear so that the novel can – like Mignon – 'werden' ('become'). As Kaiser puts it: '[Keller] buries himself in his mother-novel and emerges from this grave as a figure of masculine authority, as an author.'[47]

Furthermore, the combination of a masculine circularity and a feminine one, the count's mansion and the mother's death, produce twin circularities of law and desire which, although they condemn Heinrich to death, permit the novel to live as an aesthetic artefact. The second version ends in accommodation, but also contrives to maintain both masculine and feminine circularities, and thus sustain the Goethean model on a deeper level. The masculine determination is now commitment to the Republic. This is clearly a return to Heinrich's father's values, but it is not a devaluation of the count's: on the contrary, since, although a German nobleman, he is also an ardent Republican. It is also true that the return to the father of the second version has a counterpart in the first, where it is constituted not by an espousal of political and social responsibility, but by an association with the other determining characteristic of the father, namely early death. Heinrich's death is thus replaced by different forms of paternal circularity, and his mother's death is elaborated by the return, and subsequent death, of Judith.

Nevertheless, Keller clearly is relativising his courtly episode, and thus distancing himself somewhat from Goethe (although he does not invalidate the episode completely, and insofar as he does distance himself from the *Lehrjahre* model in his handling of the episode, he is distancing himself from the contemporary idealistic construction of Goethe, and not from the Goethe of his own, and Heinrich's, deepest subjective experience). It is, however, extremely significant that while the first version 'corrects' the Goethean synthesis by employing the model of the unsocialisable Mignon, the second version upsets the Goethean synthesis by employing the motif of un-aesthetic accommodation, the model of socialisation. Thus the terms of the *Lehrjahre*'s well-known ambiguity are the terms of the very hesitation inscribed in Keller's revision of his novel. This oscillation between the pure – incestuous – origin of art, and its transcendence in socialisation, between desire and law, is, again, itself a mark of the aesthetic as it is achieved in the *Lehrjahre*.

Yet this last defence of the novel's closeness to the *Lehrjahre* model, and of its assured aesthetic closure, is already an argument against it. Since this 'oscillation' does not take place within one text, but between two versions of one text, it indicates not a closing, but an opening of a work which seeks closure but fails to find it. The uncertainty about the relation between the artist theme and the representation of subjectivity continues to trouble what should be the finished aesthetic artefact, which otherwise derives its definition and identity from the certain resolution of that very problem. To put it another way, what troubles Keller throughout the composition of his novel is whether subjectivity and form are in fact compatible. The preface to the first version defends its subjective authenticity, but denies that it is a 'streng gegliedertes Kunstwerk' ('strictly organised work of art', XVI, p. 2). In 1854, long before the revision, Keller was already thinking about putting the work into a 'gemeingenießbare Form' ('a form which will appeal to all').[48] And even after the second revision has been completed, Keller still feels that the biographical form of the novel is fundamentally unpoetic.[49]

It is as though even at the end of the composition process, the question of 'das Dichterische' is still a problem; it is still as though the poet, in 'betraying' his subjectivity by being a poet, is somehow telling tales out of school.[50] The revision can be seen as a very determined effort by Keller to confer form upon subjectivity. The marked shift away from Jean Paul and Romantic subjectivism towards Goethe himself as literary authority is an indication of this, as are the increased use of symbols, the chapter headings and other devices which tighten the construction of the whole and increase the sense of control exercised by the author. Yet, despite the thesis of Laufhütte, there is a mismatch between this heightened but mute artistry and the prominent mundanity of the new fictional narrator, as though artistic and moral functions were striving apart. The struggle for 'abgeschlossene Form' ('closed, finished form') which Keller experienced in the revision led him to consider abandoning form altogether in favour of a fragmentary composition, as the only means of rescuing the unrepeatable authenticity of the original version.[51] As it is, there is an excess of zeal in the revision which suggests that Keller is not striving to give form to subjectivity, but striving to repress it. Hence, for instance, the anathema he reportedly declared upon anyone reprinting the first version,[52] or the new violence with which Eriksohn, in the second version, does not just mock and denounce Heinrich's great doodle, but actually tears it up, as if to stop once and for all the deleterious self-indulgence of what it is impossible from our perspective not to see as an anticipation of painterly abstraction.[53] There is a shrillness in that gesture, that slight amendment between texts, which expresses the endangering of the aesthetic modelling rather than its assured fulfilment.

Alongside the aesthetic, there is also an economic dimension to the novel, as recent studies have emphasised.[54] I will now, finally, seek to relate this to my theme, which will involve also addressing the central question of realism in Keller's novel.

The question of form with which we have been dealing is also a question of representation. Keller's aesthetic uncertainty in the matter of his 'Schicksalsbuch' (book about, and also representing, his destiny)[55] reflects the question: what is the appropriate form in which to represent a subjectivity? Putting it another way: what is the appropriate way of establishing the authority which oversees and underwrites the spaces of the public and the private and the thresholds between them? Keller repeatedly doubts that there is such an appropriate form, that the subjective is always subversive of form, a transgression of the public/private distinction, a 'telling tales out of school'. One's own subjectivity is and remains a 'notwendiger Zufall' ('necessary accident'), a contradiction in terms, which can never happily be accommodated in aesthetically valid form.[56] On the other hand, his novel, both in his lifelong commitment to it and in its enduring power and artistic richness beyond his personal enmeshment, belies this doubt.

I have tried to show the thematic function of this debate itself in the novel, and the central role of Goethe within it. The doubt, in a way, comes to structure the novel, and thus to resolve itself in favour of the aesthetic. But that is of course not the whole story: it is a sign of the remarkable richness of this book that 'the whole story' is continually slipping out of one's grasp. If one takes the case of Goethe, then, one can easily demonstrate, that, as well as the aesthetic literary construction of the subject, there is an alternative line of what one might call pragmatic subject construction in the novel.

Keller is as concerned with the physical and commercial reality of the works of Goethe as he is with their spiritual import. When Heinrich returns from the momentous Tell festival, there the fifty volumes are, bound together, on approval from one of the bookdealers who exploit his addiction to reading and expenditure. But this realistic foregrounding does not preclude our sense of the reality of Heinrich's subjectivity, manifest as it is in precisely the activities of reading and expenditure. These volumes are too expensive to buy, so once they have been passionately perused, some of them twice, they have to be returned. This is a neat reversal of the theme of art ownership we have noted in other texts, and which reappears here too, in its usual form, at the count's mansion. Heinrich's relation to these volumes is not defined only in their negative facticity, or the commercial strings attached which he is unable to break. It is also defined positively in relation to them: the subjective experience of reading these things is clear from the way the volumes overflow when Heinrich unties the bundle, spilling out onto the bed and onto the floor: the physicality of these works is exploited to convey superabundance instead of dead weight. There is also an intimacy and intensity in the reading of the works, during which the snows of winter pass unnoticed, signifying with great economy the utter irrelevance at this point of the objective world. The episode is at once materially determined and suffused with the warmth of real pleasure.

If the novel turns on Goethe, this line of pragmatic subject representation covers a spectrum which reaches from the pre-Goethean echo of Rousseau and the moments of unhoused subjectivity proper to Moritz, to the post-Goethean prevalence of the circulation of money as a determining factor of reality. Moreover, it is not always possible to separate the pragmatic line from the aesthetic one, as indeed the example of Goethe shows. Our image of Heinrich's subjectivity is largely the effect of a whole series of catastrophic public moments, the very wrongness of which makes visible the subjective life whose manifestation they are, 'the perpetual failures of my encounters with the outside world', as Heinrich himself says (III, p. 196).

Examples are Heinrich's secret letter to Anna, confiscated by the wind, and the consequences it has; the episode of his father's pew; his treatment of Römer; and his first attempt to paint commercially, featuring (in the second version) a motif from his own experience ('the deeper feeling [Innerlichkeit] of my initial design', VI, p. 36), which is deformed by the advice of, and then stolen by, a more experienced and cynical professional.

The interconnectedness of the pragmatic and the aesthetic is at its most clear in the episode of Heinrich's expulsion from school. This is the most fateful of the events on the threshold of the private and the public. Heinrich adopts by chance of circumstance the Patrician role of public leader which stands in no relation to his real social identity,[57] being rather an extension of his own heroic self-image, itself nourished by the reality of lack of social standing. In contrast to the episode of the lies in which Heinrich had produced a surprisingly effective public persona, this time he himself, like Anton Reiser to whom the same sort of catastrophic misunderstanding occurs, falls victim to the misrepresentation. This then feeds into the aesthetic dimension of the novel, since it condemns Heinrich to the search for an unconventional path to adulthood and responsibility, which turns out to be landscape painting, itself a question of differing modes and possibilities of representation. This in turn leads us to the heart of the problematic relation between the artist theme and the representation of subjectivity which structures the novel. The episode at the same time offers a perfect pragmatic example of how an authority responsible for the threshold between the private and the public – in this case the educational system, and behind it the canton and the state – can fail, since it is precisely the inadequacy of the school authorities (as in *Anton Reiser*) which derails Heinrich's otherwise healthy and conventional development.

This 'pragmatic' line of subject construction is what gives to the novel its much-celebrated realism. The novel is 'sustained by two kinds of novel discourse – that of the *Bildungsroman* and that of the realistic novel'.[58] Keller's representation of historical reality arises as the other of subjectivity, rather than in the heterogeneity of several competing subjectivities or equally (in)valid voices, such as those speaking in Immermann's earlier *Epigonen*. At the end of the long dream sequences, in which Keller seeks to find literary means to articulate the real relation between interiority and reality, a poem occurs, the first stanza of which conveys something of this subjective focus upon the objective world:

> Klagt mich nicht an, daß ich vor Leid
> Mein eigen Bild nur könne sehen!
> Ich seh durch meines Leides Flor
> Wohl euere Gestalten gehen.

Do not accuse me of seeing in my suffering only my own image! I can see your figures clearly enough through the veil of my suffering. (VI, p. 137)

In the first version, the poem is attributed to Heinrich by the third-person narrator; in the second it is attributed to a third person by the first-person narrator. Either way – and of course the oscillation is highly revealing – it conveys a sense of a realism borne out of the overcoming, however marginal, of narcissism. (The first version had 'meinen grauen Flor' [XIX, p. 179], rather than 'meines Leides Flor', thus recalling the narcissistic 'grey' web of Heinrich's monster abstraction.)

Keller includes in his fiction a parodic and critical treatment of a sub-Goethean idealism, but the episode at the count's mansion is integrated into the guiding thematic opposition of his book. Keller was ideologically committed to finding one voice, and wrestles to combine the first person, his starting point, with an impersonal authoritative voice. His problem, like Goethe's, is to reconcile different registers within one stable aesthetic hierarchy. Renate Boeschenstein argues that it is Goethe who supplies Keller-Heinrich with the single voice, the 'Hochdeutsch' (standard [high] German), which gives him authority to write. The authority of Goethe and that of Heinrich's father, who also spoke only 'Hochdeutsch' (III, p. 13), confirm each other, combining to sanction Keller-Heinrich's writing of his own life, his own first person, as literature, the voice of the aesthetic.[59]

In a sense, then, the realism generated by the pragmatic representation of subjectivity is contained by the aesthetic. This is true even within the realistic-historical terms the novel generates. The co-operation between Lee senior and Goethe in allowing the faint and threatened first person to speak gives the clue: it is a binary opposition between Switzerland and Germany, which, with the novel's characteristic structural perversity, draws order from discordance.

This guiding opposition is clearest at the end, where the Goethean German ideal ending is in balance with a Swiss pragmatic one. The moral apparatus of the Republican Swiss ethos swings into play to relativise the class-based German ideal. But throughout, Heinrich's subjective fate has been played out between these two historical actualities. 'Only one more oar's length and Heinrich could set foot in this country, whose name filled him with obscure longing and anticipation' (XVI, p. 40), we read of Heinrich's arrival on German territory in the first version. But pragmatic Switzerland and idealist Germany also switch roles in a complex thematic symmetry: Switzerland is the ground of Heinrich's subjectivity, its countryside the seat of his love of the landscape, while Munich is the actual, urban location in which this can be converted into objective achievements. The basic movement of the book is from Switzerland to Germany and back again, but then the closure of the novel itself, in either of its forms, is a return to aesthetic Germany.

The realism of the book, reaching its climax in Heinrich's dream on the threshold of his return home, is the mediation of the ideal for the real and the real for the ideal. Keller writes Germany for the Swiss and the Swiss for Germany. The Romantic dream form becomes the vehicle for the expression of Republican virtues. And as for the problem of the subject, in this perspective it is resolved by defining the subject's function as that of aesthetic service. The author of the text (as opposed to the author within it) enjoys a precarious authority at this point of mediation between Germany and Switzerland, which provides a language in which to speak of the complex relations between private and public.

At the end of the second version the meeting with Judith embodies the compromise Keller sought to the problem of representation, as already formulated clearly enough in the maxim from the *Lehrjahre*, to the effect that words are good, but unable to say what is best of all (*Lehrjahre*, p. 496). The ideal configuration of the count's mansion cannot stand unrelativised, even though it embodies a coherent world view based on the amalgamation of Keller's autobiography and Feuerbach, to give a result not incompatible with the Goethean ideal of half a century earlier. It is thus corrected by the Swiss ending, in which a former love returns, but with whom no formal union takes place, since this would be again to confuse the representation with the real thing, to forget that reality is always ahead of representations. Hence the non-union between Judith and Heinrich is another formal sign of the aesthetic unity of the text itself. The reality of experience – 'she had probably seen and tasted too much of the world to have faith in a full and complete happiness' (VI, p. 324) – is thus rather movingly represented in the motif of this renunciation. The public form of marriage can never capture the private moment of fulfilment the way the vulgar imagination and the popular novel thinks it can. The private moment is subjective and real at the same time, 'und auf die Dauer kommt es ja nicht an' ('and the permanence of it does not matter', VI, p. 168).

The whole problem of the representation of subjectivity is enclosed in the contradiction that form without duration is difficult to imagine. The Goethean answer is the organic concept of 'Dauer im Wechsel' ('permanence in change'). But this classical synthesis is threatened in Keller by the most radical formulation of the pragmatic line of subject representation, which goes beyond the grey area in which the discourses of realism and *Bildung* sustain each other, to challenge the ideology of the aesthetic in the name of the market.

Is reality always ahead of representations? There is a post-Goethean doubt here which is consciously set out in Keller's novel by juxtaposing the model of Schiller with the contemporary news story about 'revalenta arabica', the marketing of flour as a health food (in the chapter called 'Modes of Living'). Schiller's life is the perfect example of the aesthetic ideal:

> This man, escaping out of the circle for which family and the princely ruler destined him, abandoning all that according to their design was to have made him happy, stood on his own feet in his early youth, doing only that which he could not help doing, and actually by means of an aberration, a wild and extravagant robber escapade, procured air and light for himself; but as soon as he had won these, he proceeded to improve himself without ceasing, working from within outwards, and his life became no less than the fulfilment of his innermost being: the logically correct crystallising of the ideal which lay in him and his period. (VI, pp. 40–41)

The subjective inner life breaks upon the world without being anything other than true to itself, overthrowing the existing authorities, establishing its objective effectiveness in the form of art, but then immediately replacing the defeated biological and political fathers with a father generated from within itself, who reconnects the rebellious, but now free, subjectivity with the objective world, with life and history. What is more, the commercial repercussions of this consonance of inner and outer are wide-ranging, since there is a Schiller industry involved in the manufacture, distribution and circulation of this spiritual property, which materially supports many souls. The ideology of the aesthetic cannot be spelled out like this without becoming a parody of itself. The nakedness of the model, which is usually veiled, not revealed, by irony, is here occasioned by the proximity of an equally baldly stated alternative model of the relation between subject and object.

The historical case of 'revalenta arabica' seems to have been essentially a health-food confidence trick. It was an early triumph of marketing, in which flour prepared, packaged and promoted as a remedy for a wide range of ailments brought its deviser a fortune in the Europe of the early 1850s. Although it is widely distributed, and generates money and employment for more souls than the works of Schiller, unlike them, it has no essence, no inside at all. The involvement of subjective human experience, the point of significant labour, occurs at the other end of the process, as it were. The movement and circulation does not spring from a subjective force entering the world of empirical causality and animating it with its own life: on the contrary, values of industriousness, order and efficiency spring up as the effect of an originally arbitrary input. (One might add that those who felt better for taking the preparation were similarly enriched and involved.) Here reality seems to follow representation rather than vice versa.

The Heinrich of the narrative, before whose mind's eye these ironically extreme possibilities pass, cannot decide the morality of it, and my conclusion on the text as a whole is that it offers its own complex and ambiguous statement on the question. But the very notion of subjectivity as an interiority, however partial and problematic, is evidently under attack here from a notion of the world as market, in which representations are as true as they are effective. The catastrophic dealings Heinrich has with the world throughout threaten to undergo a basic shift of connotation if seen in this alternative light: no longer an indication of an imperfectly realised subjectivity, but indications that subjectivity is an effect of the circumstances in which it happens to become visible. For Marx, all these instances of the 'Veräußerung' of fragments of interiority would have been concentrated into the moment of labour as the interface of subject and object, formalised under the economic rubric, and called alienation. Certainly, economy – the circulation of equivalent exchange values, rendering identity arbitrary – is the most extreme expression of the pragmatic dimension of the novel. Jochen Hörisch in his deconstructive study of Keller's novel, a study which goes further than Marx because it abandons the notion of the subject's interiority, sees (perhaps extravagantly) Keller's novel as the last novel which can be understood independently of economics ('gar das Autodafé einer Dichtung, die transökonomisch sich zu verstehen versuchte').[60] The great theme of the novel is 'the loss of immediacy caused by the necessity of exchange (Tauschzwang)'.[61] The logic of exchange is the value which prevails in the realm of representations, and which ultimately mediates the subject to itself, effectively constituting it. When trying to sell some of his work, Heinrich discovers that his choice of landscape motifs is unfashionable not because he has chosen naively though honestly, on the basis of his own subjective perception, but because he has chosen features which he had already unconsciously internalised from a now out-of-date style (VI, p. 54). But it is more than just a question of styles: the subject already mediates itself via style, and what the style is, is decided by the market.

It is difficult to deny the extent to which the economic determination has sunk into the dimensions of the aesthetic which nevertheless still structure the novel and its construction of subjectivity. If we cited above the formulation 'Verschwendung an sich' as a poetic expression for pure subjectivity, a subjectivity daring to imagine itself as imaginable without an objective counterpart (as perhaps Schiller had, in composing *Die Räuber*), then we now need to recall that it is 'die Leidenschaft . . . des unbeschränkten Geldausgebens' ('the passion for unlimited expenditure of money', III, pp. 157–158) which gives rise to the coining of that memorable evocation of pure subjectivity. Conversely, to spend one's own subjective gifts recklessly is to incur debts and guilt at the same time. This involves the maternal dimension, the dimension of incest, in the economic dimension. The guilt of incest, and the debts incurred by excessively subjective behaviour, are linked in German in the word 'Schuld'. In the first version we read of the hopeful young aspirant setting off: 'He was now left to his own devices and free to draw whatever pleased his carefree heart into the circle of his fate. . . Had he been a king of this world he would probably have squandered many millions, but as things stood he could do no more than squander what little he possessed, his own and his mother's lives' (XVI, pp. 27–28).

The novel in both versions remains predicated upon the guilt of the debts of the mother, which vitiate the aesthetic dimension on the level of plot, but not on that of form. Subjectivity, linked by definition with the life of the mother, is inseparable from economy; it can only express itself in those terms, and the dimension of economy places demands which cannot be ignored: to do so is to incur at once both kinds of 'Schuld', and thus fail to appropriate a social persona at all. Heinrich's mistake is not just to want to become an artist, but to aspire to an impossible surmounting of the inevitable demands made by economic reality. In Muschg's words: 'Green Henry imagines his future as a synthesis of commercial success and artistic vocation.'[62] He wants to live on credit, without ever having to pay it back.

If the economic model comes to inform the maternal dimension of the aesthetic in this way, there is a parallel invasion on the masculine front. The motif of art ownership, to which we referred above and which occurs in many of the texts in my study as a sign of masculine possession of the maternally inspired artistic impulse, is here displaced by that of the manufacture of art, an awareness of art as commodity. Although this too implies masculine power, it is not the 'representation' of the post-feudal style, which as we shall see reaches its apotheosis in *Der Nachsommer*, but a more arbitrary involvement in the circulation of money, in which, as with the 'revalenta arabica', inherent value is overridden by exchange value, and which simply subverts the symbolic and political meaning of inheritance (XIX, p. 80). The commodity aspect of art is thematised in a variety of ways in the novel, from Habersaat's painting factory, to which Heinrich's mother sends him to begin his education, to Heinrich's attempts to sell his paintings so that he can eat. Heinrich himself finds himself suspended between the world of aesthetic formation and the world of worthless tat, between his 'Lehrjahre' and the sphere where 'the glory of painted tea-trays and box-lids begins' (IV, p. 43).

These products are what we would now call 'Kitsch'. The word first came into currency amongst art dealers in Munich in the 1860s and 1870s, between the two versions of Keller's novel. It has been argued, as we have seen, that Kitsch is what becomes of the aesthetic ideal of Goethe and Schiller in the increasing divergence betwen private and public worlds of the nineteenth century. (The humorous inflection given to the account of the significance of the life of Schiller reflects this progression exactly.) Where once public and private had been combined in an ideal of harmony between individual self-determination and collective consensus, the realities of nineteenth-century capitalism curtain off individual lives from the historical and political horizon, creating the space of 'everyday life' in which the wider concerns of society and economics are cut down to conform with the immediate experience and needs of the private individual. In this truncated experiential sphere, the commodity addresses and confirms the individual subject as once the aesthetic artefact had done. But where the aesthetic had in its nature effected a fusion of individual and universal, bonding pleasure and reason for the space and time of a necessary form, Kitsch offers no more than immediate sentimental confirmation of the inauthentic autonomy of consumption.

Keller's own novel is not Kitsch, but it is written in conscious awareness of its own nature as commodity as well as spirit, and thus in awareness of and resistance to the danger of the threat of becoming Kitsch. It is particularly vulnerable, since, with its autobiographical origin, it is bound to give form, representation and a viable public face to the private reality of subjective life, and thus to risk producing an inauthentic fabrication of the authentic fusion of feeling and reason such as the *Lehrjahre* was held to embody. The second version of *Der grüne Heinrich* exhibits, as we have seen, a clenched determination to increase the formal control of the first version. On the other hand, as we have also seen, Keller toyed with the idea of relaxing the aesthetic vice to offer his work as unfinished, and although he had in mind the unfinished masterpieces of Goethe and Schiller, we detect an anticipation of modernism in the temptation to refuse the closure of representation. It is the producer and purveyor of commodified art, the Kitsch merchant Eriksohn, who reacts violently to the subversion implied by Heinrich's vast doodle, the artistic elaboration of a non-public existence. Keller's novel seeks to occupy a third position, neither that of the merchant nor that of the narcissist, seeks, one is tempted to say, to maintain itself between Kitsch and modernism. This is a precarious endeavour, and accounts for the novel's insecurity about its status as a representation, but it is also in that precariousness that the novel's uniqueness lies: the fugitive life of the subject among the forms of two ages.

CHAPTER FOUR

Heinrich von Ofterdingen and *Der Nachsommer*

Friedrich von Hardenberg's novel *Heinrich von Ofterdingen* (1802) and Adalbert Stifter's novel (he called it a 'narrative' or 'story' ['Erzählung']) *Der Nachsommer* (1857) could hardly be more different from one another. Yet it is the surprising similarities between them which are most significant in our context.

Hardenberg, known by the pseudonym Novalis, lived from 1772 to 1801. In his short life he both had practical experience – he was a trained administrator, working towards the end of his life in the administration of mines – and made an enormous contribution to the moment of early Romanticism. He knew most of the other leading personalities of the time personally – Goethe, Schiller, Hölderlin, Friedrich Schlegel, Jean Paul, among others – and was significantly formed in his intellectual identity by a profound study of the post-Kantian idealist philosopher Fichte which Novalis undertook in the years 1795 and 1796.

Coming from a pietistic background among modest Saxon nobility, Novalis came to centre his religious experience upon the traumatic loss of his child fiancée, Sophie von Kühn, from tuberculosis in 1797. Love and death become the key terms in an extraordinary personal mystical philosophy in which Hardenberg's remarkably broad learning found restless assimilation. His work is the site of a dynamic combination of philosophy and science, literature and religion, for which the programme of universal interactivity is as important as the various components.

Heinrich von Ofterdingen is divided into two parts. Only the first part, 'Die Erwartung' ('Expectation'), is finished. It is the account of a journey made by a youth, later to become the eponymous medieval poet, whose historical identity was to have become important in the unwritten later part of the novel. This first part includes songs and poems as well as interpolated narratives, of which the most extensive is the complete *Märchen* ([fairy] tale) which closes the book. Heinrich starts from his parental home in the company of his mother to go to her home town of Augsburg, where he meets and falls in love with Mathilde. On the way he encounters merchants, crusaders, miners and a hermit, all of whom contribute to Heinrich's development as a poet. The fairy tale (told by Mathilde's father, Klingsohr) and the end of the book mask Mathilde's death, which has taken place once the second book begins. The second book, 'Die Erfüllung' ('Fulfilment'), of which only about seventeen pages exist in finished form, gives an account of Heinrich as a pilgrim who sees a vision of his dead beloved, and engages in two weighty dialogues. The register of the writing changes, contriving to open a mythological perspective.[1] Tieck appended an account of how his friend had intended to finish the work, based on conversations between them and on some still extant though inconclusive fragments, which may be consulted in the standard edition of Novalis.[2]

Novalis's novel has become most famous, perhaps somewhat unjustifiably, for the symbol of the blue flower. Heinrich dreams of it in the opening sequence, and was destined to pluck it, had the book been finished. Largely as a result of Heine's derision in his essay of 1833, *Die Romantische Schule*, the blue flower has become the quintessence of early Romanticism.[3]

Der Nachsommer by Adalbert Stifter (1805–1868), although often associated with the literary and cultural style called 'Biedermeier', is probably better introduced as *sui generis*. 'There is perhaps nothing else resembling it in European literature.'[4] Stifter himself was an Austrian of humble background. His story is a little like that of Keller. Stifter began as a landscape painter, beginning to publish short stories only in the 1840s. In 1847 he was still described in a lexicon of artists as a painter who also wrote 'belles lettres'.[5] As with Keller, there was a parallel civil service career – Stifter was for many years a school inspector – which was in conflict with his creative work. While Novalis was able, despite or even because of the French Revolution, to identify himself with what he experienced as an historically significant juncture, Stifter, recoiling from the events of 1848, could not. Nor did he have in Austria the objective circumstances which enabled Keller in Switzerland to develop a positive political identity. Stifter's long novel is a defensive response of German middle-class literary culture to the disorder of the year of European Revolutions.

What is so distinctive about *Der Nachsommer*? This is obvious to any reader of the novel, yet difficult to summarise. Basically, it adopts an extraordinary attitude to experience, which throws into confusion our usual sense of the relative positions of narrator, reader, world. A narrative voice plays over the objects and events of a narrative with uncanny detachment, fashioning an incantation out of the material of ordinary experience. Perhaps even the word 'voice' is misleading, since an important monograph on the book is based upon the divorce of Stifter's text from the voice, its constitution as a material space of letters.[6] Nevertheless, through this unique narrative disposition a particular story is perfectly, indeed exceptionally, apparent. A young man of modest independent means, engaged in a general programme of geological self-education, encounters a household in the course of one of his annual excursions to the mountains. This household, and the householder himself, then become, after the protagonist's own home, a second family in which his education unfolds meticulously and organically. At the house he also meets the woman he is to marry. The character constellation of the novel is very regular: the protagonist's family is echoed by his host in the country, and a related estate where a woman lives with a son and a daughter. The host and the woman of the neighbouring estate are not married, yet they are the subjects of the Indian summer of the title. At a late stage in the novel we are given a retrospective account of their story, which explains their closeness to one another. There are various servants, and the narrator of the story marries the daughter of the country dwellers. A simple indication of the strangeness of this text is that this narrator-protagonist is unnamed until almost the end of the book (hence one's reluctance, in summarising, to use his, or anybody's, name).

Novalis quite explicitly conceived his novel as an answer to Goethe's. There are other literary models: Wieland's collection *Dschinnistan oder auserlesene Feen- und Geister-Märchen* (1786–1789) and

Goethe's *Märchen* (1795) both contributed to Novalis's conception of the *Märchen*, and it has been argued that the work as a whole belongs in the literary tradition of allegorical journeys to Jerusalem.[7] But many disparate literary possibilities, from the medieval sources of the plot and characters to the Indian play *Sakuntala*, are combined in the work, and the authority or paradigm for literary combination with which Novalis worked was the novel, and *the* novel was *Wilhelm Meisters Lehrjahre* ('Roman schlechtweg, ohne Beywort', II, p. 642). While the overriding importance of the link to Goethe's novel has never been doubted, its exact nature is complex and possibly contradictory. It has certainly been the topic of a great deal of scholarship.[8] Novalis was preoccupied with Goethe's novel from its appearance in 1795 until his death. In his first responses Novalis expressed enthusiasm and appreciation, seeing in the novel a paradigm of poetic practice and achievement.[9] Later, however, he seemed to turn against it and condemn it for its anti-poetic nature, for siding with reason and common sense against poetry (famously, for instance: '*Wilhelm Meister* is really a *Candide*, directed against poetry', IV, p. 323).

The reason so much scholarship has been devoted to this particular literary historical relation is that it is situated at the heart of the Romantic preoccupation with the significance of literature. If Goethe's novel seemed to Novalis to be 'a pure novel', the significance of the novel to the young Romantic generation (in German 'Romantic' contains the word for 'novel') explains why this was so important. The novel was theoretically extended to become a universal writing in which literature and philosophy became indistinguishable. Novalis's own theorising about the novel attributed to the genre the function of a path to knowledge of the self and of the world.[10] It was part of the preoccupation of early Romantics and post-Kantian idealists (like Fichte) alike to think and act through to its farthest limits the implications of the new subjectivity introduced by Kant's critical philosophy. This is not to condemn this epochal preoccupation as subjective in a banally limiting sense, but to insist that the problem of subjectivity (as self-knowledge in its relation to freedom) was its crucial concern, and that it tended to turn what in Kant was a constitutional delimitation, into a positive moment. Partial subjectivity was its starting point, the 'Gefühl schlechthinniger Abhängigkeit' ('feeling of absolute dependency') of which Schleiermacher spoke.[11] And its aim – or so it can reasonably be argued – was the apotheosis of subjectivity as the animation of truth and reality.

For Novalis, as for Hölderlin, the partialness of the subject, of which nobody can be ignorant ('The reality of pain is the reality of common, raw consciousness', writes Novalis, III, p. 404), finds its theoretical definition as a guarantee of fullness: to be partial is to bear the inextinguishable mark of wholeness.

In his modification of both Fichte and the *Lehrjahre* in the light of his own preoccupation with poetry, Novalis accepted and affirmed, in the case of the *Wissenschaftslehre* as in that of Goethe's novel, a system with a strong anthropocentric universalising tendency which is prominently braked or placed under limitation – but removed the brake. In the case of Fichte, this limitation is that actual human experience (rather than theoretical knowledge) of the centrality of the subject is restricted, following Kant, to the experience of moral freedom ('Through the moral act, the self may attain objective validity because it is no longer determined by the object but, instead, determines it according to standards valid for all possible selves').[12] In Fichte's system the subject, which is called the 'Ego', is placed at the centre, but knows itself only in a constant de-centring, a dialectic relation with that which is not the self, the Non-Ego, everything it defines itself by not being. This activity takes place against the horizon of an absolute, a final self-identity, which Fichte calls the Absolute Ego. In this scheme, one might say, the peculiar trick of the *Lehrjahre* (the centre occupied by the non-central) is formulated philosophically. Novalis removes the brake from Fichte's system by admitting the possibility of direct experience of the paradox of subjective centrality. The subject's oneness with the cosmos can now be experienced passively, by revelation, as well as actively, as for Fichte, in moral engagement.[13]

In the *Lehrjahre*, the Romantic revolution initiated by Goethe with his magisterial work of art is, for Novalis on second thoughts, arrested by what he called 'Oeconomie' (practical, not just financial, management, the practical configuration of causes and effects).[14] Goethe had betrayed poetry: 'I can see so clearly in Meister the great art with which poetry is destroyed by itself' (IV, p.

323). *Heinrich von Ofterdingen* is then the proper 'poeticisation of the novel', started, but not finished, by Goethe. The close association Novalis wished to convey between his novel and Goethe's is evidenced by his wish that his own work should appear in exactly the same external format as that in which the *Lehrjahre* had been published by Unger in Berlin.[15] It is also easy to see how both authors use shifts in stylistic register, for instance from realistic narrative to symbolic narrative, but to different ends and with different effects.

Heinrich von Ofterdingen is thus itself a continuation of Novalis's working out of his deeply felt and complex response to the *Lehrjahre*. The figure of Klingsohr, the father of Heinrich's beloved, is said by some commentators to recall Goethe, and has an important place within the economy of the novel. It is even possible to situate the *Lehrjahre* in the dense allegorical space of Klingsohr's *Märchen*. If Fabel is the representation of 'poesy', then her progress might be seen as that made by a transhistorical quality through the vicissitudes of a history of various forms, towards the point at which form and content are no longer separable from one another. Poetry, so the implication might be from the perspective of early Romantic literary history, was liberated by the advent of the novel from the straitjacket of genres,[16] and took up residence for a while in the form of Goethe's *Lehrjahre*, which Novalis did identify, at least at first, with 'Poesie' itself (II, p. 643), and as the quintessential 'Roman'. Thence this spirit is passed on to the form of *Ofterdingen*. Oskar Walzel established the artistic debt Novalis owed to the *Lehrjahre* in this regard.[17] But the baton is passed on even within the work, in the form of the *Märchen* it contains, but which already points beyond it, to the dissolution of all forms. (For Novalis, *Fabel* was quasi synonymous with '*Märchen*'.)[18] Fabel's sojourn in the underworld would then allegorise the moment of the *Lehrjahre*: the spirit of poetry spins (the connection to 'narration' is possible in German as it is in English) in the dark, temporarily, but cheerfully enough, forced to content herself with a single shaft of light from the world above (perhaps the intimations around Mignon and the Harper, possibly Natalie), but nevertheless in visual contact with the constellation of the Phoenix, the sign of certain renewal. Even if the Enlightenment in the form of the 'Schreiber' imagines it has recaptured Fabel when the scribe descends to the underworld (I, p.

303) in other words, even if it appears for a passing moment that Poesie has been subjugated by 'Oeconomie' in Goethe's stewardship – this is an illusion brought about by the distortion of unilinear chronology, and Fabel has no difficulty in successfully completing her negotiation of the underworld. It is noteworthy that Mignon's funeral takes place in the 'Hall of the Past', at the entrance to which sit two granite sphinxes. Fabel encounters a living sphinx on her descent into the underworld and, like Oedipus, succeeds in answering the monster's riddles. In Goethe's refraction, Mignon must die, whereas here that death is transcended, not decorated by the dispositions of Reason.[19]

The link between Stifter's novel and the *Lehrjahre* is not so well defined and familiar an academic topic as that between Novalis and Goethe. But it is nevertheless firmly established in literary history that *Der Nachsommer* 'clearly aspires to the succession of Goethe'.[20] Although the *Bildungsroman* tradition as a self-conscious element of German literary history had not yet come into being in the 1850s, Stifter's novel is and was then unmistakably a novel of German classical *Bildung*: Risach physically resembles the greatest theorist of *Bildung*, William von Humboldt, and the novel is evidently about an education which is more than that, being an organic development towards the integration of the subject in the world. As in *Der grüne Heinrich*, the works of Goethe as physical entities, as properties, provide a certain aura in which the artistic, the moral, the real and the ideal are simultaneously present as they otherwise might have been only in the productions of religion.[21] The intertextual orientation upon Goethe is thus as clear, and of the same order, as that perpetuated by Dilthey and his successors when they established the institution of the *Bildungsroman* as the German novel form after the first unification of Germany. The heroine's name (Natalie), and the echo, in the 'Hall of Marble', of the 'Hall of the Past'[22] are also distinct references to the Goethean paradigm within the text, as is the crucial thematic importance of a Shakespeare play (not *Hamlet*, but *King Lear*).[23]

Stifter saw himself as an aesthetic heir of Goethe's, saying in a letter to his publisher, Gustav Heckenast, in May 1854, that although he was himself no Goethe, he was nevertheless a kindred spirit, sharing the same ideals of purity, high-mindedness and simplicity.[24] It was Goethe's more stylised, consciously aesthetic works, *Iphigenie* and *Hermann und Dorothea*, which most attracted Stifter, and thus the aesthetic element in his novel of young masculine development is more evidently foregrounded than in Goethe's own novel on that theme. At the same time, the relevance of the aesthetic to Goethe's novel will by now have become clear: the novel embodies rather than advertises it, and Stifter's strong commitment to it thus simply brings out more strongly a tendency already present in the *Lehrjahre*. The emphasis upon the moment of 'Entsagung' (renunciation) in Stifter's novel is a reminder that for him *Wilhelm Meister* meant the *Wanderjahre* as well as the *Lehrjahre*, and Stifter's utopian projection recalls the 'pedagogical province' of Goethe's later novel.

The most salient point about the historical relation between the two books, and one upon which literary historians are likewise agreed,[25] is that Stifter is a latecomer. His espousal of Goethe's cause, and not just Goethe's but that of the whole 'Humanitätsideal' (including notably the thought of Herder), is anachronistic. History has moved on, and Stifter, in defending the classical moral values and conception of autonomous subjecthood, is speaking out of time, which accounts for the massively defensive style and content of his aesthetic-didactic intervention. One might equally speak of a programmatic refusal to intervene.

Der grüne Heinrich combines the *Lehrjahre* model with contemporary history. This was not to distort or alienate the model. It was simply to develop one aspect of it, within an overall consonance of presupposition about the subject and art. The *Lehrjahre* also addressed history, but crucially related it to a larger aesthetic formula. While the original version, the *Theatralische Sendung*, was recognisably set in the later eighteenth century, the revision is noncommittal as to the matter of date. History is represented in the final novel not just as a configuration of prevailing circumstances, the multiple effects of causality, but as a moment of possibilities, of possible new social and economic permutations. Keller reviews the power of the novel, and of the individual subject, to sustain mutually confirming form in the face of his experience of historical circumstances.

A further aspect of this is that Keller writes with a real popular audience in mind. Nobody was more shrewdly attuned to (though by no means enslaved by) the literary market place than Keller. Goethe, himself the author with *Werther* of one of the most popular novels of European literary history, in writing the *Lehrjahre* transformed the popular novel into high art, using its properties and business ironically. His position in this regard is thus curiously poised between the popularity of his earlier work and the resigned but defiant hermeticism of the later. Novalis and Stifter, on the other hand, turn to the novel not in order to tap its popular potential, but to tap its artistic potential. Novalis perceived how Goethe had ironically exploited what then could still be called 'the romantic' (i.e, having to do with 'Der Roman', the protean and unstable popular novel form), but resented the ironisation as a trivialisation of the deeply serious thing that he understood by the word Romantic.[26] Stifter hoped to continue the work of Goethe in writing for the improvement of readers through art, but was deeply disappointed by the (hardly surprising) popular incomprehension which met the publication of his novel, and was anyway quite conscious of writing against the expectations of the readership of his time.

What *Heinrich von Ofterdingen* and *Der Nachsommer* have in common in this context is that they develop the aesthetic component of the *Lehrjahre*. They do not ignore history, since that would have been unthinkable in the intensely historically minded nineteenth century (and, in another sense, is impossible anyway), but insofar as they are actually both historical novels, they are so in order to evade being genuinely historical, which is to say realistic. *Heinrich von Ofterdingen*, as has been argued, is in a sense an historical novel about the Middle Ages,[27] but this thematisation was for Novalis a way through and beyond pragmatic history; what he was after was 'The meaning of history' (I, p. 340). *Der Nachsommer* is set somewhere in the first half of the nineteenth century so as to antedate the 1848 revolutions. This avoidance of the topical is anticipated in the *Lehrjahre*'s refusal to acknowledge the French Revolution.

Neither *Heinrich von Ofterdingen* nor *Der Nachsommer* is realist in style. It has been said of them both that they repress history, and history returns as style, like a neurotic symptom.[28] Certainly, both texts exhibit the dominance of style combined with an aesthetic distancing of history.

As with history in general, so with its inner driving logic: money. The radically subversive role of the modern culture of exchange and the circulation of money for the aesthetic model of subjecthood is prominent in *Der grüne Heinrich*. The *Lehrjahre*, in its combinatory genius, accommodated the economic developments of its time within its own, aesthetic, economy. Both *Heinrich von Ofterdingen* and *Der Nachsommer* recognise (as they must) the increased importance of exchange value rather than use value in the life and definitions of their times, but seek to transvalue it. Although a miner in *Ofterdingen* says of gold nuggets that they lose their charm once they have become commodities (I, p. 244), we likewise read of the merchants' approval of the circulation of goods and capital: 'Money, activity and commodities stimulate one another, driving one another on in rapid circulation, and the country and the towns flourish' (I, p. 206). Nor is this affirmation only an economic matter: the image of money is astonishingly closely related to the agent of poetic transformation in Klingsohr's *Märchen*, Fabel. Her poetic potentiality enables her, as money enables the merchants, to move in vastly different realms, and to mediate them to one another in a mutually fruitful way.[29] Furthermore, it can persuasively be argued that the entire concept of signification upon which *Heinrich von Ofterdingen* rests (or moves) is an analogy with the function of gold as the universal equivalent.[30] Although, in other words, Novalis resisted the triumph of 'Oeconomie' in the *Lehrjahre*, he was in favour of the dynamism which resided within the market system, but the market system understood in a more-than-historical way, as a universal motor of transformation:

On the mercantile spirit. The spirit of trade is the spirit of life. It is the epitome of great spirit itself. It motivates and combines everything. It awakens countries and towns – nations and works of art. It is the spirit of culture – of the perfecting of the human race. The historical spirit of trade – which slavishly follows the particular requirements and circumstances of a given time and place – is nothing but the bastard of the authentic, creative spirit of trade. (III, p. 464)

This is a transformation or potentiation of the sort of value of which Lothario in the *Lehrjahre* would certainly have approved, but which (in Novalis' opinion) Goethe as maker took too literally.

For Stifter it was more probably fear of the market system which led, as Russell Berman argues, to the figures of a different sort of exchange system (Berman is considering the contrast between Stifter's book and the hugely popular contemporaneous work by Gustav Freytag, *Soll und Haben* [1855], which accommodates a story of individual male development in the economical and political setting of the mid-century):

> Even more than Freytag, Stifter is worried by the process of destabilization unleashed by a market economy. Yet while the realist Freytag limits exchange by holding onto the heterogeneous correctives of nationalism and the aristocracy, Stifter transforms the character of exchange itself. In his hands exchange loses the excited dynamic that brought the world together in a 'poesy of commodities' . . . and the individual actors in the exchange lose their atomistic mobility. Instead, exchange becomes a highly formalized ritual, pervaded by a rigorous conventionality and designed to ensure the stability of a society threatened by catastrophic disorder.[31]

Since both texts resist or stylise and transform history in these ways, there is a peculiar attraction in dealing with them in tandem, although they were written fifty years apart. They are parts of a single moment, for all the traces of political and economic circumstances they betray.

To treat these texts together is first of all to address their differences. In form they are almost perfect opposites. Novalis's text is unfinished. This is because the poet died before he could complete his project, and Novalis scholarship no longer entertains the notion that the book was inherently unfinishable.[32] On the other hand, it is not an exaggeration to say that, on the evidence provided by Tieck and by the various notes Novalis left about how he intended to continue his novel, the project is enormously ambitious. Not only does it aim to achieve 'transfiguration' (I, p. 344, p. 347), and the 'revelation of poesy on earth' (I, p. 341), and to tell how Heinrich 'divines the meaning of the world' (I, p. 344), but the vastly ambitious project, when finished, was to be only the first of a series of seven, as Tieck reported (I, p. 359). Perhaps, despite the confidence of some modern scholarship, Thomas Carlyle can be forgiven for doubting whether, on the evidence, 'strictly speaking, it could have been completed'.[33] There is an impetus within it and intrinsic to the questions it raises which points forever beyond. Indeed, the literary fragment as a genre was programmatic for early Romanticism, expounded by Friedrich Schlegel as the form best able to express the enormousness of a theme which could only be diminished by enclosure within finished form.

Der Nachsommer, on the other hand, is, like the furniture and other artefacts represented in it, nothing if not perfectly finished. It conveys an overwhelming sense of artistic control in its formal organisation. Closure is its hallmark, just as open-endedness is that of *Ofterdingen*. *Der Nachsommer* has a uniform and unmistakable narrative style throughout, with only one, structurally intensely considered and equally intensely crucial, variation in the penultimate of the seventeen chapters. Every chapter, including the aberrant one, bears a uniform title consisting of a noun and a definite article. Novalis displays, in contrast, a deliberately disparate range of literary modes: dream, parables, poems, *Märchen* and myth, as well as third-person narrative.

These contrasting formal properties reflect, of course, the contrasting concerns of the two novels. Crudely put, it is an opposition between subject and object. Against the background of idealist philosophy, preoccupied as it was with the nature and status of self-knowledge and the relation of that to moral freedom, Novalis elaborates the notion that the world is within. In a famous fragment in the *Blütenstaub* collection, he says:

> is the cosmos not within us? The depths of our spirit are unknown to us – the secret path leads into the interior. Eternity and its worlds, the past and the future, is within us, or nowhere. The external world is the shadow world, it casts its shadow into the world of light. Now everything within seems so dark, solitary, formless, but how different will it appear to us when this eclipse is past and the shadowy mass gone. (II, p. 419)

In the early Romantic view, partial subjectivity becomes an article of faith. Poetry is the objective realisation, the trace in the material world of the journey of the subject to itself – that is to say, to the realisation that it is identical with the entirety of creation. The recognisable historical world is a stage through which poetry must pass on its way to itself. Novalis's project is to make everything which is strange familiar.[34] In practical terms, the role of the poet and his poetic work is to anticipate future states of the world.[35] The novel is thus part of that progress toward another state of the world. It is the fulfilment of a high duty, and becomes therefore in a sense the site of freedom, the authentic activity of the subject – or its objective trace – in the working out of the world. 'The spirit of poesy is not restricted to the literary arts, nor even to art itself. It pertains to all areas of human endeavour, since it re-defines the relationship between self and world from the perspective of freedom.'[36] It is a point of exchange between what Fichte termed ego and non-ego, and in this inter-animation it anticipates oneness. This is likewise the plot of the novel: a poet's journey through the historical world, towards and beyond his own vocation in the 'apotheosis of poetry'. It anticipates its own transcending in the *Märchen*. This involvement in significant process extends also to the reader. The objective trace of the poet's subjectivity is re-animated by the subjectivity of the reader who in turn becomes poet.[37]

If Stifter starts out from subjectivity, it is from its dangers. He introduces his story 'Turmalin' (1852) by telling the reader that he will learn from it

> what can become of a man if the light of his reason becomes dimmed, if he strays from the inner law which leads unfailingly to do right, gives himself over unconditionally to the intensity of his pleasure and pain, loses all firm ground, and strays into circumstances of which we are scarcely able to make sense.[38]

Although there is mystery in the depths of subjectivity, it is not (as with Novalis) the mystery in which the secrets of the universe are locked up, but an accompaniment to perdition. The great danger for the subject is to cease to understand 'die Dinge', the objects of the world. Elsewhere Stifter spoke often of the need to understand 'die Forderung der Dinge' ('the demands made by things'), and in the novel there is talk of 'the innocence of the things outside ourselves' (p. 213). *Der Nachsommer*, more than most of Stifter's other works, concentrates upon how the world could be if people did seek themselves not by the route of introspection, but precisely by the route via the things of the world, because only in that way can the distorting pressure of the appetites, of subjective desires and emotions, be corrected to allow individual subjects to find and fulfil themselves in their true place within the objective order of creation. This is why Stifter's novel has a powerful interest in itself being finished, being itself a thing, by surrender to which a reader may take a detour to his own moral being.

It will be evident that this identification of *Heinrich von Ofterdingen* with the subject and *Der Nachsommer* with the object is an over-simplification. In the words from the introduction to 'Turmalin' quoted above, there is a curious tug between interiorities, an 'inneres Gesetz', which connects the individual with the universal moral law, versus an 'Innigkeit' which leads astray. Stifter condemns a false subjectivity, while never doubting any more than Novalis that the truth lies within, if only one can find it. Similarly, Novalis is intensely aware of the dangers of a false or narcissistic subjectivity, allegorising it in the dalliance between Eros and Ginnistan in Klingsohr's *Märchen* as a kind of short circuit in the pursuit of the absolute, in which Eros is downgraded to Cupid.[39] If Uerlings can say of Novalis's novel that it is 'simply put, very largely a novel about the subject–object problematic',[40] then something similar might be said of Stifter's novel. Both novels are part of a culture which is deeply preoccupied with the philosophical and moral status of the subject, and although each text favours either subject or object in its literary construction of (masculine) subjectivity, it is characteristic of the mirror symmetry between the texts, as well as a logical necessity, that they include the object with the subject and vice versa.

There is a symmetry here of central relevance to my argument. A minor but persistent tradition of scholarship is devoted to the question of the curious parallels between the two works, some of it aimed at establishing conscious influence of Novalis upon Stifter.[41] This specific question of influence remains inconclusive, and matters perhaps less than the shared broad cultural context, which extends over the conventional boundaries of literary history and classification.

The focus of this shared cultural context is the common intertextual relation to the *Lehrjahre*. Certainly, even in the framework of their relationship to Goethe's novel there are important differences. They divide along the thematic lines one would expect: Novalis seeks to transform and transcend Goethe, Stifter to strengthen and consolidate him. But the determining thematic strategy of Goethe's novel as I have expounded it is retained. Both texts, that is to say, exhibit structures of mutually supporting masculine and feminine circularities (inheritance and incest) which unite law and desire in aesthetic *form*, the significance of which is to define and speak for the nature and value of the individual human subject.

The maternal dimension of *Heinrich von Ofterdingen* is clear enough not to need too much labouring: '*Ofterdingen* must be the only novel in world literature in which the hero is constantly accompanied by his mother.'[42] The dream, with which the book opens, is a representation of the journey within.[43] It contains a passage which expresses perfectly the way in which female figures come to embody male desire in all the novels in the wake of the *Lehrjahre* with which I am concerned:

'new, hitherto unseen images arose, and they too flowed into one another, becoming visible beings about him, and every wave of the lovely element nestled against him like a tender (zart) breast. Charming girls seemed to be dissolved in the waters, becoming momentarily embodied at the touch of the youth (Die Flut schien eine Auflösung reizender Mädchen, die sich an dem Jünglinge augenblicklich verkörperten.)' (I, p. 197)

This dream goes on to confirm the importance of images of women in the figuring of masculine desire in the apparition of the blue flower, which folds open to reveal 'a delicate (zart) face'. This distillation of longing is then connected with the voice of the mother, which breaks into the dreamer's consciousness at this precise moment (I, p. 197).

As the author of a monograph on Novalis has remarked, 'Heinrich's dream is an ideal case study for a psychoanalyst.'[44] Desire and the mother are thus linked from the beginning in the economy of the book. This picks up and radicalises the intimations of incestuous longing which animate the *Lehrjahre*.

Novalis's text brings together, much more explicitly than the other texts we have considered, the basic incestuous orientation upon the mother and the general use of woman figures to structure plots, and with it masculine subjectivity. Heinrich meets Mathilde (whose name begins with a maternal syllable) on a journey made in the company of his mother to her home town of Augsburg. When Heinrich sees Mathilde he recognizes her face as the face of the flower in the dream (I, p. 277), so that both Mathilde and his mother are associated with the same deepest yearning. The account of the first encounter between Heinrich and Mathilde unites them in a 'symbiotic primality'.[45] Klingsohr's *Märchen* tells of the burning of 'the Mother', a death which functions as a structural anticipation of Mathilde's. Both are in fact the overcoming of death. The Mother's ashes are put by Sophie into a bowl on the altar at the end of the *Märchen*, and everyone partakes of them, in a secular version of Holy Communion (I, p. 312). Mathilde's death is associated with the entry into myth initiated in the second part of the novel. All women figures now seem interchangeable (recalling the image from the dream quoted above), and one of this succession of embodiments, Zyane, in answer to Heinrich's question 'Where are we going?' gives the reply in which the essence of circularity is concentrated: 'Immer nach Hause' ('we are always returning home', I, p. 325).

As in Hölderlin, it is in the experience of love that it is possible for ordinary mortals to have direct rather than theoretical experience of the absolute. In Diotima and Mathilde the form- and meaning-giving properties of women characters in this type of masculine text are taken to the limit. Hölderlin (in this respect as in others) is the more extreme in his impossible attempt to dispense altogether with the masculine dimension, while Novalis retains the masculine circularity in a strong commitment to aesthetic form, despite postulating the ultimate priority of the feminine.

To Novalis, on the other hand, to imagine that one can find satisfaction by giving in to the immediate promptings of desire, is to confuse the immediacy of subjective desire with its true philosophical and religious significance. Where the other novels distinguish between an illicit, unsocialised, incestuous desire which threatens form and a permissible, socialised one from which form is derived, Novalis distinguishes between the *illusion* that the deepest desires are incestuous, and the truth that *even deeper* lie feelings which transcend incest and reach towards a oneness of which desire for union with one's own mother is only a faint echo in the individuated historical self. Thus Eros is seduced by Ginnistan in the body of his mother, with the effect that he regresses to childishness, sexuality is reduced to promiscuity, and an indirection occurs along Love's true path. Love is trivialised in this lack of self-restraint, which appears to be the result of the deepest stirrings of the subject, *appears* to be the ultimate consummation of incest, but of course isn't, since Ginnistan only appears to be the mother. In Lacanian terms, the mother becomes the 'signified of desire', and incest the imaginary erasure of the lack which in fact inhabits all desire.[46]

For Novalis, then, the circle of incest has quasi-religious dimensions (in this he is close to Hölderlin). But this feminine circularity is nonetheless complemented by a masculine one (in distinction to Hölderlin), as is the case with the *Lehrjahre* and its other cognates. The novel as we have it (although not as it was planned) starts and ends with Sylvester, whom Heinrich refers to as 'excellent father' (I, p. 332). Sylvester in 'The Fulfilment' also serves the function of taking us back to Heinrich's actual father, since Heinrich's father was known to Sylvester in the past. He explains the particular nature of Heinrich's father, as a man gifted but too attached to the ordinary sublunary world to develop his gifts beyond the mundane, and who remains thus only a craftsman, not an artist. In this capacity he is very like Wilhelm Meister's father, who, as we saw, in modest ways anticipates the new fathers of the Society of the Tower. This parallel is all the more compelling when one considers that Klingsohr, the father figure Heinrich finds waiting for him in Augsburg, is an intensified version of his own father as the proponent of the craftsmanlike elements within the work of the true artist as opposed to the mere dilettante (I, p. 282). He is an artist *and* a craftsman.

Klingsohr bears some relation to Goethe. He occupies in *Ofterdingen* the structural position occupied by the Tower in the *Lehrjahre*. He represents the authority which will help Heinrich to become what he is. The fact that Ofterdingen is a poet, which the book makes unambiguous, is also a link to Goethe – albeit a negative one, since it is the most obvious opposition to the model of the *Lehrjahre*, in which of course Wilhelm thinks he is an artist, but learns that he is mistaken.[47] At the same time, the figure of Klingsohr contains something of the ambiguity Novalis felt about the *Lehrjahre*, since Klingsohr's lessons about poetry are Goethean in tone;[48] indeed, it has been suggested that the figure of Klingsohr bears a physical resemblance to the historical Goethe (see I, p. 270). We note the 'clear, masculine relations' which characterise his behaviour (ibid.). As Molnár writes, 'there is good reason to believe that Goethe's craftsmanship, his ability to execute, to realise genius fully rather than imply its potential in fragmentary flashes proved to be a decisive impetus for Novalis's own emergence as an artist and, one might add, as a man'.[49] Novalis derived from his intensive study of the *Lehrjahre* 'a composite ideal of man and artist, which he came to consider his future vocation'.[50] It is thus precisely the Goethe of the *Lehrjahre* who accommodates a need for a masculine, mastering presence in the representation of the subject. The presence of Goethe as an authority, a father figure, within a text anticipates *Der grüne Heinrich*.

As with the *Lehrjahre*, the protagonist receives his bride from the milieu of his higher education: in this case, in close consonance with *Der Nachsommer*, from the very hand of the father figure. This configuration points towards a convergence of masculine and feminine determinants within the masculine protagonist and the work in which his subjectivity is realised, and therefore adumbrates the motif of androgyny. In *Heinrich von Ofterdingen*, as in the *Lehrjahre*, a tendency towards a union of male and female properties can be discerned. The nature of the union between Heinrich and Mathilde is expressed in a poem which Tieck put at the head of the fragment of the second book, with the title *Astralis*. Astralis is the name of the mythical being whose birth is the result of the symbolic union of Heinrich and Mathilde. In the poem, Astralis, mention of whose gender is avoided, tells the story of his or her own conception, in which and in the result of which the parents are fused (I, p. 318).

As Sara Friedrichsmeyer puts it: 'Heinrich and Mathilde have actualised the Urbild of androgynous totality.'[51] Furthermore, despite the association of Heinrich's mother, Mathilde and other female figures (see I, p. 348) with the blue flower, at its first appearance the face revealed within it is not gendered ('ein zartes Gesicht'), and so bespeaks a promise of oneness which transcends gender.

Heinrich Drendorf too receives his bride from a second father figure,[52] and on the day of their wedding the Peruvian cactus *Cereus*

Peruvianus flowers, which it does so rarely that only a few people in Europe have ever seen its precious single white flower (p. 826). Not only does this motif recall the blue flower of Novalis's text, but it contains an allusion to androgyny too, since the sexual connotations of the opening of the cactus unite male and female in a symbolic androgyny.[53] The extraordinarily enhanced value of social ritual and exchange in Stifter's novel make of this marriage something more than just a mundane union. Indeed, it is suggested that Heinrich Drendorf himself might aspire to the state of androgyny (p. 819).[54] The implication of androgyny, and the strong formal dependence upon a woman figure to round out the text (in this case her name is the same as that of the analogous figure in the *Lehrjahre*), are thus clear enough in *Der Nachsommer*.[55]

On the surface, however, the motif of incest is missing. Yet it is all the more powerfully implied, because the movement of the text as a whole is towards a blending of families into a single large family[56] in which exogamy remains a foreign concept: 'My sister did not yet know that men sought to please her, and she paid them no heed. For my part, when it occurred to me that my sister must one day have a husband, I could think of no other suitable candidate than a man in the likeness of our father' (p. 184).

The problem of incest, which seems to have been so naturally overcome, announces itself in an untypical moment of disturbance in an otherwise uniformly tranquil text.[57] On hearing of her brother's betrothal, Klotilde's reaction is to fall on her brother's neck and to burst into tears (p. 592). In the discourse of the *Nachsommer* this is a reaction of operatic proportions. It signals a dysfunctional moment within the kinship system set out by the novel: if Heinrich marries (which of course he must for the system to function) the perfect family is broken open: the love between brother and sister is problematicised by the explicitness of the sexual implications of *choosing* a partner, rather than pre-existing in a complete, hermaphroditical system. Heinrich's mother is clear-sighted about the need for this excess of sexual implication to be dealt with: 'Klotilde will have to change the nature of her affection towards you' (p. 590). Klotilde, on the other hand, can see equally clearly that what is happening is not a disturbance of the status quo, but merely a repeat of it: 'My only wish (Verlangen) is that she should love you as I do' (p. 592). ('Verlangen' is rather a strong word to use in this context, and serves in German to convey sexual feelings as well as others.) The novel must contain this slight disturbance within its economy: Heinrich takes his sister for a ride in the mountains and, it has rather charmingly been suggested, explains to her the facts of life,[58] although needless to say the text reveals no such thing (p. 641) – only the intensity and privacy of discourse between brother and sister, a closed dyad to which there is access for no third party. When sister and bride eventually meet, the disturbance has been assimilated within the 'Großfamilie', and an irresistible logic suggests that Klotilde will marry the brother of her brother's bride.

The masculine dimension, in the form of the circularity of inheritance, is as prominent in Stifter's text as the feminine one is in Novalis's. The topic of inheritance fascinates Stifter and his male characters. Both Drendorf senior and von Risach display an almost voluptuous love for testamentary detail. So, for example, in the chapter 'Der Einblick' ('The Insight'), and after the narrator has come to a realisation about the value of his father's collection of art objects, he learns what is to become of it after his father's death, and a paragraph is devoted to the dispositions the elder Drendorf has made to cover all contingencies (pp. 456–457). Similarly, when Risach makes his official engagement speech, he does not neglect to provide a detailed account of his legal relationship to his 'daughter' Natalie (p. 800). So important is the securing and administering of inheritance that the size of the marriage settlement, details of which are foregrounded in the closing pages of the book, virtually constitutes the book's *dénouement* (p. 835).

There is a further aspect of the place of inheritance in *Der Nachsommer*. Stifter has constructed *two* fathers for his hero to inherit from.[59] Heinrich is surprised to discover an equivalence between his own father and the spiritual guide he has found in his host Risach (see, for instance, p. 835). The book as a whole argues for an *identity* between these two figures.

The point can perhaps be put most clearly with the aid of a simile. It is rather as if we were being presented, in Drendorf senior and Freiherr von Risach, with two diagrams of the same thing, the latter simply an enlargement of the former, serving to highlight the details of the object's real nature. And because some of the congruences are less than immediately apparent, lines are provided which lead from one point in the smaller image to its equivalent in the larger picture. The function of these lines is the same as that of Heinrich Drendorf in the economy of the novel. The motion of direction (as the lines move from diagram to diagram, or Heinrich Drendorf as he makes his seasonal trips from father to father, town to country) reveals itself as the stasis of identity, for the very *function* of the ride from image to image, from Drendorf to Risach, is to insist upon the identity of these two terminal points, and not to describe any sort of progress.

The parallels between the two men and their respective establishments are prominent and explicit (see, for instance, pp. 89, 173, 448). Most compelling of all is the revelation, in the chapter 'Der Einblick', that they have identical art collections (although the scale is different). The representative example of this strange parallel is the fact that Drendorf's father has an equivalent to the classical sculpture that forms the pride and centrepiece of Risach's collection (p. 450).

The pattern of the *Lehrjahre* and that of *Heinrich von Ofterdingen* is thus repeated: two paternal instances, one an intensified version of the other, attend the male subject, ensuring that he inherits that which will ensure the development of his full potential, whether this is worldly wisdom, the secret of the artist's craft or property.[60]

These two texts retain something of the compatibility of law and desire, and this establishes a common context with the literary construction of subjectivity in the *Lehrjahre*. *Heinrich von Ofterdingen* and *Der Nachsommer*, however, are also united in a common and highly significant divergence from the Goethean paradigm. Whereas Goethe had drawn a picture of individual development by devising all sorts of adventures and reversals for his hero, these two novels do not. This is one of the main parallels fixed upon by scholarship. The heroes of Novalis and Stifter do not seem to encounter the recalcitrance of the world. 'Novalis's writing is close to the edge of boredom, in a similar way to Adalbert Stifter's in *Der Nachsommer*, where the resistance of the world is also blocked out.'[61] The development of the two protagonists proceeds smoothly on its way without significant resistance from circumstances. One could put this another way by saying that, whereas in Goethe, and to a greater extent in Keller, the form-guaranteeing circularities of incest and inheritance are tested against determinations from reality, here they are not; both novels are, in the words of the scholar who first drew attention to the affinity between them, suspended between 'Domesticity and domesticity (Häuslichkeit)'.[62]

What the previous scholarship on this subject has, surprisingly, not stressed is that both novels *do* thematise reversal, but in a way quite unlike the neo-picaresque narrative of Goethe. Reversal is focused into one, single, devastating denial of desire, which the texts then accommodate. At the heart of each is the loss of a lover, whose name, in both cases, is Mathilde.

By the beginning of Part Two of *Heinrich von Ofterdingen* it is clear that Mathilde is no longer alive. The union between her and Heinrich had been conveyed in terms which left the reader in no doubt about its predestined nature. Now, without explanation and certainly without narrative exposition, two distinct forms of discourse, Astralis's poem and the narrative of the second part, address the significance of the union between Heinrich and Mathilde, her loss, and its transcendence. This then retrospectively links up with what now must be read as anticipations of this catastrophe, Heinrich's dream of her drowning (I, pp. 278–279), and the death of 'Die Mutter' in Klingsohr's *Märchen*.

After fifteen chapters and many hundreds of pages, in a chapter called 'Der Rückblick' (the 'Look Back', or 'Retrospective View'), the reader of *Der Nachsommer* becomes acquainted with the background to the relationship between Freiherr von Risach and his neighbour Mathilde Tarona. In their youth, Risach had been a tutor in Mathilde's parental home. The two young people had fallen in love, but Mathilde's parents, when at length they had learned of the attachment, while not in principle disapproving of an eventual union, had required a period of separation. Risach had been willing to accept this restraint, but the young Mathilde, traumatically for both parties, had accused him of a lack of passion and rejected him, experiencing his acquiescence in parental regulation as a betrayal of their love. The 'Indian summer' of the book's title is then a partial recovery of the lost possibility of love of many years before.

It does not matter that in Stifter it is Risach who loses the lover, not Drendorf, or that in Novalis the loss occurs only in code, in fairy tale or poetry, and otherwise vanishes into the hiatus between the two extant parts of the novel. The point is that the works, *as works*, in both cases turn on these episodes: they work to make good these losses in the manner of their respective stylistic repertoires. For Novalis, the death is a necessary preliminary to a higher plane of experience, the connection (in its absence) between the two parts of the novel, from one intensity of discourse to another. For Stifter the loss of Mathilde Makloden, memorably encapsulated and embodied in Risach's agonised self-mutilation with a rose thorn (p. 765), is made good by the cultivation of thousands of roses; Risach's house is called the House of Roses, and these roses are among the novel's most insistent symbols. In both cases, the catastrophe of love is brought into a positive relation with a love which is more than just a novelistic love affair: Heinrich von Ofterdingen and Mathilde's brief but profound mutual recognition prefigures apotheosis; the disaster of Risach and Mathilde is re-written by them in the positive form of the story of Heinrich Drendorf and Natalie. Both experiences of love are close, in their perfection, to religious experience. The only difference is that, with Novalis, the perfect meeting precedes the catastrophe and points forward to revelation, while with Stifter, the ideal love comes later, in the preordained coming together of Heinrich and Natalie. This is the real harvest of the Indian summer and the overcoming of that earlier loss, a loss which nevertheless, gives meaning to everything else in the novel's world.

It is thus a certain *modification* of the *Lehrjahre* model that constitutes the most striking parallel between these two texts and explains the intriguing mirror symmetry between them. This mirror symmetry can be related back to the *Lehrjahre* model, which will in turn throw light on that model, and on the general topic of the literary construction of subjectivity in the *Bildungsroman*.

To take the major point first: although both novels display the double circularity of masculine and feminine, it could hardly be clearer that in Novalis the maternal dimension predominates and in Stifter the paternal.[63]

Novalis retains Goethe's paternal model in order to transcend it.

This is clear, for instance, in the comparison between Heinrich's dream, with which the novel opens, and that of his father which is reported soon afterwards. Heinrich's father had subordinated the timelessness and universal spatiality of the dream to the unilinearity of social existence. He had climbed back into chronology, where Heinrich is destined to turn his back upon it and in reversing, dissolve it, as his father's dream knows (even if his father does not, I, p. 202). His father interprets the dream of his youth in a mundane way: 'and yet, what did the dream mean? It was quite natural for me to dream of you [Heinrich's mother] and to feel soon thereafter a longing (Sehnsucht) to possess you, since I already knew you' (I, p. 200). Chronology is king; it explains 'Sehnsucht' and orders it into the social narrative, the happy ending and mundane beginning of matrimony. Heinrich's 'Sehnsucht' is free of such social determination, flowing backwards as well as forwards and ultimately linking his subjectivity to the abolition of time.

Klingsohr too represents a value which the novel as a whole affirms but goes beyond. He is 'the father of love' (I, p. 287), who enunciates but does not embody the principle in relation to which he is a father: 'die Liebe ist selbst nichts, als die höchste Naturpoesie.' ('Love is nothing but the highest nature poesy', I, p. 287.) It is Klingsohr who produces Heinrich von Ofterdingen's *Bildungsroman*, when he interprets the story so far in terms sometimes taken as a summary of the novel as a whole.[64] But what the various strategies of the novel are really after is ways of suspending such linear, progressive, cumulative meanings in favour of global, simultaneous halls of correspondence, remote from the dimensions of time and space, in which masculine hegemony is indispensable and unquestionable.

The element which contains and exceeds the paternal is the maternal. The most radical demonstration of this comes again from Friedrich Kittler. Kittler's analysis concerns itself mainly with Klingsohr's *Märchen*, in which 'Die Erwartung' culminates. The tale completes the movement, begun by the conventional narrative, away from masculine authority. In a self-undermining gesture (I, p. 87) Klingsohr presents a work of his youth, in which the masculine order is replaced by a feminine one. 'The mother is among us, and her presence will bring us eternal joy' (I, p. 315). 'The *Märchen* completes the replacement of the father to the point of complete erasure',[65] writes Kittler. The *Märchen* is the 'Oedipal fantasy of the novel'.[66] The Romantics were the first generation to grow up in the historical family form in which the mother had the role of socialising agent. The effect of this is to privilege that space of 'Innerlichkeit' which I refer to as the partialness of subjectivity. The importance of this space is that it is the habitat of both the modern subject and the modern poet.[67] Modern poetry and modern sexuality derive their definition from the appearance, in the system of codes which organise people's lives, of this area of hitherto inchoate experience. Whereas in the *Lehrjahre* this new role of the mother was still registered, stored and legitimated by father figures, in the *Märchen* of *Heinrich von Ofterdingen* the mother herself speaks, pronouncing the dissolution of all differences and identities, in the establishment of an 'absolute family'. This maternal speech is at the same time the end of language, which depends upon differentiation in order to work.[68]

The *Märchen* anticipates something which hovers in potentiality, and the return of Sylvester after Klingsohr's narrative underlines how the moment of paternal circularity is preserved within, as well as annulled by, the progression of the plot. And indeed, these two moments, the end of the paternal order and the inauguration of the maternal, are interdependent. Kittler quotes Novalis himself: 'Alle Schranken sind bloß des Übersteigens willen da' ('all barriers are simply there in order to be crossed', III, p. 269), and points out how although this utterance appears to undermine the law, it also refounds it at the same time, since it decides the shape and form of the transgressions it demands by virtue of demanding them.[69]

In Novalis's novel, then, one element predominates over the other which, nevertheless, is enfolded within the first. With Stifter, the situation is reversed. While the masculine dimension is supreme, the male protagonist passing from one father to an identical one on his way to becoming one himself, the feminine dimension is more complementary and less subordinate than the masculine emphasis of the book might lead one to expect. Stifter actually treats women characters in a more differentiated and less stereotyped way than many otherwise comparable writers, and certainly than the Romantics.[70] While Natalie has something of the icon about her, and functions rather as a supreme possession (see, for instance, p. 818), her mother, Mathilde, is an independent woman at the time of the narrative, and a powerful and defiantly passionate individual at the time of Risach's retrospective account.

Admittedly, her defiance and passion are massively circumscribed by the rest of the text. Yet just as Mathilde provides a contrast to the iconic nature of her daughter, so, surprisingly, Risach contrasts in a certain sense to the impeccably law-abiding Heinrich. Although Risach is (catastrophically for passion) law-abiding in his confrontation with the young Mathilde, his own later role as a crucial embodiment of law in relation to Heinrich is itself, paradoxically, not without its feminine aspects. Risach's own personal history, as one is prone to overlook,[71] actually represents him as a father figure produced by the need for and the attention of mothers, having been brought up by his own mother, seeking a new mother in Mathilde's mother and finding fulfilment in a platonic relationship with the now maternal Mathilde herself. 'Risach's path is thus truly "matrilinear"'.[72] Indeed, as Schäublin also observes, 'it is remarkable . . . how motherly the two father figures, Heinrich's father and Risach, are'.[73] The entire paternal function which so unmissably imposes its structure on the book has something maternal about it, in that both men are passive conservers of nature, bringing forth its fruits rather than actively engaging in its transformation.

Moreover, the kind of inheritance represented in the unimpeded flow of money to the novel's subject and his fledgling establishment betrays something of the munificence and unconstrained quality one associates with the love of the mother. In *Der grüne Heinrich*, the mother's love was both the source of funds and the source of guilt, the two ideas coming together in the German word 'Schuld', which means debt as well as guilt. In the absence of paternal guidance, the young man squandered his maternal gifts by mistaking himself as an artist and failing to recognise the true demands of a reality which is inseparable from economics. Here, however, the maternal dimension is perfectly accommodated within the masculine.

These two texts thus complement each other in important ways.

Novalis locates an insistence upon stern discipline, formal control and manliness within an overall textual affiliation to the maternal element, while Stifter elaborates a regularity administered by and for patriarchs, from which, however, the greatest taboo of all, against incest, is exempt. In the preface to his collection of stories *Bunte Steine*, Stifter coined the term 'das sanfte Gesetz' ('the gentle law'), which conveys perfectly the oxymoronic mix of rigid legality and the sanction of longing evoked by his novel.

What are the implications of these (broadly speaking) thematic circularities, with their respective weightings, for representation itself? How do these two avowedly non-realistic texts conceive of, and themselves practise, representation?

Neither novel conforms to the conventions of nineteenth-century realist narrative: the narrative of *Ofterdingen* is relativised by other narratives and forms of discourse, that of *Der Nachsommer* is effectively slower and more ritualised than the reader coming from a realistic novel expects. This estrangement of the novelistic is a device inherited from the *Lehrjahre*. There the evident artificiality of the novelistic devices was lent an aura of significance, and this contributed crucially to the *aesthetic* authority of the text. Within this authority, it was possible to combine realistic and idealistic components, and for them to enrich and confirm each other. In taking their cue from the aesthetic aspect of the *Lehrjahre* these two texts are, however, unwilling to concede anything to the arbitrariness of extra-literary reality. The evident artificiality or literariness with which we are presented by both is an extremely earnest pointer toward universals.

For Novalis the only 'form' which really counts is the form of the new order, of which all artistic forms are *only*, but of which all *artistic* forms are *necessarily*, anticipations, 'Vor-Bilder' ('models', but literally 'advance images').[74] For Stifter the observance of form which dominates his novel implies a reverence for God's creation no longer available from other forms of aesthetic or other discourse.

Poetic practice and aesthetic observance are moral imperatives in Novalis and Stifter. If Goethe's integration of Wilhelm Meister into the world is largely dependent upon an intentional hesitation between social-moral meanings (the 'programme' of the Society of the Tower, the related symbolism of Natalie, the play with class differences) and aesthetic ones (the combining of all these in an ironic and self-consciously artificial scenario), then Novalis and Stifter subsume the social-moral sphere under the aesthetic, although without intending to devalue it. The aesthetic merges into the religious sphere in their respective constructions of erotic love.

What becomes of the subjective authenticity of autobiography? In both cases an autobiographical core is assimilated into the conceptual system which vouchsafes aesthetic access to universals. Here too, art prevails over autobiography. In the case of *Heinrich von Ofterdingen*, this is explained as follows by Molnár: 'The poet can describe nothing else but the process through which he attained the level of self-consciousness that permits the world to appear as the poetically transformed phenomenon he presents it to be.'[75]

The poet must write about his own autobiography ('for Novalis, the poet's genesis is at issue and not the poem's'),[76] how he came to be a poet; but this will already by definition be part of the larger transformation of the world. Poet, poem and moral existence are fused: the distinction between autobiography and fiction vanishes. In Stifter, the unhappy and unfulfilled life of the civil servant Risach (and to an extent of Drendorf senior), in which it is possible to recognise Stifter's own experience as an inspector of schools prevented from pursuing his own dearest interests, are only given in the context of their overcoming. This context is the book's belief in the priority of the world of objects over the clamour of subjectivity. Authentic experience is included in the book in order to be contained and transcended.

The stylisation of autobiographical experience is concentrated in the two moments of erotic reversal which have such vital function in the structures of the books. (In Novalis's case the parallel between the death of Mathilde and that of Sophie is not in doubt.) A moment in which the partialness of subjectivity is manifest also serves as the supreme moment of that which the peculiar style of the text will contain or transcend. The death of Mathilde is the invisible point from which Novalis's text spirals outwards toward the margins of creation, while the entire extraordinary construction of Stifter's text is there in order to compensate for this moment of appalling disjunction between subject and object.

In their rejection of the novel as a genuinely popular medium, and their respective transformations of the market-place reality of exchange, both works defend themselves as far as possible against the danger of what later received the name of Kitsch. Their contrasting, but equivalently extreme, styles also bear witness to the aesthetic exertions necessary to overcome the threat of a banality which, in commodified form, would become Kitsch – that is, easy representations and illusory confirmations that the world is constructed to recognise and answer to the needs of the private individual. Novalis's vision of the correspondence between subject and world, the confirmation in the blue flower of a consonance between subject and object, is the forerunner of a million false epiphanies. In its aestheticisation of the everyday, *Der Nachsommer* betrays a kinship with the practices of mass culture with which everyone is familiar today.[77]

How do these two novels construct and represent art and artists? 'Heinrich was by nature born to be a poet' (I, p. 267). Novalis's novel is all about the vocation of the poet, but this is no narrow theme: Klingsohr remarks how the function of poet is actually the essentially human. 'It is a bad thing that poetry has a special name and that poets belong to a special guild. What they do is nothing special. It is the characteristic form of activity of the human spirit. Is there not poetry and striving in all man's endeavours? (Dichtet und trachtet nicht jeder Mensch in jeder Minute?)' (I, p. 287).

Klingsohr's words might be the very inspiration of the opinion about poetry and subjectivity expressed by the young Keller quoted above (p. 130). In what does the vocation of the poet consist? We already know the answer: in the transformation of the world. The poet has a moral function in the development and exercise of his gift, which in some sense represents the potential, indeed the actual, mode of being of all subjectivities.

The ethical trajectory in Novalis's novel is towards the suspension of the subject–object relation. The poet, who, as Klingsohr observes, is really no more or no less than a representative of everybody, by achieving an external display of his inner insights effects an expression – indeed, a revelation – of the truth ('Offenbarung der Poesie auf Erden' , I, p. 341). Subject and object are thus suspended as categories ('the inner is revealed and the outer hidden', I, p. 310), for the free activity of the subject is the revelation of truth, not as the isolating privilege of self-expression for others, but as the cosmic choreography in which the self and others have their common place and movements. Expression takes on a mystic mutuality in the projected state where 'Jedes in Allen dar sich stellt' ('each particular is represented in everything', I, p. 319).

The poet has come to represent subjectivity, just as Wilhelm Meister had done, with the difference that the notion of subjectivity has been transformed, and partialness converted into a signpost to plenitude. Whereas for Weimar Classicism subjectivity in art brought the threat of dilettantism, in Novalis subjectivity can only properly be understood (or better: realised) in relation to the meaning of poetry, and, more specifically, the figure and activity of the poet. It is not a misunderstanding, but a shift in assumptions, which lies behind Franz Grillparzer's comment: 'Novalis – Deification of dilettantism. A Wilhelm Meister without his charter, caught up forever in his apprenticeship.'[78] Grillparzer was himself, somewhat like Stifter, a writer who sought to adapt the precepts and values of Weimar Classicism to changed historical circumstances. As the Goethean strictures of Klingsohr make quite clear, the charge of dilettantism is not fairly levelled at Novalis, unless one takes the 'deification' more seriously than it was intended. Within the subjective maternal dimension of poetry the masculine dimension of order and control is fully present but expressed *in its terms*, since the two father figures, Heinrich's actual father and Klingsohr, are both makers, the authors of form.

Poetry, then, is the form and content of everything in *Heinrich von Ofterdingen*. The main figure is a quintessentially creative figure, one from within whose inwardness the golden age of poetry is in the making. The status of art in *Der Nachsommer* is no less high, but there is a difference. It can perhaps best be encapsulated in the fact that in this work it is not creativity that counts, but the collecting, ownership and appreciation of art. The model of subjectivity in Stifter's text is constructed by means of two father figures, between whose identical art collections a young man moves, in a development towards his own patriarchal effectiveness. As he gradually learns to discern and appreciate aesthetic value, he moves towards the paternal position of authority. What is more, of course, he will also inherit both collections himself. Because the whole logic of the development is one of conservation and repetition, it does not matter that one can argue about who is the main figure of the novel, Heinrich Drendorf or Risach. Rhetorically, it is the *figure*, or motif, of ownership and collection which gives art its definition in this world, not the creation of art. Stifter's is the text in which that particular configuration of inwardness *and* external splendour, anticipated in the recognition between father and son in *Agathon*, is worked out to the greatest extent. As Heinrich slowly recognises the parallel between his own father's art collection and that of Risach, and as he learns also from the ripening of his own subjective experience (especially the unconscious growth of his love for Natalie) to appreciate art, son recognises father in, and himself through, the mediation of art, so that both measurable social status and inner life, the public and the private, are included in the transaction between father and son. It is a transfer of identity, which is another reason why Risach and Drendorf are in a sense interchangeable as the subject of the text: they illuminate the particular identity with which Stifter is concerned.

This moment of paternal art ownership, so characteristic for one particular dimension of the model I am expounding, is not absent from *Heinrich von Ofterdingen* either. It occurs in the 'Atlantis' story, told in Chapter Three by the merchants. Here the paternal authority towards which the poet-subject aspires exhibits the same traits as all the other father figures from Agathon senior to Green Henry's count and Gustav von Risach, in that he has loved poetry all his life, spent great sums on his collection of their works in all languages, and valued the company of poets above all others (I, p. 214).

Since all stories in *Ofterdingen* are really one, this moment takes its modest but inevitable place in Novalis's configuration too. Its absence in Moritz and Hölderlin is an indication of their significant difference from the *Lehrjahre* model.

If everything tends towards a translation of the world into the state of poetry in *Ofterdingen*, in *Der Nachsommer* it is as though everything is already art. The moment and agonies of creation lie somewhere in the past. (There is a very potent metaphor in the novel for the hidden agonies of the beautiful: the alder roots which grow on the edge of Risach's estate are crippled and tortured in aspect, because Risach cannot adequately drain the swampy region where they grow, but their very deformations produce the exquisitely flamed wood used in marquetry, pp. 135–136).[79] Art is a principle of all behaviour and all attitudes, even where it is not itself being practised or produced.[80] The culminating artistic focus of the book is the Greek statue, the marble figure with its origin in the ancient past, which survives into the present, amputated from the subjectivity which created it, like an aesthetic denial of the passing of time. The statue is the artistic equivalent in the hierarchy of values to Natalie. They stand for one another, art providing the language in which all values may be expressed: 'the marble muse is Natalie immortalised'.[81] And it is only in possession that art finally fulfils itself.[82]

Thus, art is established in a relation to the subject in two very distinct ways. In Novalis the essence, meaning and function of poetry is passed on without mediation from the mother to the son, with other masculine figures taking care of formal matters only (Klingsohr is 'the father of love', but love itself is 'the highest nature poesy', and a product of the relation between Heinrich and Mathilde, woman and poet, I, p. 287). In Stifter, already formed products of artistic genius, whose greatest value is commensurate with an ideal of womanhood, are passed on in a patrilinear manner from father figures to sons. The relations between paternal authority, subjectivity and art, and the related question of the representation, and thus the construction, of subjectivity are thematised in these ways.

The *Lehrjahre* depends upon a collaboration between the protagonist and the narrator. Together they produce what Moritz called 'der Roman eines Lebens'. The novel as an *act* of authorship is unified with the *process* of self-authorship of the hero. There is an identity between male hero and male narrator, which is disavowed on the thematic level (the protagonist is *not* an artist), but asserted in the *form* of the novel, which in its closure is offered as the work of an artist and a work of art.

It is in the nature of Novalis's understanding of the life and significance of the poet that this delicate balance between process and act will not be maintained. All acts, including the programmatically unfinished act of the text, are a pointer towards a process of which they are part. 'Everything is seed' (II, p. 563); 'to create poetry is to procreate' ('Dichten ist zeugen', II, p. 534). *Heinrich von Ofterdingen* is centrifugal, always tending outwards. Its narrative perspective, a neutral third person, from the first pages onward seeks ways of subverting itself: first in dream, then through stories, then in self-consciousness (the hero reads his own story), then by the agency of Klingsohr's *Märchen*, after which the text mutates into a different form of discourse altogether. The text is the trace or deposition in the material world of the subject's trajectory towards the Archimedian point at which the material world will yield to its spiritual condition.[83]

Der Nachsommer is narrated in the first person. But Stifter employs a very peculiar sort of first-person narration. Heinrich Drendorf tells his own story in the past, but virtually never reflects upon it from the present position logically entailed by every act of first-person narration. Whereas Hölderlin, for instance, exploits this space of reflection between a present and a past self, Stifter rather remarkably denies that it exists. The space of subjectivity which would normally open up as a result of a first-person stance is thus excluded. Heinrich Drendorf is a memory amputated from the inevitably ongoing reflection of consciousness. He is 'a speaker without subjectivity'.[84] The text appears to exist 'without any trace of inwardness'.[85] In him, *qua* device, the experiential fact of subjectivity is given, but also contained inside, a text which in this as in everything else is preoccupied with closure.

The function of self-authorship is displaced from the protagonist on to the father figures in the text. But of course their function is less to author themselves than to author Heinrich Drendorf, in whom they re-write their own lives. In doing so they redeem the inevitable partialness, failure and shortcomings of their own biographies, which bear the traces of extra-literary circumstantial reality.

Where the work of Novalis exploits its own evident artificiality to produce programmatic unfinishedness, expanding the subject towards the Absolute, Stifter's contains the energies of the subject, moving centripetally towards a consciously and defensively artificial and closed work of art. Novalis looks to the future ('Die Erwartung'), and Stifter to the past ('Der Rückblick').

The tendency of *Heinrich von Ofterdingen* is towards an ideal of orality, a full expression *beyond* the medium of representation. Novalis writes *about* the transcending of language (whereas Hölderlin *attempted* it; see I, p. 287). The final configuration of the *Märchen*, as Kittler has shown, dreams the dream of a perfect expression, without division, a speech (rather than writing) which never takes the detour around the third person of language. In contrast to the discredited *Schreiber* (scribe), Fabel's song will be an incessant spinning (recalling the connotations of the idea of spinning in Keller and Freud) from within herself: 'from within yourself you will spin for us an indestructible golden thread', says Perseus to Fabel at the end (I, p. 314). The 're-coding' undertaken by the *Märchen* thus identifies modern poetry as a 'free outpouring of inwardness', which is predicated upon the abundance of maternal love: 'Fabel's inexhaustible gift of speech is simply the reciprocation of the inexhaustible mother love which she has received.'[86] The mother rather than the father now regulates all communication, and her regulation consists in the abolition of all regulation.[87] Subjectivity no longer needs to be represented, since the division between subject and object logically implied by any act of representation has been removed.

The preoccupation of *Der Nachsommer*, on the other hand, is with the absolute inevitability of the mediation of representation, and the consequent imperative need to pay such attention to all its forms. *Der Nachsommer* is deeply conversant with this necessity of representation. It reserves its deepest reverence for it, where Novalis is always pushing for its final abolition. If Kittler was able to show how *Ofterdingen* was a writing about orality, Stifter's writing can be seen as a writing which, uniquely, restores to writing the priority denied it (according to Derrida) by western culture in relation to speech. This is the burden of Thomas Keller's study of the novel, *Die Schrift in Stifters 'Nachsommer'*, in which he argues that the text affirms its written status in the sense that it offers itself not only as a novel about space, but as itself a spatial entity, a visual, printed, thing. It therefore does not aspire to a spurious fulness which is erroneously ascribed to language by associating it with the presence of the human voice.

Each novel contains the image of the mode of representation

which it defines itself by opposing. In *Heinrich von Ofterdingen* the assured masculine narrator reappears in the person of Der Schreiber in Klingsohr's *Märchen*. He represents a form of masculine authority, associated with the written word, which opposes the new order of the world announced by the tale. It is as if that form of magisterial authority which Goethe adapted from the Enlightenment for his aesthetic end has been separated back out, and isolated as a caricature of dry rationality, in order to be disposed of. The scribe stands for control through representation. *Der Nachsommer* is a uniquely clear example of the sort of control through representation which Der Schreiber allegorises. It seems as though Der Schreiber is consigned to oblivion after his attempt to impose his divisive mastery upon the world.[88]

Novalis's discourse betrays its ideal of immediacy in relation to the scribe. This has to do with his murder of Die Mutter. The climax of the scribe's bid to gain ascendancy is the burning of the mother. In terms of the tale, this brings out most clearly both the baseness of the scribe and his followers, and their lack of understanding of the mother's central significance. Her death by fire is in fact the occasion of her transsubstantiation in the final configuration of the tale. However, the motif of the scribe's murder of the mother can be read another way. In the novel's attempt to transcend representation completely, the fundamental logic of representation appears at the margin as a figure of violence. Writing, representation, *has to* murder the mother if she is to become a symbol. As Kittler puts it: 'Only writing can undertake re-codings, which after all work by erasure and re-writing; only her killing can give to the mother the presence of a symbol.'[89]

The murder of the mother by the scribe in *Heinrich von Ofterdingen* is thus the quintessential example of that formal, symbolic violence done to women throughout the texts I am discussing, from Meister's Marianne to Keller's mother. It distils the essence and meaning of the already extreme motif of the death of Novalis's Mathilde. The death of women repeatedly confers meaning, just as the death of the mother is the source of the inner meaning of the new order at the end of Klingsohr's *Märchen*, when Sophie passes the urn containing the mother's ashes to Eros, and all partake of them and feel transfigured from within by her presence (I, p. 312).

The closest parallel to this extreme potentiation of the motif of the death of women is the nature and death of Diotima in *Hyperion*. But although that work provides an illustration of the hypertrophy of the idea of art or poetry against which the *Lehrjahre* model sought to secure itself, it is distinct from that model in that it lacks the paternal dimension which ties poetry to the common circuits of coherence and meaning. This is not the case with *Heinrich von Ofterdingen*, which replicates the *Lehrjahre* model in real and important senses. Where the extraordinarily radical Hölderlin works always on the brink of extinction – his own as well as that of the most favoured feminine image – Novalis's text, for all its massive orientation towards the mother, is ultimately a construction of the masculine poet, figuring very specifically the violence at the *heart* (Die Mutter is the allegorical representation of 'Herz') of that construction. Within Novalis's vast programme for poetry and the world we are vouchsafed an especially distinct glimpse of the way the feminine functions in the construction of the masculine subject.

Helmut Pfotenhauer defines the common moment between these two texts as not only a refusal to allow space to the multifariousness of extra-literary reality, but as a shared violence of representation.[90] It is curious that the particularly masculine and controlling *Der Nachsommer* does not depend upon the death of women within its economy. The image of the form of representation that it itself opposes is the figure of Roland, the painter. Apart from the zither player from the mountains, Roland is the only character in the book who is genuinely gifted as an artist. By the same token he threatens the regulated calm of the *Nachsommer* world. He is nomadic, he paints an incommensurately large, wild painting (like Heinrich Lee's doodle, an anticipation of abstract modernism), and he is seen casting desiring glances at Natalie. The dangers of subjectivity as a disruptive and anarchic force are thus associated with artistic creativity ('Roland was an uncompromising supporter of innovation, even if it meant the overthrow of everything', p. 521).[91] The view of poetry as a potentiation of subjectivity through and beyond itself towards a transformation of the world, which is associated with Novalis, is here rigidly circumscribed. Risach expresses the need to control this undeniable but potentially destructive talent, whose fire will only consume him if it is not directed outwards at the creation of works of art (p. 834).

These two texts reproduce the *Lehrjahre* model in polarised form. There are two aspects to this. In the first place they both polarise the model itself. On the one hand we have the harmonious coincidence of law and desire in the main narrative and its masculine protagonist, on the other a moment of catastrophe, in both cases the loss of a woman called Mathilde, which represents precisely the opposite: the failure of law and desire to coincide. The partialness of subjectivity, the essential autobiographical moment, the resistances of reality, all are stylised in both cases into a single motif. The *Lehrjahre* blends reversals and fulfilments into an integrated artefact in which law and desire confirm each other as the principle of the aesthetic, informing hero and text.

The second way in which the two texts polarise the model (and this is what distinguishes them from each other) is that they each take one component of the Goethean synthesis and seek to make it predominant, while nevertheless maintaining the force of the synthesis. It is this stylistic extremism which in both cases acts to compensate and make good the devastating moment of loss at the heart of the economy of each text. Both texts are bids for totality within a model which ironically and paradoxically, but with an authority *deriving* from this irony and paradox, foregoes totality. Both seek to repeat, but this time incontrovertibly and absolutely, the *Lehrjahre*'s gesture of speaking of subjective partialness with aesthetic authority.

Because both texts are limit texts in this sense, it is certainly not a coincidence that both texts have been read as precursors of modernism (despite the distance in time between them – another indication that we are dealing with a unified moment across a large historical span). In both cases it is only the operation of an extreme style which staves off the collapse of the Goethean model: the Romantic metamorphoses of Novalis, the repetitions of Stifter. They bring out clearly, as Keller's novel had done in a completely different way, how the stylistic neighbours, as it were, of the aesthetic model are Kitsch on the one side and fragmentation on the other. Helmut Pfotenhauer can argue that Heinrich von Ofterdingen in its vast project wishes to provide a framework within which all the things of the world will fall into place, as part of the universal order disclosed by poetry. An aestheticised encyclopedia, in short. But this totalising and, as Pfotenhauer argues, unfinishable project comes close to being indistinguishable from that modernism for which the things of the world are resistant and discrete fragments without a unifying context, particulars with no universal, and for which encompassing and sustaining beliefs exist only as 'a heap of broken images'.[92] Similarly with *Der Nachsommer*. As the Swales urge persuasively throughout their monograph,[93] in Stifter's cataloguing and inventorying a vision of plenitude and a nightmare of clutter coexist and trouble each other. In these terms, then, both texts are situated on the same boundary with modernity, a modernity defined in such works as *Ulysses* and *The Waste Land* as the post-historic falling asunder of mythology and facts.

In a sense, these two peculiar works of literature are twin deconstructions of the *Lehrjahre*, [94] dismantling its irony, revealing all its components and constitutive circularities. For instance, the traumatic loss of a desired object, the mother, powerfully suggests the Oedipal theme, pointing up how that theme is, as it was for Goethe and Freud, the foundation upon which possibilities of successful social and aesthetic self-authorship are based. In these two works, taken together, bound to one another for all their divergent thematic and stylistic tendencies by an insistent symmetry, we can read in decoded form how interiority and regulation, incest and inheritance, female and male, defy all contradiction to combine and become the literary construction of modern, masculine, aesthetic subjectivity.

CHAPTER FIVE

Der Zauberberg

The success of *Buddenbrooks* (1901), one of the best-selling German novels in the first half of the twentieth century, brought Thomas Mann (1875–1955) fame and prestige as a chronicler and representative of his time. He cultivated this reputation by word and deed until his death, against the background of the catastrophes of modern German history.

Mann was born to a patrician family in Lübeck. His early work was in the style of *fin de siècle* decadence, much influenced by Nietzsche, but *Buddenbrooks* embedded this thematic complex in a full-blooded realism of the nineteenth-century sort. Until the outbreak of the First World War, Mann continued to work at the theme of the Artist as a problematic focus of the problems of civilisation, work which culminated in *Der Tod in Venedig* (1912). With the War Mann's aesthetic preoccupations necessarily became engaged with political ones, and he aligned himself with a 'Germanness' which he opposed to the liberal humanism of the western democracies in *Betrachtungen eines Unpolitischen* (*Reflections of a Non-Political Man*, 1918). The progress of the War and its aftermath caused Mann to reconsider again the cultural meaning of his aesthetic, and to seek, in *Der Zauberberg* (*The Magic Mountain*), the text with which we are here concerned, to blend it with the spirit of democracy. Forced into exile by the advent of National Socialism, he found himself once more compelled by historical circumstances to revise his thematic preoccupations. The years of exile produced *Joseph and his Brothers* (1933–1943), a reformulation of the neo-humanist message by recourse to a mythological refashioning of the Bible story of Joseph in four massive volumes. Mann's reckoning with the German catastrophe, a return to his preoccupation with the role of the Artist and the essence of 'Germanness', but now in an ambivalent tragic mode, is *Doktor Faustus* (1947). Having survived, as it were, the conclusion of his own artistic biography as he conceived it, Mann returned, with *Felix Krull* (1954), to the ludic Nietzscheanism which had inspired the beginnings of that text in 1910.

After the Second World War Mann lost the prestige of representativeness in a Germany seeking to reforge a cultural identity. He never returned to live in the country whose voice he had claimed to be before the entire free world throughout the war years. His standing as a representative of European culture in the United States, however, remained very great. The publication of those of his diaries which he did not burn, in 1979, and of a greater fraction of his voluminous correspondence, giving information about his private persona (including, notoriously, his own homosexual tendencies and his ungratefulness to the benefactor who made his opulent lifestyle in California possible), have further modified the representative status Thomas Mann enjoyed during the first half of the twentieth century. Nevertheless, it is still hard to imagine that Mann will ever be regarded as anything other than one of the greatest writers in German.

Mann gives an account of the genesis of *Der Zauberberg* in a lecture given before Princeton University students in 1939 (XI, pp. 602–616).[1] It had its autobiographical origin in a visit Mann paid to his wife in a Swiss sanatorium in 1912, and was first intended to be a humorous counterpart to *Der Tod in Venedig*. The monster essay *Betrachtungen eines Unpolitischen* then intervened to bear the weight of all the intellectual soul-searching engendered in Mann by the First World War. The novel itself, when Mann returned to it after the War, took up the central problems and dilemmas of the essay, but without the earnestness of that work,[2] in a spirit of play which included a parody of the *Bildungsroman* tradition.[3]

The novel's hero goes to visit his cousin in a sanatorium in Switzerland. The novel manipulates its readers with exceptional virtuosity, and one of the most brilliant of these effects is the way in which Hans Castorp is drawn into the world of the sick, just as the reader is drawn into the world of the novel. Convinced, largely by his own unconscious inclination, that he also is suffering from tuberculosis, Hans Castorp eventually stays on the mountain for seven years, leaving only when it becomes necessary to fight in the First World War. His stay on the mountain is an account of his exposure to ideas, which are embodied in characters who retain enough charm and idiosyncrasy to entertain the reader, without ever ceasing to be the obvious embodiment of a point of view. Hans Castorp's story 'certainly makes use of the means of the realist novel, but it is not one itself. It continually goes beyond realism by symbolically intensifying it, making it transparent upon the intellectual realm of ideas (das Geistige und Ideelle)' (XI, p. 612). As well as Hans Castorp's cousin Joachim Ziemßen (who represents certain aspects of the German national character), the doctors, and a swarm of minor characters, there are Settembrini and Naphta, who speak for Enlightenment humanism and irrational reaction respectively; Clawdia Chauchat, who represents sexual enchantment; and Mynheer Peeperkorn, the embodiment of patriarchal authority.

Hans Castorp is reminiscent of Wilhelm Meister in that, programmatically ordinary in himself, he is at the centre of a whole world of meanings. He is as perfectly realised and modulated a representation of the partialness and yet centrality of the liberal human subject as any we have yet encountered in this study.

This work has many superb qualities which one can only indicate here in passing. It not only thematises time in much-advertised ways, but does it by manipulating the reader's sense of it with marvellous control. The ironic tone of the narrator is also a perfect instrument for the pleasurable direction of the reader's sympathy and expectation. There are perfectly controlled climaxes, most notably the end of the first half of the work, at which point, on Carnival night, the hero has the one and only sexual encounter of his seven-year stay. The alert reader will notice innumerable number games,[4] and the educated one a plethora of allusions and parallels, from *Tannhäuser* and *Faust* to the mythical figure of Hermes. It is a work of wonderfully urbane culture, distilling artistic coherence from a display of sheer superabundance of information and formulations.[5]

The novel ends on a quiet note of hope, despite the progressively negative indications which gather towards the conclusion in the run-up to the Great War. Hans Castorp is last seen embroiled in the reality of fighting in the trenches, probably doomed to die. But the reader is left with the question whether one day love will arise from this 'universal feast of death'?

With *Der Zauberberg* we seem to enter a new conceptual universe. If Stifter's novel was tinged with the dusk of Schopenhauerian pessimism, Thomas Mann's cultural and intellectual landscape is unthinkable without the effects of Schopenhauer and Nietszche. They are its condition, not merely in the sense that Mann himself read these thinkers, but in the sense that their thought had become common intellectual currency, effectively challenging the anthropocentric world view of the literary model which is the subject of this book. Their thought also articulated doubts about the production of meaning, so that the assumption of metaphysical coherence, which attends the texts dealt with so far like an invisible safety-net, is no longer so easily made. The more likely assumption will now be that meaning is relative and ethics precarious.[6] As Mann put it himself in the argument of *Betrachtungen eines Unpolitischen*, 'Geist' (mind, spirit) has been overthrown by 'Leben' (life). Without this sort of expectation, Mann would not be able to thematise the making of sense itself with such paradoxical assurance in *Der Zauberberg*.

Der Zauberberg had its origin in the atmosphere of the self-conscious problematic 'aestheticism' of the *fin-de-siècle*. An account of Mann's own, offered in reply to an enquirer in the 1930s, explains what happened then:

> The many ideas and ruminations about the problem of Man, the human problem itself, including politics, all the thoughts occasioned by my inner experience of the War, had crystallised around the original plan. The narrative proved as absorbent as a sponge . . . and in the work of many years the grotesque Novelle I had planned became the two-volume portrait of the epoch with all its philosophical, even mystical, aspects. It was curious enough to witness how a plan so modest in conception developed, how even the image that the author himself had of his work gradually changed. Quite unintentionally I had joined the succession of 'Wilhelm Meister', to whom I had scarcely given a thought.[7]

The figure of Goethe now came to take the strain of a need to embrace a general humanism without abandoning identification with Germany. The novel about the sanatorium becomes aligned with Goethe's paradigm unintentionally, although it started out as something quite different. And it still contains an entire Romantic and post-Romantic thematic structure, as defined in Mann's words on Novalis: 'never has a more intimate combination of disease, death and desire been expressed in poetry' (XI, p. 849).

Nevertheless, there can be no doubt that Mann's novel belongs to the context of this study. Not only did Goethe provide the vital link to a German tradition, he provided one also to the realm of autobiographical experience. Mann's early view of autobiography had been that it implied shameful self-disclosure and must be resisted and overcome. It was 'telling tales out of school', and invited ostracism. One of his basic, formative and recurrent experiences, thematised repeatedly in his works, is the terror of being laughed at, of the status of outsider.[8] That Mann was articulate about the partialness of subjectivity is compellingly clear from the following passage: 'The deepest and most dreadful sufferings on earth are not those which are most picturesque or gruesomely conspicuous; there are pains and torments, humiliations of the soul . . . wounds tended by no human hand and which no public charity can reach, inner mutilations, without honour, decorations or heroism' (XII, pp. 475–476). Setting to one side for a moment the unattractive context in which they occur,[9] these lines are remarkable for the autobiographical intensity with which they are written, and for the importance that the lack of a public aspect plays in the intensity of the suffering invoked.

It was from Goethe that Mann derived a concept of self-authorship which empowered autobiographical discourse.[10] In 'Von deutscher Republik' ('On the German Republic'), Mann referred to the Goethean ethos in a characteristic phrase as 'autobiographisch-selbstbildnerische[s] Bekennertum' ('an autobiographical, self-forming culture of confession', XI, p. 831). In the essay 'Goethe und Tolstoi' (1921), which was intimately bound up with the composition of *Der Zauberberg*, Mann expressed clearly the transition from the notion of autobiography as self-indulgence to that of autobiography as self-authorship:

Goethe somewhere calls Wilhelm Meister his beloved likeness ('geliebtes Ebenbild'). How can this be? Is it permissible to love one's own likeness?

Shouldn't any man who is not afflicted with incurable vanity become conscious, by contemplating his own likeness, only of his own need to improve himself? Yes, this is precisely what he should do. And it is precisely this sense of a need to improve and perfect oneself, this awareness of one's own self as a duty, a moral, aesthetic, cultural commitment, that finds objective expression in the hero of the autobiographical novel of formation and education (Bildungs- und Entwicklungsroman). This awareness is concretised in a *thou* in relation to which the poetic *I* can become guide, formative influence, educator – identical with him and yet at the same time superior to him in the degree that Goethe, with paternal affection, calls Wilhelm, whom he has produced from within himself, a poor dog – a phrase full of feeling both for him and for himself. (IX, pp. 149–150; cf. XI, p. 615)

Mann's formulation here recapitulates much of what I have said about the *Lehrjahre* model. It is a representation of subjectivity, springing from an autobiographical source, in which the partialness of subjectivity, its 'need to improve and perfect oneself', is objectified in an inscrutable blend of socio-moral and aesthetic values, in such a way that the original subject bifurcates into, on the one hand, an objective image of partialness in the figure of the protagonist, and on the other, a narrative authority in relation to which the trajectory towards self-perfection is adumbrated. Together, these instances point to the submerged assumption that the form of a novel and the form of a life are mutually guaranteeing and legitimating. As Mann says elsewhere in the essay: 'With wit and feeling (Geist und Empfindung) any life can be made into a "novel" ("Roman")' (IX, p. 72).

Harold Bloom's famous theory of poetry sees the poetic process born in rivalry between strong poets and their stronger precursors: 'Mann's swerve away from Goethe is the profoundly ironic denial that any swerve is necessary. His misinterpretation of Goethe is to read precisely his own parodistic genius, his own kind of loving irony, into his precursor.'[11] The key principle of the model here at issue, on the other hand, seems to be one of inheritance from father to son. This gentle transmission is nowhere better characterised than in Mann's appreciation of Keller. Mann discovered Keller's work comparatively late in life, but when the time was ripe, he voraciously read it all, perfectly ready to receive it, just as Keller tells us in *Der grüne Heinrich* he had done with Goethe's (X, p. 849).

Mann remembers and celebrates the act of filiation by which Goethe's authority enters into Keller's text, and associates himself with it by a similar one from his own life. Thereby a mythology of acts of reading opens up, in which a writer is absorbed by a superhuman but spontaneous effort of concentration on the part of a successor, a moment of appropriation located in an area between fiction and autobiography, and by means of which Goethean authority – the authority to inhabit and represent one's own subjective being as potentially perfectible – is passed down the literary generations.

Der Zauberberg, in its controversial identity as a *Bildungsroman*, bears the marks of both these determinations. If Goethe was Mann's 'Vater-Imago'[12] then his relationship to him no doubt showed signs of Oedipal ambivalence.[13] The *Lehrjahre* succession is here acted out self-consciously on the level of cultural history. The novel is both parody and renewal. It is both a powerful appropriation of a pre-existing model, a 'Wilhelm Meisteriade' or 'Wilhelm Meisterchen',[14] and the announcement of a subjectivity as partial as any other such representation in this book. The novel itself, one of the most evidently magisterial literary and cultural acts of the twentieth century in German letters, is poised between a sense of its own modernity, its originality – which is what Bloom's poets are always doomed to seek hopelessly in combat with their fathers – and its place in a continuum, 'patriarchal authority as the necessary complement to self-representation',[15] a safe place in which the subject, the ground of originality, may prosper under the aesthetic authority established by its cultural forefathers.

This is indeed a strange and paradoxical negotiation of the problem of authority. What is inherited is the authority to establish a space in which authority may be suspended. In this space is the protagonist. For Mann as well as for Goethe, the protagonist is in some sense representative of subjectivity in its partialness and vulnerability. From this starting point, Mann's re-animation of the model twists in and out of the Goethean paradigm upon which it depends, towards a fresh centralising of the familiar de-centred subject. It aims to repeat the original Goethean act of aesthetic authorisation, but at the level of public and historical consciousness. Goethean authority is figured, in a lecture on Freud, as proceeding from within the newer writer's own unconscious (IX, pp. 498–499; we recall how Mann declared that he had arrived within the Goethean paradigm without any conscious intention), so that the historical horizon is discerned in the very depths of the subject, describing in a single sweep its obscurest impulses and its most distinct literary-historical representations.

By reinstating the authoritative voice of the narrator, absent from the novel for more than a century, Mann makes another important allusion to the *Lehrjahre*. His narrative voice enjoys what Weigand describes throughout as 'sovereign irony', speaking in his own person and with omniscience about the story of his, 'our', hero. This is a conscious return to the narrative manner of the eighteenth century, and as such includes within its irony the ability to accommodate this allusion to the past as both a parody, a conscious game with the past, and a renewal of its specific aesthetic-moral authority. 'Mann . . . viewed Goethe's irony in *Wilhelm Meister* as a master stroke of genius and in a sense sought to emulate this virtuosity of style, albeit in more "modern" form.'[16]

Hans Castorp is quite consciously foregrounded as ordinary yet, in that extreme ordinariness, representative: 'A man lives not only his personal life as an individual but also, consciously or unconsciously, the life of the epoch and of his contemporaries' (III, p. 50). If the questions adumbrated in the depths of subjective interiority as to the final meaning of our efforts and actions in the world receive (at whatever level of consciousness, or even on the unconscious level) no answer, only 'hollow silence', then this will not fail to leave its mark on the subject. 'And so he was indeed mediocre, albeit in a very honourable sense' (ibid.). Mann is repeating here the Goethean gesture of placing the de-centred subject at the centre, but the gesture is now made ironically explicit, enriched by Romantic irony, in which subjectivity per se becomes susceptible to an infinite potentiation, a direct connection not only with the reality but the ideality of the objective world.

Hans Castorp parallels on the common or private level the representativeness of his author on the patrician or public-historical one, 'identical with him and yet at the same time superior to him'. 'In the end it is not the novel that is historical, but I', said Mann in a letter to his publisher in 1926,[17] subtly shifting the meaning of 'historisch' from 'about the past' (as in 'the historical novel'), towards 'belonging to history' – thus combining in himself, as distinct from the humble individual historicity of Hans Castorp, private and monumental dimensions of history.

For all his sovereignty, however, the narrator, the author of the text, is dependent upon the subject, upon whom the sovereignty is exercised and becomes manifest. Thus the contract between the partial subject and the narrative authority of which I spoke in the context of the *Lehrjahre* is repeated, but at a higher level of self-consciousness. The key configuration of author-in-the-text and author-of-it is repeated in particularly pure form. Hans Castorp is revealed in a process of self-authorship by the authority of the narrative voice, whose justification is that it reveals precisely this.

Der Zauberberg certainly enjoys a differentiated and by no means straightforward relation to the *Bildungsroman*. It was part of the official culture of the genre from its publication; it leans on the *Bildungsroman* as being quintessentially *German*, and is thus much more self-conscious about its generic status than any other of the novels discussed in this book. Furthermore, it ironises this genre as much as it leans on it. The debate about the status of the novel in this regard has been correspondingly varied and inconclusive.[18]

Perhaps the most sober assessment of *Der Zauberberg* – based on an impeccably thorough knowledge of Mann's biography and the attendant circumstances to be expected from a critic who was the sometime Keeper of the Thomas Mann Archive – is that it 'remains a decadence novel, with counter-impulses (ein décadence-Roman – mit Gegenimpulsen)'.[19]

Now this might very well be an unanswerable case for the exclusion of Mann's novel from the *Bildungsroman* canon as it is stereotypically constructed in terms of the harmonious and happy development of an integrated personality ('he does not take up any profession, he finds no Natalie, he does not found a family; activity, a child, a family – all are missing').[20] As far as my own understanding of the model is concerned, however, Wysling's formulation is simply a rather grudging description of exactly the configuration that concerns me. If Mann is seeking to fold Goethe upon Nietzsche, if he is seeking to extract a human distillation from a view of *Leben* which in some ways resists it (or seems to), and to do this in the form of a novel, then his text becomes a site of convergence and divergence under the sign of the human, in a way not radically dissimilar to Goethe's.

Mann's and Goethe's novels are bound by a counter-historical assonance, in that they both seek to formulate humanist responses to massive world-historical convulsions which interrupt the process of composition. Both authors began their novels within the perspective of an early engagement with problematic subjectivity. They then returned to them after, in Goethe's case, the French Revolution, and in Mann's, the First World War. They try to elaborate the initial impulse in such a way as to offer a response to the cataclysmic intervention of history commensurate with the commitment to humanity implicit in their subjective and problematic beginnings. Moreover, both works are in some sense discursive counter-models to developments in contemporary discourse which responded to these seismic moments in ways not so commensurate: in Goethe's case, to what would become Romanticism, and in Mann's, to Expressionism.[21]

The term *décadence* in Wysling's formulation might seem to trouble this parallel between his concise formulation and our model, but in fact it confirms it. In *décadence* we have the descendant of that partial subjectivity with which we have been occupied throughout this study. Mann has inherited and internalised (his version of) the Romantic solution to the problem of subjectivity, and this supplies him with a fully thematised representation of subjective partialness, in the imagery of disease, desire and death, of music and the dark side of life etc., but then latterly in the guise of Germanness also.[22]

The wholesome transcending of individuation which was the true purport of Novalis's turn towards inwardness (as well as the purport of his interest in disease)[23] has become much less wholesome through the refraction of Schopenhauer, Wagner and Nietzsche, though no less seductive. Mann, in the post-war situation, must both associate himself with and distance himself – in 'counter-impulses' – from this sort of inwardness, from the 'aestheticism' of the pre-war days.

Thomas Mann's conscious, ironic and willed return to the Goethean model from a position of post-Romantic 'Ästhetizismus' which threatens it is perhaps most evident in one particular aspect of Hans Castorp's ordinariness. Hans Castorp is prominently *not* an artist. In this he is as much a paradigm of the model as Wilhelm Meister himself. Hans Castorp's status as a non-artist is clearest from the perspective of Mann's works as a whole, in which as a rule the focal figure, from Tonio Kröger to Leverkühn, tends to be an artist. Where we expect problematic self-projection, we find in this instance an engineer. Moreover, Mann orphans his hero at the age of seven, so that the habitual thematisation on the basis of parental attributes, which goes back to Mann's own parents and Goethe's rhyme about his parents (cf XI, p. 98), is avoided. The nuclear family as the ground of the artist is removed, and Castorp is cast as the sort of new man Spengler envisaged for the new age, when he wished that 'people of the younger generation should turn towards technology not lyric poetry, the navy rather than painting'.[24] Internal evidence also crisply confirms Hans's Spenglerian modernism. Although he shows some talent for painting as a young man, he has only a good-natured smile at the suggestion that he might follow this vocation, and no intention at all of living the eccentric life of the artist on the breadline (III, p. 51).

Yet the whole thematic slant of the book is away from this prosaic characterisation towards something much closer to, but never quite, an artistic character for Hans Castorp. He becomes an artist in the appropriation of experience.[25] As Weigand puts it, 'Thomas Mann's irony scores its most surprising point, perhaps, in the transformation of this simple young man into a genius in the realm of experience.'[26] Hans Castorp agrees: '"There are two paths to life: one is the regular, direct, honest one. The other is bad, it leads through death – that is the path of the genius (das ist der geniale Weg)!"' (III, p. 827). The ironic context in which this declaration occurs illustrates the point perfectly: Hans Castorp both is and is not a genius.

Clearly, Mann saw him in this way too: 'The modest hero of my novel is on occasion called "life's problem child". We artists are all life's problem children, but nonetheless children of life for all that.'[27] Is Hans one of them or is he not? The point is deliberately moot. It is also relevant to report the evidence pointing to a parallel in Mann's mind between Novalis himself (the archetypal artist but also a practical scientist) and Hans Castorp, found by Steven Cerf in Mann's annotations to Georg Brandes's *Die Romantische Schule in Deutschland*. For instance, Mann underlined the anticipated similarities between the poet, as depicted by the Danish critic, and Hans Castorp: 'a fascination for one's own physicality, heightened by sickness, and a subsequent need both to express love for another individual and to reject restrictive forms of reason'.[28]

In the terms of Mann's own claustrophobic thematic household, we are dealing with a typical modulation of binary oppositions to suit a particular rhetorical demand. 'If we may say that it is German to be a *Bürger*, then it is perhaps even more German to be something between a *Bürger* and an artist', Mann had declared in *Betrachtungen eines Unpolitischen* (XII, p. 111). This is to express in his conceptual vocabulary exactly that co-operation between an aesthetic authority and a prosaic subject required to lend competence to the authority and aura to the subject. The types must be distinct in order for their identity to be significant. Hence, the complicity between narrator and protagonist must, as in all the texts with which I have dealt (apart from the Romantic one, for the reasons given), be kept secret. The common representativeness of Hans Castorp could never itself result in the self-evidently splendid achievement of the novel, *The Magic Mountain*. But the quality of the protagonist and that of the author are nevertheless continuous with one another, merging first in Germanness, and then in humanity. They are part of a single identity, but different, united by an irony thanks to which it is possible to propose a model of representative humanity which nevertheless – in a sense as obscure as it is certain – is animated by the spirit which gives rise to art.

The partialness of subjectivity is, however, not so easily redeemed after Schopenhauer, for whom its only redemption is extinction. Yet of course Schopenhauer is not for Mann the last word on the subject. With Nietzsche and Freud, Mann is part of the continuing history of the 'ideology of the aesthetic', which in the aftermath of Schopenhauer has to 'go back to the beginning and think everything through again, this time from the standpoint of the body itself'.[29] The Schopenhauerian dismissal of the charmed circle of humanism means that Mann must orchestrate his Goethean construction of subjectivity in relation to the insistence and otherness of the body.

The body, in the form of desire, is accommodated within the aesthetic model with which we are by now familiar via women figures and the thematisation of incestuous desire. Erotic energy and aesthetic form, the body of the subject and the body of the work, are consonant. There is no unmanageable tension between the ability to represent, which is to say, transmit masculine meanings (inheritance) and the truth of subjective desire, which is the ground and principle of subjective partialness (incest), since they combine in the accommodation of the aesthetic. In *Der Zauberberg* the picture is complicated by the presence of the post-Schopenhauerian body, the site of mere blind striving, as a perpetual relativisation of all human constructions.

Mann's humour is at its best when it 'thematises' that which is by definition resistant to such domestication – the body in its brute material facticity. The motifs from Novalis – disease, desire, death – are refracted in the simplifying apparatus of Hans Castorp's earnest moral consciousness. 'Krankheit macht den Menschen viel körperlicher, sie macht ihn gänzlich zum Körper' ('disease makes people much more physical, it makes them nothing but body', III, p. 251), thinks Hans Castorp while reflecting upon the naked body of his cousin, who is undergoing his monthly X-ray. The setting of the novel is a metaphor for the universal priority of the body. It is one of the distinguishing aspects of the parodistic relation of Mann's book with *Wilhelm Meister* and its tradition that Mann's book is set in a sanatorium among a cast of characters who are all ill. In disease one sees more clearly the body's insistent refusal to coincide with the products of the mind, of social, historical or philosophical consciousness. Hence Joachim's beauty, ambition and pride are simply countermanded by the priority of his body as a site of sickness. Hence also, Settembrini's persistent illness is the condition of all his loquacious idealism, and mocks it. Krokowski explains how, since nobody is ever perfectly healthy, health is a term with no stable referent in nature. The concept of health and the true state of bodies simply do not map on to each other. Hans Castorp himself is rescued from his conventional beginnings by being mischievously placed upon the non-existent borderline between sickness and health. Situated there, he finds a loophole through which to escape the otherwise ubiquitous containment imposed upon the body by concepts.

Hans Castorp's physicality, resisting definition upon the borderline between the two categories of sickness and health, is also a site of unsocialised desire. Mann makes an ironic symbolic link between the mark on Hans Castorp's lung and his erotic affect with regard to first Pribislav Hippe and then Clawdia Chauchat. His present condition is related to his feeling for Clawdia in a way too subtle to be described as cause and effect (see III, pp. 182–183).

Like disease, desire enjoys an oblique relationship with the matters of the mind. The similarity between Chauchat and Hippe's eyes is more than similarity, it is identity: '"Similar" was not the right word – they were the same eyes' (III, p. 206). Although the occasions, in the objective world, and in the world of mental constructions, are different, the unity and continuity of desire underlies them, negating the successive moments of chronological time, and establishing an absolute priority in relation to the different identities of the social: homosexual, heterosexual, Hippe, Chauchat; as well as to the concepts of morality and philosophy.

Hans Castorp's grandfather is laid out in state after his death, and in this form seems to have assumed 'for all time his true and adequate shape' (III, p. 42). In other words, his death is taken up into the world of representations, where social and religious significance is conferred upon it very specifically by means of ritual and conventional symbolisation. At the same time, all these social meanings have another, different meaning, in that they conspire to mask the brute physicality of death, to which no cultural values attach, the material side 'which could not be called beautiful or pious or meaningful, not even sad' (III, p. 43). A non-symbolic fly lands on the corpse, to be shooed away by an old retainer 'mit einer ehrbaren Verfinsterung seiner Miene' ('a seemly look of disapproval'), a semi-social gesture employed to cover the gap in social meaning opened up by this intrusion into it of the body as 'nothing but body and naught else besides' (III, p. 44). The same verbal signal, the same 'ehrbare Verfinsterung', recurs as Hans Castorp's reaction to the sound of noisy lovemaking coming from his Russian neighbours on his first night at the Berghof. Here too, evidence of the material reality of the body crosses the boundaries erected by culture to contain it.

Thus, the body, in this post-Schopenhauer world, will be irreducibly distinct from all representations and constructions placed upon it. The Goethean 'counter-impulse' insists that although mind and body are split off from one another in this way, they are not without significant relations of a sort. Hans Castorp's position as a mind plus body, as more and less than intelligence, within a set of values oriented upon the future, resembles Wilhelm Meister's function as a whole human being, including, but also exceeding, consciousness. And, as with Goethe, Hans Castorp finds and maintains a place in his relation with the object in ways which recall the familiar circularities of incest and inheritance.

A vital aspect of the rivalry with Goethe implicit in *Der Zauberberg* is the parody of the entire 'woman' theme. Whereas before it had been a sort of secret determinant within masculine subjectivity, Mann now holds it up for all to see. In the *Lehrjahre* and its cognates, the inner regularity and meaning of a masculine life is expressed and figured in relation to women. Hans Castorp's fevered and impassioned exaggeration in the Walpurgisnacht scene sums it up: '"je t'aime," he babbled, "je t'ai aimée de tout temps, car tu es le Toi de ma vie, mon rêve, mon sort, mon envie, mon éternel désir . . ."' (III, p. 476). More than a century of male pathos and profundity seems to stand revealed in this intoxicated infantile babble. Mann's trick is to make even more excessively visible what has always been excessively visible: the figure of women who have carried and embodied the inner meaning not of themselves, but of the masculine protagonists. And what better motif for this excess of excessive visibility, this devouring appropriation by the narcissistic male gaze, than Hans Castorp's fixation with the X-ray photograph of his beloved? At one point Mann considered a different eventual outcome of this special affair: 'New idea for the relationship with Clawdia: she doesn't come back at all. Having possessed her, he waits for her, with nothing but her X-ray, for seven years.'[30] Hans Castorp's fixation becomes a function of his simplicity, and that simplicity appears for a moment divested of its quality as the object of indulgent narrative affection and the focus for humanitarian pathos, becoming instead naked mockery of the banality behind the idealisation of woman in patriarchal bourgeois culture. It is the extremely sharp edge of Mann's Goethe rivalry, and it is not at all surprising that Mann decided against this solution.

Mann is not, in fact, overthrowing this idealisation, or at least its function, at all. The main function of Clawdia Chauchat is to embody the physicality in which Hans Castorp's subjectivity is grounded, and to make sure that this physicality has its life in the representation of subjectivity with which, albeit on an extremely high level of ironic self-consciousness, Thomas Mann presents us. Hans Castorp remains on the mountain because his whole subjectivity is engaged: Clawdia Chauchat binds him in his innermost being to the experience of the mountain, which also includes philosophical, artistic and ethical dimensions. The arrangement is thus not fundamentally different from that whereby Wilhelm Meister's whole involvement in the processes of his life, the orientation of his entelechy, *Daimon*, 'son rêve', 'son sort', etc., was conveyed by the incest strand which issued in Natalie, which is to say, by the woman theme, the notion of 'le Toi de ma vie'.

Of course, in Mann the love interest vanishes abruptly half way through the book. This is an important deviation from a model which generally manages its final aesthetic resolutions in some reference or other to the woman theme. As Hörisch observes, 'Marriage for Hans is not even worth a fantasy, as it still had been for Green Henry.'[31] The point here, however, is that although Clawdia Chauchat does vanish, and comes back a changed woman, the load-bearing structural dimension of the woman theme is firmly in place. Hans Castorp stays on the mountain because of a vague yearning for her return, although not in as crass and unrewarded a manner as Mann once envisaged. Furthermore, as Weigand pointed out, when she goes her thematic role is taken over by Naphta. Naphta verbalises the body into a sort of intellectual system, and by this very process of verbalisation and intellectualisation, reduces it to a term in an abstract polarity in relation to Settembrini, who continues to argue for the primacy of Enlightenment rationality. This reduction to the purely verbal is then corrected by the arrival of Mynheer Pepperkorn.

Mann thus contrives both to ironise the woman theme to the point of parodistic dismissal, and nevertheless to retain the structural circularity of masculine sexuality in his representation of masculine subjectivity. He trumps even Novalis, for whom the murder of the mother in the act of representation was the condition of the apotheosis of masculine subjectivity. In Mann's version, 'Das Weibliche' becomes at last no more than simply a moment in the dynamics of masculine subjectivity. Once the object of desire has been 'possessed', as Mann puts it in his diary entry, the woman figure is subsumed in the banality of ordinary sex, while masculine erotic orientation is distinguished from this specific heterosexual and parodistic attachment, and is free to stand for a more generalised masculine eros, such that, for instance, Exner can write of Hans Castorp's learning experiences: 'All learning is erotic in nature; pedagogic eros fills us with desire for novelty (Neu-Begierde) and the longing for love.'[32]

This has to be seen against the background of Mann's homosexual inclination. Clawdia emerges into distinct definition as the paradigm and parody of all *Bildungsroman* women from a series which is predominantly masculine. First there is Pribislav Hippe, then there is Naphta and then there is Mynheer Peeperkorn. It is they who carry and modulate the sweep of masculine desire within the overall representation of subjectivity. Moreover, Clawdia Chauchat herself is given in distinctly non-feminine terms (as has been shown in detail by Karl Werner Böhm),[33] only being presented as unambiguously female when she returns in the encompassing significance of Mynheer Peeperkorn as the female to his male.[34]

The recent studies of Mann and sexuality have revealed a general pattern of development which is of immediate relevance to the theme of sexuality in *Der Zauberberg*.[35] As Mann said in a now notorious diary entry of 1919: 'For me there is no doubt that the "Reflections" too are an expression of my sexual inversion.'[36] The effect of Mann's homosexuality in the works up to and including the *Betrachtungen*, and his turn towards democracy, seems to have been to feed into his identification with a strong masculine militaristic Germany, a sort of *Männerbund* mentality, in a way with which Freud was completely conversant,[37] and which has been investigated in its most extreme manifestations in Klaus Theweleit's massive study of post-First-World-War *Freikorps* literature, *Männerphantasien*.[38] This rather aggressive form of homosexual identification is perhaps still to be discerned in the parody of the idealisation of heterosexual eros centred on Hans Castorp's attitude to Clawdia Chauchat. But precisely during the later stages of the composition of *Der Zauberberg* (especially in the thinking behind 'Von deutscher Republik' and 'Über die Ehe', 'On Marriage', 1925) Mann developed towards supporting a notion of bisexuality, in which the feminine is incorporated into a masculine perspective.[39]

After Clawdia's departure the incidence of bisexual and hermaphroditic images increases,[40] and the novel's thematic development is towards an androgynous ideal which corresponds to the Republican tendency of the work as a whole. The motif of androgyny, which is another of the recurrent emphases of the texts with which I am dealing, is set to play a central role in the aesthetic resolution of the novel, despite the apparent distancing from the mother/woman incest theme with which we have become familiar in our other texts.

After 1900, after Nietzsche, writes Friedrich Kittler, the mother/woman, 'the enigma at the origin of all discourses, is played out'.[41] It is no doubt an aspect of the post-Nietzschean, twentieth-century constitution of Mann's novel that the enigma at the heart of subjectivity and its representation is no longer that of incest and the pervasive presence of the mother. Clawdia deconstructs into versions of homosexual desire, instead of feeding into the universal mother. To this extent, *Der Zauberberg* belongs to a different 'discourse network' from our other texts, which all fall under the sign of the mother. Nonetheless, the fact that there is an enigma at the heart of this representation – indeed, that it has a heart at all – links Mann's text with the discourse system of the previous century. And it is safe to assume that homosexual desire, seen as the representative example of unsocialised and transgressive desire rather than as a term of difference or diversity,[42] in the end also falls under the sign of the mother.

In the 'Snow' chapter Mann is visibly adumbrating his neohumanist, Goethean theme, the more abstract expression of which came in the contemporaneous essay 'Goethe und Tolstoi'. Despite the strong homoerotic tones of the 'snow' dream (the two sides of the dream are mediated by 'a handsome boy', III, p. 681, while, as Böhm observes, 'the repellent aspects are illustrated by women'),[43] its function is to be part of that development towards the androgynous harmonisation of male and female, of law and desire, in terms of which the novel seeks to articulate the possibility of hope. The fundamentally content-neutral sexual orientation upon Hippe-Chauchat, which is the deepest lure of the mountain for Hans Castorp and the reason he stays there, has illustrated the morally questionable nature of his encyclopaedic promiscuity in the first half of the book. Insofar as these researches, which have led him to doubt the enduring significance of the human form and the final semiotic authority of the line between organic and inorganic, are coloured by desire, they are bereft of the moral responsibility which is articulated in the famous italicised maxim (III, p. 686). The thrust of the 'snow' episode is to connect Hans Castorp's desire with the law. It is the fantasy of a benevolent super-ego, a 'sanftes Gesetz', possible only within the charmed circle of the aesthetic.

Hans Castorp prominently forgets the dream maxim vouchsafed him in this episode, but that suggests that the insight sinks from his consciousness into deeper realms of his being. We all forget dreams, but dreams are at the same time a phenomenon in which the mind and the body enjoy a privileged and mysterious relationship. The *Lehrjahre* too is organised to show that a subject is more than the sum of its consciousness. Another related similarity with the aesthetic model of the *Lehrjahre* consists in the device of offering a maxim, only to relativise it again. Castorp's insight is denied outright authority, but not completely undermined. It is allowed to hover.

Clawdia Chauchat returns in the company of Mynheer Peeperkorn. The pencil (the humorous symbol until now of the convergence of desire and representation that facilitates the passing of subjectivity into objective relations) is no longer necessary to represent the alliance of the phallus and signification, because this is embodied in Peeperkorn himself: 'for he regarded himself as God's wedding organ (Gottes Hochzeitsorgan)' (III, p. 867), a walking penis which self-destructs when it ceases to work, a topic upon which the usually inarticulate Peeperkorn becomes uncharacteristically eloquent (III, p. 784). Life is a supine and aroused woman, and a man must respond at all costs to this 'Herausforderung'. Nothing is worse than the failure to do this;

impotence is 'das Ende, die höllische Verzweiflung, der Weltuntergang' ('the end, hellish despair, the destruction of the world'). The failure of the male organ is the collapse of all meanings.

This character is given as the masculine answer to the feminine enigma posed ironically in the cat-like Clawdia Chauchat. She subsists as an open invitation to Man. At once rapturous and terrifying, narrow-eyed and mocking, this 'Weibliches' is the ground and condition of masculine meaning. If Clawdia's door-slamming wittily represents the tear in the fabric of civilisation that so fascinates and engages Castorp, Peeperkorn is the man to close the door behind her, by his force and presence overmastering, but also honouring, the life of desire, present in every human disposition despite the admonishments of reason. He is what Hans Castorp would need to be in relation to Clawdia Chauchat, if his vague but persistent and powerful yearnings were to resolve themselves unproblematically into a social and existential masculine identity.

Yet Hans Castorp is evidently not a *rival* of Peeperkorn's. His desire is not engaged in this way. Instead, the return of Clawdia Chauchat in the company of Peeperkorn is the occasion for Mann's naive protagonist to apply the ethical responsibility, which was crystallised in the 'snow' experience, to a collective context. His 'Sympathie mit dem Organischen' ('sympathy with the organic', III, p. 832), his notion of a love now brotherly and collective rather than somatic and personal, manifests itself in an alliance with Clawdia Chauchat in care of Peeperkorn, whose condition is troubling. Paradoxically, a secret compact is made to protect the personification of strength. The complex question of subjective desire is resolved by the narrator in a typical passage glossing the 'Russian kiss' with which Clawdia Chauchat and Hans Castorp seal their alliance: 'in God's name let the meaning of love waver. Its very wavering is the meaning of life and humanity' (III, p. 832). Similarly, at the end of the section 'Mynheer Peeperkorn (Continued)', Castorp and the Dutchman declare a fraternal bond (*Duzbruderschaft*), and the euphoria of transgression, associated from the beginning of the novel with the 'Vorteile der Schande' ('the advantages of shame'), that is, with dropping out of the community, is here associated with forming collective bonds.

The nature of this engagement with others can only be gauged *ex negativo*. In his infatuation with Pribislav Hippe and its resolution by the loan of a pencil, Hans Castorp, half consciously, had accommodated his authentic stirrings by sublimation within a social and ethical system of which, in his deepest places, he could not approve. Here, however, is an engagement with a set of problems regarding the relation of desire and community which are completely explicit and visible. In order to elucidate, we need to turn to the question: 'What does Peeperkorn mean?'

Extravagant claims have been made on behalf of Mynheer Peeperkorn by Mann's commentators. Some have seen him as his author's 'greatest creation',[44] others have responded to the promptings in the text to see him as hyper-significant, 'the self-identification with the living presence of the creatively divine',[45] an embodiment of Pan, or a superimposition of Dionysos upon Christ.[46] The presentation of the Dutchman as a 'personality' as such, much celebrated by Hans Castorp (for instance, III, p. 809), also invites one to interpret and decode. But this very excess of meaning, this extremely obvious invitation to an orgy of hermeneutic activity, is surely itself one of the significant things about the figure of Peeperkorn: he is a parody of meaning, a sense of the excess and over-availability of ambitious exhaustive interpretations in the wake of Nietzsche. It is in this sense that Hörisch talks of the 'unbounded over-determination' of the scene at the waterfall, where the Dutchman evokes, to cite only the most conspicuous allusions, Christ and Dionysos, Plato, Dante, Goethe and Nietzsche.[47]

Like Clawdia Chauchat, Mynheer Peeperkorn is a principle of meaning made visible, and in its explicitness made ridiculous and relativised. The patriarchal law, predicated upon the phallus, is exposed. How anyone can read the lengthy passage about impotence being the ethical secret of the world (III, p. 784) as anything other than a huge joke it is hard to guess. Goethe's phallic tower also loses its mystery and authority once it has been revealed to the reader and to Wilhelm Meister himself.

And this is the point: at the moment of revelation, responsibility passes onto the subject himself to live ethically. The only maxim is that there are no maxims of universal applicability. It is not a question of knowing, but of doing, and thus being. What Hans Castorp's example will mean in concrete terms is unknown and unknowable, since it lies in the future. The same applies to the synthesis of middle class and nobility implied in the *Lehrjahre*, which lay beyond existing circumstances, but, as Lukács hoped, present within them as a potentiality.

What *is* clear, however, with Goethe as with Mann, is what the future will *not* be. Mynheer Peeperkorn does (about this there can hardly be debate) represent European colonialism, traditional authority and an aggressively heterosexual, patriarchal view of the world. The colonial connection is made by inventing a colonial Dutch character to occur at this thematic juncture. A Frenchman or an Englishman would, in Mann's post-*Betrachtungen* intellectual cosmos, have involved a host of irrelevant connotations. The Dutch colonial expatriate, with his stage-native Malay manservant and his tropical fever, is calculated to call up associations of the colonial ethos. The connection to traditional, non-democratic forms of authority is made not only by the evident depiction of Peeperkorn's personal charisma, his nature as a 'personality' around whom lesser natures gather and find their subordinate place, but also by the exceptionally prominent use of royal or imperial adjectives to describe him, so that it is impossible not to associate him with the European ancien régime, as it had survived anachronistically until the Great War. Thus, when Peeperkorn dies, and Clawdia says 'c'est une abdication' (III, p. 867), it is hard not to make the association with a prominent imperial abdication, itself the result of a war which might indeed be described as 'das Ende, die höllische Verzweiflung, der Weltuntergang'.[48]

Mynheer Peeperkorn's ridiculous machismo is thus given specific historical definition by these associations. This is an order of power and of meanings which is at an end. It destroys itself out of its own nature. Mynheer Peeperkorn commits suicide with poison in a device of his own invention because he can no longer be the Man to Clawdia's Woman. That system is at an end. Mann himself spoke of the insight arising from the trauma of the war, which had opened his eyes to the fact that 'we can no longer live and write as hitherto' (XI, p. 657).

The order which Peeperkorn embodied is translated from a

condition of meaning, in the shape of the power structures of patriarchal Europe, into itself a meaning among meanings, 'symbolic rather than real' (III, p. 867). But the power and authority of that old order, an order which Mann continues to revere, passes into symbolic currency and becomes renegotiable. Hans Castorp, whom Mynheer Peeperkorn more than once calls his son, does not dismiss this order; indeed, he is deeply implicated in it. Castorp is almost an embodiment of continuity: 'Hans Castorp's "loyalty"... consisted... in a certain heaviness, slowness and obstinate patience of temperament, a fundamental tendency to feel respect for conditions of duration and stability; and the longer they lasted, the more respect he had for them. He also inclined to believe in the permanence of the particular state or circumstances in which he happened to find himself...' (III, pp. 171–172)

This subjective internalisation of continuity will, or might, subsist even when the objective order is in as profound a mutation as is suggested by the tragedy of Peeperkorn's self-annihilation. Hans Castorp functions, one might say, as a sense of continuity without content. He is perfectly primed and placed to inherit from the dead king his power and authority, but in a changed configuration, in a new form. In Mynheer Peeperkorn is rendered visible what Hans Castorp, as an ordinary young man in the *Flachland*, has not been able to see, namely the nature of the objective historical world in which his subjectivity has been constituted. What will replace the forms of this world is, as we said, unknowable. But it is the motif of inheritance which makes it possible to express the difficult notion of a succession which is also a transformation. This is Mann's modulation of the patrilinear relay, of the motif of inheritance, with which I have been recurrently concerned in this book.

The second chapter of the novel presents a miniature of the nineteenth-century German world of patriarchal succession which is the immediate historical context of our theme of inheritance. 'Children and grandchildren watch so that they may admire, and they admire in order to learn and to develop (ausbilden) what lies pre-formed within them from their forefathers ('was erblicherweise in ihnen vorgebildet liegt', III, p. 39). In *Der Zauberberg* this system is given as belonging to the past. The baptismal bowl, 'that symbol of family continuity',[49] belongs to the world Hans Castorp, already a little adrift from orderly generational succession by the fact of being an orphan, forswears in committing himself and his modest private income to the Mountain and the other promptings of his nature, made flesh in the figure of Clawdia. Mann had written an account of the end of succession and generational coherence in *Buddenbrooks*. In *Der Zauberberg*, it is taken as read: we are firmly in the post-Nietzschean, post-World War world. Yet the symbolically named Mann was not adumbrating the end of patriarchy. He was adumbrating, rather, its reformulation. In the *Betrachtungen* he had enquired rhetorically: 'what would mankind be like deprived of its masculine component?' (XII, p. 463), and in the speech on the German Republic he could still quote Goethe with approval to the effect that 'objectively, the masculine is the purer and more beautiful expression of humanity' (XI, p. 848).

In thrall to Clawdia Chauchat, Hans Castorp feels intensely disoriented: 'And it was paternal authority for which Hans Castorp's heart now felt an uneasy need' (III, p. 209). It is Mynheer Peeperkorn who eventually supplies this authority, a figure foreseen as a major structural necessity before Mann happened upon Gerhard Hauptmann as his model (IX, p. 814). As in all the other texts I have examined, there is a father figure at hand to ensure the coherence of the representation of the masculine subject. In this instance there is the complicating circumstance that what the father figure leaves to his heir is the end of father figures as we know them. But the thematic import is perfectly clear: Hans Castorp does not replace Mynheer Peeperkorn as Clawdia Chauchat's lover, he 'refuses the role of the "manly" man, dictated to him by a bourgeois and traditionally sexist society, and becomes a human being'.[50]

The nature of Hans Castorp's succession is carefully specified by Mann. There is a counter-image, an image of the masculine partial subject as disaster, unworthy of any succession, as unaccommodated as ever Anton Reiser was. This is Ferdinand Wehsal, whose name in German has connotations of miserable whining. He too is hopelessly in love with Clawdia, the eternal feminine fantasy, but unable to progress beyond the somatic obsession which distorts and vitiates his thoughts and his personality ('"Life is desire and desire is life"', III, p. 855), and which annihilates him in unsuccessful rivalry. He represents what Hans Castorp rises above in his concern and respect for Mynheer Peeperkorn: 'Our hero was no Wehsal . . . It was simply that he was not a "hero" at all, which means that he refused to allow his attitude to masculinity to be defined in relation to women' (III, p. 797). Hans Castorp himself defends his unwillingness to perceive Peeperkorn as a rival:

> That would of course be very masculine, masculine and gallant, in the social sense. But with me it is different. I am not at all masculine in the sense that I see in another male nothing but a rival. Perhaps I am not masculine at all – certainly not in the sense that I involuntarily called 'social', I don't exactly know why. (III, pp. 811–812)

Presumably this form of manliness is associated with a society which Hans Castorp now, although only rather dimly, is rejecting, and an alternative to which his new, tentative, but strong gender identity implies.

Hans Castorp's attitude to Mynheer Peeperkorn is not pusillanimous. Mann's protagonist tells the hoary Dutchman, with a precise circumspection which has rubbed off on the hero from his author, exactly what passed between Clawdia Chauchat and himself. He makes every effort to tell the truth (III, p. 843), although it is difficult, since what happened, happened only on the margins of what can be encoded in terms of, to use Hans Castorp's term, 'das Gesellschaftliche' ('the social'). Although this courage cannot be narrated without irony – such is the narrative arrangement of the novel – it remains courage nevertheless, and there is a significant moment at which the baton of patrilinear succession passes before our eyes: 'They looked into each other's eyes, the grand old man and the insignificant young one, the one continuing to hold the other by the wrist' (III, p. 842).

While Hans Castorp refuses to construct himself in the terms which situate Mynheer Peeperkorn and Clawdia Chauchat in relation to each other, saying that 'I should feel boastful and tasteless if I called myself a "man", although Clawdia is certainly a woman' (III, p. 845), he nevertheless enters a double alliance with them without betraying his subjective authenticity. Clawdia Chauchat seeks his company and support because she values his humanity, and the old man also responds to his honesty, although Hans Castorp has refused the Law, which would demand rivalry and confrontation. This is the culmination of the construction of his subjectivity in such a way as to respect its authentic drives and at the same time posit a new form of community as a possibility arising from the destruction, but not the betrayal or dismissal, of the old.

This complex moment of transmission takes us back to the complex relation between Mann and Goethe, since Mann is here confirming, but also varying, the central moment of inheritance from the *Lehrjahre* model. Since the time of the *Lehrjahre*, the concept of authority, of the source of inheritance, has always also included the figure of Goethe himself. There are thus elements of Goethe in Peeperkorn: the problematic link to 'nature' is one such, as indeed is a whole series of parallels to the Goethe of the contemporaneous essay 'Goethe und Tolstoi',[51] and Peeperkorn's eating and drinking, as well as his fear of death, are moments attributed by Mann to Goethe in *Lotte in Weimar*.[52] It is Eckhard Heftrich who notes that at the moment of mutual recognition quoted above between the grand old man and 'der unbedeutende junge Mann', Mann is inconspicuously bringing his own name into play.[53]

Mynheer Peeperkorn's core experience is a horror of being laughed at, of the dreadful humiliation he sees as the inevitable and justified consequence of impotence. His authority is thus predicated upon a refusal or transcendence of weakness, which is analogous with Mann's own entry from a state of partialness into the world of public representations, by means of judiciously modulated 'radikaler Autobiographismus'. It also defines the complex form of authority implied in the subjective culture of Goethe, both as I have explained it in relation to the *Lehrjahre* model, and as Mann himself repeatedly saw him, in terms of 'autobiographisch-selbstbildnerisches Bekennertum'. The father figure whose bequest to his heir is that there should no longer be father figures is thus not as paradoxical a phenomenon as it seems. What is inherited, as I asserted above, is the authority to establish a space in which authority may be suspended prior to its reformulation.

The form of authority Mann wishes to transform includes both the authority Goethe himself transformed in his empowering of subjectivity, namely the non-ironic authority of arbitrary power (cf. III, p. 615), and the authority with which Goethe replaced it, namely the ironic authority of the aesthetic. Yet the authority with which Mann wishes to replace these others is itself derived from Goethe, as the essay 'Goethe und Tolstoi', and the whole later development of Mann's thinking and public pronouncements, suggest. Mann's position is undoubtedly contradictory: '*Der Zauberberg* might be described as an attempt to bury the dead law with dignity; it is of course also a powerful wish for its resurrection.'[54]

In this context it is of more than just anecdotal relevance that Mann used Gerhart Hauptmann as the model for that 'structural necessity' (XI, p. 597) ultimately expressed in the figure of the bibulous Dutch coffee planter. In caricaturing Hauptmann, whose name is as punningly apposite as Mann's own, Mann is destroying his only rival for the succession of Goethe as the great representative German writer.[55] Mann was thus clearing the decks of one rival before the defining moment of measuring himself against Goethe himself. Indeed, by thus 'finishing off' Hauptmann, Mann both proves himself worthy of the succession (and thus emulates Goethe) and avoids the direct confrontation with Goethe himself, for whom he expresses reverence in this very act.

The relation of Castorp to Peeperkorn and of Mann to Goethe thus seems to be one which settles Oedipal rivalry on a conscious level. Potential rivalry, potential conflict, is set aside in the name of a greater good.[56] Castorp commits himself to an active engagement of his own desires with a Love which is socially fertile; Mann invokes Goethe in the cause of a new humanism which will be conducive to political progress. Of course, this apparent resolution of Oedipal male–male rivalry is undercut or ironised by the issue of homosexuality.[57]

But this is in fact the point of Mann's version of the co-operation of the twin circularities of incest and inheritance. The return of Mynheer Peeperkorn as the Man to Clawdia Chauchat's Woman means that the Law is sanctioned by Desire. The two are no longer at odds, as they had threatened to be; 'the limitless advantages of shame' can now be put to the service of a new humanity, just as the forces implied in the figure of Mignon become available for public effectiveness in the alternative incestuous figure of Natalie. The double alienation of the Goethean model, namely, first, that desire is specified in the particular form of homosexuality (rather than generalised as incest), and secondly, that the content of the inheritance is the end of inheritance, is made good in the double alliance Hans Castorp makes with the two characters, in relation to both of whom desire and law are mutually confirming. In making that alliance, Hans Castorp defines his identity clearly enough as the heir to this configuration, whatever form of responsibility that inheritance will entail. This was no clearer in the case of Wilhelm Meister at the end of the *Lehrjahre* than it is for Hans Castorp after the departure from the screen of the two larger-than-life characters. The end of the order of meaning and values signified in the excessive visibility of Peeperkorn and Chauchat, their grotesque or caricature qualities, implies the beginning that their heir will or might personify.

Mann attempts with gender roles what Goethe had attempted with social ones. Hans Castorp's subjectivity is defined not in relation to middle class and aristocratic qualities and attitudes, in a new, utopian, combination, but in relation to gender qualities and attitudes. Mann spells this sort of thinking out in 'Über die Ehe', where he argues that the 'patriarchal authoritative relationship between parents and their children' (x, p. 203) belongs to the past, and youth itself has taken on certain feminine qualities. Mann then argues in favour of an androgynous universalisation of homosexuality,[58] uniting the qualities of masculine and feminine. An oxymoron admirably encapsulates the contradiction and pathos of modern bourgeois culture: 'das Ewig-Menschliche aber ist wandlungsfähig' ('the eternally human is capable of transformation', x, p. 206). By this political indirect route (the reflection about gender identity and gender roles also played an important part in 'Von deutscher Republik'), Mann as it were rediscovers the androgynous ideal of alchemy that lurked within the humanism of the *Lehrjahre*. Hans Castorp too displays a fascination with the '*lapis philosophorum*, the male–female result of the combination of sulphur and mercury, the *res bina*, the androgynous *prima materia*' (III, p. 705).

The resolution which the representation of subjectivity enjoys in Hans Castorp's alliances with Peeperkorn and Chauchat does not, however, coincide with the end of the novel. Five sections follow the departure of these two characters, during which a debilitating drift sets in. The end of the novel is brought about by the intrusion from outside of the Great War. There is no happy ending.

The model with which we have become familiar in this study would lead us to seek in the formal closure of the novel as a whole the final guarantee of the representation of subjectivity. This aesthetic equipoise we would expect to offer the stabilising corrective to what is otherwise necessarily represented by means of a constitutive openness to relativisation. Is this view sustainable in Mann's case?

There is a perfectly explicit development of the theme of form in the novel, which it will suffice to sketch out here, since it is well known.[59] Coming to the magic mountain from a background excessively dependent upon external form and formality ('Überform'), Hans Castorp discovers the delights of transgression ('Unform'), of which he had earlier only had fleeting anticipations. Despite the instruction of Settembrini, Hans Castorp explores the possibilities of formlessness to the point where the arbitrariness of all forms threatens to dissolve an educative process into a sense that the very boundary between organic and inorganic has no compelling moral implication. The actual progress of Hans Castorp's educational journey, however, leads him safely through these dangerous realms, until he is able to affirm all the more resolutely the vital link between form as a general proposition and *human* form. This occurs principally in the 'Snow' section and the dual pact with Clawdia Chauchat and Mynheer Peeperkorn.

That this thematic development was in Mann's mind is borne out by the tendency of the contemporaneous essay 'Goethe und Tolstoi'. The 'Sympathie' section of that essay ends with a commitment to 'the human form' as the epitome of all human disciplines: 'it is, as Goethe said, "the non plus ultra of all human knowledge and deeds", "the alpha and omega of everything known to us"' (IX, p. 149). The long essay, and particularly this commitment to the horizon of significance established by the human form, seems to confirm that the central orientation of the novel itself is towards a Goethean valuation of form as something essentially human.

This confirms the presumption about form which we are led to make on the basis of the other texts in this study and in terms of the model by means of which we have sought to understand them. Indeed, Mann sometimes offers the very paradigm of that view of the function of form. In the thematic climax of the 'Snow' section, for instance, we read: 'Form too consists only of love and goodness' (III, p. 686), and in 1925 Mann offered the following definition: 'Form is . . . a mediation blessed by life between death and death: between death as formlessness (Unform) and death as an excess of form (Überform), between dissolution and petrification; it is measure and value, it is man (der Mensch), it is love' (XI, p. 371).

This strong linkage between form and humanity could be a motto standing over all the texts dealt with in this book. The novel form and the form of a life are in some sense analogous. As if to confirm the sometimes only subconscious presence of this nevertheless determining assumption, Mann significantly misunderstood a line from Oscar Wilde, reading Wilde's 'To love oneself is the beginning of a lifelong romance' to mean: 'Liebe zu sich selbst ist immer der Anfang eines romanhaften Lebens' ('love for oneself is always the beginning of a life that resembles a novel', X, p. 559).[60]

But although Mann and *Der Zauberberg* seem to offer the culmination to the theme of the significance of aesthetic form as the last arbiter in the representation and consequent guaranteeing or empowering of partial subjectivity, there are in this case, as will be evident, severe problems.

I have already touched upon one problem about the formal dimension of the novel. It has recently been argued by Hans Wysling that the novel is actually formally deficient, showing all too clearly the span of time over which it was composed, and the different needs engendered by the changes in circumstances over that long period. For Wysling, the novel follows a line, to use Mann's own terminology, from 'Form' to 'Unform'.[61] In answer to this we can reaffirm, now with more thematic evidence, that although Mann's novel might not meet the criteria of that *Bildungsroman* which never existed in the pure form from which Mann is accused of deviating, it actually meets our formal expectations, shaped by the other texts we have read, remarkably well. The relationship between narrator and partial subject, the circularities of law and desire, are, as we have shown, as structurally indispensable as ever, albeit at a very high level of self-consciousness.

Closure, whether impeccably achieved or not, is a formal characteristic of the work. All the more so against the background of a modernism which notoriously resists closure. We shall return to the actual question of the novel's conclusion, but it is important to emphasise the commitment to closure implied in Mann's retention of what every reader will experience as conventional narrative. Like Thomas Mann, and at much the same time, James Joyce began to write with the sort of deadpan irony which eases language away from its naturalness, from its moral embeddedness in social realities, placing it disorientatingly in quotation marks.[62] Joyce, however, as everybody knows (Mann knew it too) developed his practice in radically different ways, and specifically away from the conventional unilinear narrative which Mann never completely abandoned.

The end of the novel sees Hans Castorp vanishing into the holocaust of the Great War. It is as though the 'Snow' experience is about to be repeated, but this time with an uncertain outcome, and in circumstances in which the nightmare aspects of Hans Castorp's dream have become historical certainty, while the love and goodness pitched against them are reduced to a tune on the hero's lips. This tentative image of hope represents a sort of summa of subjective potential at its most positive, but its effectiveness in reality is unknown. Yet this ending is an especially structured openness. Mann knew from early on that the end of the novel upon which he unexpectedly found himself embarked would be the war. 'That the outbreak of war was an ideal ending for the novel is perfectly clear in retrospect',[63] writes the most recent editor of Mann's novel, and although Mann does not express himself quite so infelicitously, it is clear that the outbreak of the war clarified the overall progress of the work on the novel, relieving Mann himself of the need to invent a conclusion.

This ending provided the setting for the sort of uncertainty which animates the close of the *Lehrjahre*. Whereas there marriage is announced but deferred, here the resolution is not marriage but the projection, however endangered, of what might come about after the war. It is the notion of a republic which might emerge from the devastation, based upon the same symbolic androgyny (replacing the strongly gender-defined order of Peeperkorn's tottering monarchy) which is the deeper meaning of the union of Wilhelm and Natalie. It is no coincidence that Mann (in 1925) wrote a piece on marriage, in which he contrived to see in it the sort of synthesis of body and mind which characterised the (classical) notion of the aesthetic as well as Mann's own hopes for a German Republic (x, p. 207). The political implication of *Der Zauberberg* had been formulated in distinctly analogous terms in 1919: 'The essence of the new idea is the conception of Man as an amalgam of spirit and body (eine Geist-Leiblichkeit). It is . . . the renewal of the Christian state of God, but in humanist terms.'[64]

As early as 1915 Mann talked of the structural necessity of ending the projected work with the outbreak of war. He wrote to a friend that the hero of his story was like the figure from a fairy tale 'for whom seven years pass like days, and the end, the resolution – I see no other possibility than the outbreak of war. This is a reality that the storyteller cannot ignore.'[65] Thus the historical configuration not only gave Mann the ideal ending for his novel, it also virtually forced upon him the solution to the problem which had dogged Keller, namely combining the *Bildungsroman* with history. The protagonist is subtracted from history for seven years, and the problem is itself thus prominently ironised – another aspect of the high level of self-consciousness upon which this novel works. But the return of history, in the implacable reality of the war, re-integrates the entire problematic into history by the formally pre-eminent moment of its ending. The structured openness thus extends to uncertainty about whether history or aesthetic form has the final word.[66] Post-realist confidence about the ability of narrative to accommodate history converges with the Goethean freedom to prevaricate within the realm of the aesthetic.

It can be objected that the representation of subjectivity offered by the work as a whole is severely threatened by the fact that Hans Castorp is marching off to virtually certain extinction in the trenches. But this seems to be the most decisive indication of all that the novel is resolved in aesthetic form. No reader actually feels that the preceding 800 pages are annulled by the possibility that Hans Castorp will die. The novel, on the contrary, engages death, just as it engages the war, for its own formal resolution, by closing upon the very uncertainty of whether the hero will live or die. For the *form* of the novel it really doesn't matter. Indeed, the form defines and constitutes itself because it does not matter. The novel is something aside from these sharp distinctions and hard questions of practical existence. One sees clearly at this point how little the novel has to do with an authentic awareness of death, despite its insistent thematisation of it. Indeed, to thematise death is necessarily to domesticate it. We are reminded of the paradoxical relation between Novalis and Stifter: it is significantly Novalis, in many ways Mann's guide in the thematic composition of *Der Zauberberg*, whose work is informed by Eros despite his central structural dependence upon the theme of death, while Stifter's inclination is towards Thanatos, although, uniquely among these novels, death is entirely banned from the surface of his plot. In his revealing exaggeration, and the shadow it casts, Stifter makes plain that the true 'sterbefreier Raum' ('deathfree space') is the space of the model which we are examining, which does not engage with curtailment and otherness, and which depends upon the subject at its centre. Kowalik argues that Hans Castorp is not a true Nietzschean crusader of the spirit, in that he never actually confronts the reality of loss, despite his many claims to the contrary.[67] Although she exempts Mann himself from this charge of Nietzschean 'resentment', it seems to me in the context of my argument that Mann too evades the final implications of Nietzsche's ethical imperative, an unblinking confrontation with adversity, in favour of the 'sterbefreier Raum' of the *Lehrjahre* model. The peculiar ideal of the *homo dei* provided by Naphta and taken up and cherished by Hans Castorp is precisely the paradoxical idea of Man defined by Foucault as at once the subject and the object of knowledge: 'der Mensch selbst mit seiner religiösen Frage nach sich selbst' ('Man himself with his religious question about his own nature', XI, p. 657).

Therefore, in my view neither the war nor the specific extinction of Hans Castorp needs to be held substantially to detract from the role of *form* as final arbiter in the representation of subjectivity. It is rather to the contrary. But there *is* a threat to this function of form, and its immediate source is Mann's characteristic ambivalence about the meaning of form itself. The willed formal integrity of the *Lehrjahre* mutely underpinned the aesthetic authority by means of which partial subjectivity was represented as central despite and because of its partialness. In Mann, the question of form, in its ambiguous relation to the morality of legitimating authority, threatens to be self-undermining in its high degree of self-consciousness. The larger context of this is the post-Schopenhauer, post-Nietzsche world in which, for all his cultivation of the uses of tradition, Mann finds himself, and in which all representations are relativised.

The ambivalence of form is probably Mann's favourite theme. Indeed, it is more than a theme, because the theme of the artist engenders artistic self-consciousness, which in turn entails self-conscious art, which shifts the stable discourse of mimetic realism towards the state of self-referentiality. Play on form is the threshold between conventional realist representation and self-referring discourse upon which Mann loves to dwell and hesitate. 'And does form not have two faces? Is it not both moral and immoral at the same time?' (VIII, p. 455). If aesthetic form derives its subtle authority from an otherwise or elsewhere impossible equipoise of law and desire, Thomas Mann maintains that equipoise again and again in his works in order to afford glimpses of its impossibility outside the self-referring dome of his own willed artefact. Form balances between the two 'deaths' of excessive form and the complete absence of it, and contrives perpetually to be about these two things.

Børge Kristiansen takes this view to its logical conclusion in his original and much-praised study of *Der Zauberberg* in relation to Schopenhauer's philosophy. He argues that, despite the entire humanist programme explicit both in the book and in Mann's claims about it, the work is actually grounded in a Schopenhauerian dismissal of all social and cultural forms as mere constructions upon a basis of undifferentiated will, mere blind striving. The value of form is thus reversed: 'The irrational does not achieve form, rather form (das Gestaltete), as far as possible within the framework of a novel, is made transparent upon the irrationality of its primal ground.'[68] The stylistic procedure of the book consists for Kristiansen in 'the invalidation of the world of forms by consistently unmasking it as illusion'.[69]

If it were not for the quality and consistency of Kristiansen's argumentation no one would take this 'strong' reading of the novel seriously, since Mann was so evidently much more ambivalent (how could it be otherwise?) than Kristiansen will allow. But he nevertheless has a point, namely that there is a quality in the order of representation engaged by Mann which has a tendency towards the dissolution of all forms as mere illusion. Whereas in Keller the relativity of representations and their detachment from any authentic source in interiority was dimly adumbrated as part of the novel's realism, in Thomas Mann these things have become the condition of representation: Mann can retain conventional narrative structure and the comportment of realism because he knows that they ironise *themselves*. He plays with this on all levels of his text, a text which teases the reader with the possibility that it is undermining itself. The significant detail of the colour of Pribislav Hippe's (and Clawdia Chauchat's) eyes is significant not because it symbolises anything specific, but because the way in which it is given introduces indeterminacy into the text. These eyes are always given as 'blue-grey or grey-blue' (for instance, III, p. 170). The apparent precision of the narrator is the opposite of what it appears to be: which of the two colours is the noun and which the adjective, which the master and which the slave, which the form and which the content? The order of authority, or the hierarchy, upon which grammar (and thus meaning) depends is overthrown. The point is so obvious and so lightly made by Mann, that it is embarrassing to labour it in this way, yet to do so is to describe how the text consistently and characteristically makes fun of its own functioning.

One hesitates to write about irony, especially in the context of Thomas Mann, unless it is absolutely necessary; but perhaps it is permissible to compare and contrast this effect, which is ironic, with Goethe's irony in the *Lehrjahre* by saying that the latter endows the conscious artefact with life, while the former perpetually promises to take it away again.

This undecidable quality also affects the entire construction of meaning offered by the novel. It is obvious enough that Mann both employs and discards Naphta's and Settembrini's arguments, but he does the same thing with the entire construction of the novel.

The question: which is form and which is content? defines the constitutive ambiguity of the work. Does the form of the work become the content represented by a neo-humanist ethic, or do the pertinent issues around this ethical question actually come to rest in a formal completion, which alone justifies them? The last word on Castorp's moral state is not a word at all, but a song, namely the *Lindenbaum Lied*: the focus of the section 'Fullness of Harmony', and the tune on our hero's lips as he heads towards extinction. The function of the song is to allow something beyond words to be the centre of personal identity. This feeds into the humanist ethic of the novel, matching irreducible interiority up with a general proposition, and thus fulfilling the conditions of the aesthetic. Yet in the dimension of music, the Schopenhauerian dimension, all articulated meanings threaten to become pure composition. Mann said, with a note of informal arrogance and humour which suggests sincerity, 'Der Roman hat nicht Komposition, er ist eine – halten zu Gnaden!' ('The novel does not have composition, it is one – if you please.')[70]

Similarly with the concept of time. Like irony, this is a much-advertised aspect of the novel, and one hesitates to recycle the copy. But clearly, the novel, on one hand, claims to be historical in that it formulates the old world against the challenge of the new, while on the other again and again it suggests its own timelessness. Hippe and Clawdia are identical across time; Hans Castorp's 'Umkommen' in the snow evokes a timeless circularity; and Peeperkorn's suicide by artificial snakebite recalls the motif of the snake biting its own tail (the embodied phallus destroys itself by the use of a phallic machine), to which allusion is made in the 'Snow' section, and which is an immemorial symbol of infinity. In the end, the novel itself enjoys an impossible status as both a contribution to humanist republicanism and a timeless artistic moment, not caring whether Hans Castorp lives or dies.

Many critics have formulated this undecidable quality of *Der Zauberberg*: 'in a work of art constructed by analogy with music nothing may be unambiguous . . . music is ambiguity as art';[71] 'Thomas Mann's novels no longer have any unambiguous themes.'[72] What is important for my argument is that the vital link between humanity and form is thereby weakened. Mann's version of the *Lehrjahre* model is less stable than the original. Instability is essential to the original model, since it is a quality of the partialness of subjectivity. But, taken to the extent to which Mann takes it, as a result of his own disposition as well as the prevailing cultural and philosophical climate, the subject himself threatens to disperse into a Lacanian effect of differences. Meanings are just an endless play of binary oppositions, entailing nothing but each other: I mentioned how the final scene recalls the 'Snow' section. In doing so it emphasises the reversibility of that insight: the image of the integral human body entails a counter-image of its dismemberment. Neither has priority, and the play is the thing.

The maxim in italics which gives the message and the hope of the book recalls the use of different 'languages' by Goethe in the *Lehrjahre*. To different languages were accorded different functions, which combined to establish the de-centred subject at the centre of discourse. But the maxim in Mann is hugely exposed. It is not that Hans Castorp forgets it; indeed, as I argued, this is what the attentive reader of such novels might expect. It is more that it is suspended between linguistic versions of 'Überform' and 'Unform'. The speaking of languages other than one's own is a recurrent condition of speech in the novel. Settembrini and (presumably) Naphta are not native German speakers, although they are articulate to excess. When Hans Castorp really wants to say something important, he says it in French, and tends towards meaningless babble. Peeperkorn is also a non-native German speaker, but the main point about him is that he destabilises all linguistic projects. Just as he is an ironic destabilisation of representation, by being so many meanings rolled into one, so he is articulate, inarticulate and gifted with a musical turn of phrase (see III, pp. 840–841).[73] He is a language dysfunction, the point at which an order of meanings, arranged around the primary significance of the phallus, ceases to operate. (The only subject he is really articulate about is the significance of impotence.) All the characters have a more than *vraisemblable* verbal facility, and, as has been observed, abnormal verbal memories. Everything is in quotation marks, and there is no access assured to the interiority in which all quotations originate. Language threatens to become disembodied. The maxim falls into Hans Castorp's pre-conscious interior, and we have no way of knowing whether it forms part there of a developing moral identity, or becomes simply a junction traversed by the traffic of the unconscious in arbitrary directions.

This is the point: the integrity of the subject is not clear, not even in the complex and contradictory form with which we have become familiar. It is undermined and threatened by the order of representation. The aesthetic made possible a certain form of authority, a certain possibility of narrative and representation, which Mann here relativises at the same time as he uses it, just as he did with realism in *Buddenbrooks*. The aesthetic means a certain alliance between law and desire, a place where they overlap and mutually confirm, in the name of the masculine subject; and in Mann the relation between them becomes unstable. Even in Novalis, where the ultimate identity of law and desire could be glimpsed, this very ultimate identity, this very teleology, stabilised them in relation to each other and in relation to the agency of the effective masculine subjectivity which is always finally that of the Poet. In Mann there are many examples of this instability of law in relation to desire, from the light in the eyes of the model pupil Hippe, through the passion of Hans Castorp's 'besoin d'ordre' (III, p. 467), to the quasi-erotic attraction between Hans Castorp and Mynheer Peeperkorn or, perhaps most destabilising in our context, between the narrator and his protégé.[74] This relation is an indeterminate one, between homosexual appreciation and narcissism, and this disturbs the central authority upon which the model as I have described it depends. If the author of the text nurses secret desires, and the author in the text, the subject, is the object of them, the crucial distinction (and relation) between public and private is eroded.

It now remains to link what we have said about Mann's novel to the theme of representation conceived as exchange rather than as a construction of subjectivity. It will be clear that this notion of language as a system of exchange, a swapping of symbolic counters rather than a guarantee of the richness and priority of interiority, guides Mann's text, despite the superficial conventionality of his procedure. The exchanges between Settembrini and Naphta are precisely that, an exchange of linguistic acts which, before our very eyes, drift free of referential anchorage.[75] But the thoroughgoing bracketing of all meanings, and the famous operations of irony, make the whole linguistic cast of the novel that of a composition of circulating meanings.

What is odd about Mann's otherwise encyclopaedic novel is that there is one sphere which is conspicuous by its absence, namely the economic one.[76] In Keller one could see rather clearly how there was a link between the rise of a sense of the abitrary nature of signification, which established itself in the following, post-Saussurean century, and the circulation of money as a determining dimension in the composition of what we perceive, and are subordinate to, as reality. It is odd, therefore, that there should be no hint of this link in *Der Zauberberg*. Where are its effects? They are there, it seems to me, in the novel's status as commodity, which is not just a matter of sales figures, but also of Mann's own very shrewd sense of the contemporary literary market place. The economic theme is driven out of the explicit world of the novel because it is all-conditioning upon the implicit level. There is a polarisation between the thematic and linguistic effects of modern reality, on one hand, and the economic ones on the other.

To explain the point further: Mann expressed astonishment at the – extraordinary – success of his novel on publication. But it is hard to believe that, preoccupied as he was with his public profile, he did not have a very shrewd sense of a readership for his works – his diaries record carefully the success of readings he gave of his work in progress – and make decisions in composition which were deeply influenced by these considerations.[77] Broch and Musil objected to his success and felt that he was selling short the high earnestness of modernism, with its commitment to opacity and distance from the market place.[78] As we have seen, Mann retained conventional narrative, as he retained conventional characters and conventional language. He also retained conventional themes, and, as I have tried to show, the established structure of the *Lehrjahre* model beyond the superficial play with the cliché of the *Bildungsroman*. He retained, in other words, 'literature' as the educated German or European reader would understand it.

But this is literature as commodity, not as the new medium of guiding truth it had been a century before. Whereas in 1800, as Kittler proposes, the central 'Aufschreibesystem' was Literature, which came from the secular soul and spoke to the secular soul, in 1900 there were just a series of systems, discourse networks which were constituted by the machinery which supported them, whether the 'writing machines' of new technology (about which there is a better pun in German, on 'Schreibmaschine', than is unfortunately available in English) or the physiological mechanisms and reflexes which produce speech and writing.[79] The real point about the universally high level of self-consciousness in Mann's work, in relation to almost every single aspect of the model I am expounding, is that this ironic exposure is an act of product identification: this is culture, our German culture, our deep, historical, perennial problems and so forth. Thus does Mann avoid the dangers of Kitsch which wait in ambush for anyone trying to peddle the ideals of Weimar in the age of mass reproduction. He produces the commodity Literature, miraculously surviving (enticingly revealing glimpses of its timelessness) into the age of the media and the catastrophic problematicisation of the human subject (advertising the attractions of the individual human subject, without being able to force any one to buy it), aware of itself as only one discourse among others.[80] One last time, in ironic suspension, these themes and dilemmas can be put out in exceptionally urbane formulation. Where Hanno Buddenbrook the poet was unable to succeed his father in the world, Thomas Mann became the real continuer of the family business, exceeding his father in wealth and prestige many times over (cf. XI, p. 556). We return to the strategy of Goethe in writing *Wilhelm Meisters Lehrjahre*, a strategy which in a sense is here reversed: whereas Goethe exploited the popular novel to make it serious, Mann exploited the serious novel to make it popular. Readers ever since, among whom I include myself, have had ample reason to be profoundly grateful to them both.

Conclusion

A conclusion can consist of a summing up of what has gone before, but it can also seek to define the outline of what is being concluded. My view is that the *Lehrjahre* model finishes with *Der Zauberberg* and had already been replaced for this century by other and more various variations upon autobiographical discourse. In the light of this finality, I therefore prefer to adopt the second sort of conclusion, and finish by referring very briefly to the hugely influential modernist writing of Franz Kafka. In doing this, I wish simply to sketch the boundary of the world I have been mapping in the pages above. *Anton Reiser* and *Hyperion*, the reader may recall, were also included with the same defining function in mind.

In Kafka's case one can no longer talk of a liberal humanist discourse or liberal humanist attitude to the subject. The genderedness of his discourse is not tacit, but explicit: the impossibility of the son's relating, by succession, rivalry, inheritance, identity or whatever, to the father is the condition of his writing (this is explained in the autobiographical *Brief an den Vater*). The circle of incest (witness, for instance, the roles of the mother and the sister in *Die Verwandlung*) has become first a trap, then a hope raised only to be extinguished. If it is true that Kafka's work is 'die kunstvolle Inszenierung des eigenen Versagens' ('the artist's staging of his own failure'),[1] then the failure remains failure and is neither symbolically transcended, nor transcended by symbols, as it would have been in a *Bildungsroman*.

Kafka's relation to classical German literature is in general one of significant negation. Goethe, the literary giant who bestrode the tradition of German literature, threatened to bar

Kafka's literary achievement, just as his father's mere existence barred his son's development (Kafka likened his own 'development', 'Entwicklung', to that of a bad tooth, rather than a humanist 'Bildung').[2] The oppressive authority of Goethe's unchallengeable greatness threatened to freeze Kafka in a state of partialness.

A diary entry illustrates perfectly Kafka's attitude to the tradition I have described in this book:

> Full-length silhouette of Goethe's complete figure (ganze Gestalt). Something repellent about the sight of this perfect human body, since you could not imagine this level of perfection being surpassed, yet it appears at the same time contrived and arbitrary. The upright posture, the hanging arms, the slim neck, the bend at the knee.[3]

Goethe's whole significance is compacted into the form of his body: his constitution as an individual is both unsurpassable and circumstantial. Indeed, it is the conjunction of completeness and particularity which now nauseates Kafka. Previously this conjunction defined the aesthetic and the *Bildungsroman*: the sensuous particular and the universal; subjective partialness transfigured, the apotheosis of the Individual. But what had once been a necessary and constitutive conjunction is now 'arbitrary', and as such the very antithesis of the aesthetic. Autobiography is blocked from the public domain; Kafka's *Letter to his Father* was never sent.

Kafka was therefore obliged to devise a different way of imagining a public existence, for a body of work as private as his own, from that offered by the *Lehrjahre* and its cognates. (Kafka was far from sure that his writing belonged to the public domain in any defensible sense, and directed Max Brod, as everyone knows, to burn his unpublished work. Even the few works published in Kafka's lifetime left him full of doubt.) Kafka addressed the problem in a couple of diary entries about 'minor literature'. What he had in mind was the literary reality and commerce of a small nation or linguistic group, which has to sustain itself against the threat from a larger one. Yiddish and Czech literatures would be examples.[4] Great literatures, he mused, are deformed in their relationship to the real life of people, because they have been, as Kafka puts it, 'perforated by talent', made to conform to the contours of an individual genius, which exercise a normative, though ultimately arbitrary, influence. The example of the great talents of great national literatures on one hand demoralises others and on the other provides a pathway into the public literary sphere for the epigone.[5] 'Minor' literature furnishes the possibility that 'the differences between fathers and sons can become worthy subjects for public debate, national shortcomings can be represented in a manner that is very painful, to be sure, but also liberating and deserving of forgiveness'.[6]

Kafka himself could only dream of participation in such a literature and of such a liberation, since his own language was German and he 'had to make the best of it'.[7] The community which would transform his personal isolation into a common cause did not really exist, although he was preoccupied, especially in later life, with a search for one. But in a sense his own writing does mimic his own conception of minor literature by remaining true to the partialness from which it springs, just as such a small literature remains true to the unfinished but living processes of its own community. He finds ways to be a 'stranger within his own language'.[8] Kafka's writing makes a grim virtue of total exclusion from a powerful public sphere, to the point at which it might (just) become a contribution to the project of an alternative one. The full context of Pasley's admirable phrase, quoted above, was as follows: 'In order to achieve something genuinely praiseworthy, wouldn't it be necessary to break free of the common run, and show by means of the artist's staging of his own failure the need for a complete restructuring of the whole show?'

In contrast to the positive aesthetic construction out of subjective partialness of the *Bildungsroman*, Kafka works with the artistic value of negation. One of Kafka's most memorable aphorisms, after all, reads: 'Our art is dazzled blindness before the truth (ein von der Wahrheit Geblendet-Sein). The light on the recoiling distorted face is true, nothing else.'[9]

Kafka's work therefore, in all its famous enigmatic refusal of meaning and resolution, in its glimpses of subjectivity vanishing and possibly escaping, concludes our story by negation. Writing of the power of belief, Kafka said: 'In this negation it assumes form'

('In dieser Verneinung bekommt sie Gestalt'),[10] and the same words might be held to apply to his version of 'Litteratur', which as a matter of historical fact has entered the public domain, and has done so as the – specific and significant – negation of Goethe's 'ganze Gestalt', of *that* form, of the *Bildungsroman* and its culture.

Notes

INTRODUCTION

1 For a recent and comprehensive survey of writing about the *Bildungsroman* see Todd Kontje, *The German Bildungsroman: History of a National Genre* (Columbia, 1993).
2 *Novalis Schriften*, edited by Paul Kluckhohn and Richard Samuel, second edition, 4 vols. + 1 Begleitband (Stuttgart, 1960–1988), I, third edition (of this vol. only), p. 325.
3 For a clear account of this complicated and notoriously confusing topic, see the Introduction to Michael Metteer, *Desire in Fictional Communities* (New York and London, 1988).
4 Morgenstern's claim to this invention was established by Fritz Martini, 'Der Bildungsroman. Zur Geschichte des Wortes und der Theorie', *DVjs*, 35 (1961), 44–63.
5 Karl Morgenstern, 'Bruchstück einer den 12/24 Dec 1810 zu Dorpat im Hauptsaal der Kaiserl. Universität öffentlich gehaltenen Vorlesung über den Geist und Zusammenhang einer Reihe philosophischer Romane', in *Dörptsche Beyträge für Freunde der Philosophie, Litteratur und Kunst*, edited by Karl Morgenstern, III (Dorpat and Leipzig, 1817), pp. 180–195, p. 195.
6 Morgenstern in a letter to Falk, 1 December 1796, cit. Martini, 'Bildungsroman', pp. 51–52.
7 Thomas Mann, *Gesammelte Werke*, 13 vols. (Frankfurt, 1960, reprinted in paperback, 1990), X, p. 195.
8 Terry Eagleton, *The Ideology of the Aesthetic* (Oxford, 1990), p. 262.
9 See, for instance, Peter Bürger, *Theory of the Avant-Garde*, trans. Michael Shaw (Manchester/Minnesota, 1984), pp. 35–41.
10 These words are quoted from the *Oxford Companion to German Literature*'s entry on the *Bildungsroman*.
11 Mann, *Werke*, IX, p. 150.
12 Andrew Bowie, *Aesthetics and Subjectivity: from Kant to Nietzsche* (Manchester and New York, 1990).

13 This is the subject of the study of the *Bildungsroman* by Michael Beddow, *The Fiction of Humanity. Studies in the Bildungsroman from Wieland to Thomas Mann* (Cambridge, 1982).
14 Peter Dews, *Logics of Disintegration* (London and New York, 1987), p. 155.
15 See Terry Eagleton, 'Self-Authoring Subjects', in *What is an Author?*, edited by Maurice Biriotti and Nicola Miller (Manchester, 1993), pp. 42–50, and Dews, *Logics of Disintegration*, pp. xiv, xv.
16 Bowie, *Aesthetics and Subjectivity*, p. 67. For a contemporary philosophical defence of this position, see Thomas Nagel, *The View from Nowhere* (Oxford, 1986).
17 *Novalis Schriften*, II, p. 138.
18 Bowie, *Aesthetics and Subjectivity*, pp. 77–78.
19 Principally in the essay beginning 'Wenn der Dichter einmal des Geistes mächtig ist', formerly known by the title 'Über die Verfahrungsweise des poetischen Geistes'. Friedrich Hölderlin, *Sämtliche Werke*, edited by Friedrich Beißner, 8 vols. (Stuttgart, 1946–1985), IV, 1, 1961, pp. 241–265.
20 Bowie, *Aesthetics and Subjectivity*, p. 71.
21 Ibid.
22 See Hans Jörg Sandkühler, *Friedrich Wilhelm Joseph Schelling* (Stuttgart, 1970), pp. 90–91.
23 I am grateful to Andrew Bowie for bringing this parallel to my attention.
24 Bowie, *Aesthetics and Subjectivity*, p. 97.
25 Ibid., p. 95.
26 Clemens Heselhaus, 'Die Wilhelm-Meister-Kritik der Romantiker und die romantische Romantheorie', in *Nachahmung und Illusion*, edited by H. R. Jauß (Munich, 1964), 113–127, p. 114.
27 Martin Swales, *The German Bildungsroman from Wieland to Hesse* (Princeton, 1978).
28 For Schelling, and Manfred Frank, on the significance of limits, see Bowie, *Aesthetics and Subjectivity*, p. 91.
29 This topic is dealt with more fully below: see pp. 169–170, and note 8.
30 See Bowie, *Aesthetics and Subjectivity*, pp. 99–100, and Hölderlin's letter of 1 January 1799 to his brother quoted there, which is to be found in Hölderlin, *Sämtliche Werke*, VI, pp. 302–307, p. 305.
31 Rolf Selbmann, *Der deutsche Bildungsroman* (Stuttgart, 1984), p. 11.
32 Karl Philipp Moritz, *Schriften zur Ästhetik und Poetik*, edited by Hans Joachim Schrimpf (Tübingen, 1962), p. 148.
33 Cit. Heselhaus, 'Die Wilhelm-Meister-Kritik der Romantiker', p. 118.
34 *Novalis Schriften*, II, p. 563.
35 Ibid., p. 599.
36 See below, pp. 128–129.

37 See Hans Wysling, 'Thomas Manns Goethe-Nachfolge', *Jahrbuch des freien deutschen Hochstifts* (1978), 498–551, p. 535.
38 Mann, *Werke*, x, p. 559.
39 Eagleton, *The Ideology of the Aesthetic*, p. 263.
40 Hubert L. Dreyfus and Paul Rabinow, *Michel Foucault: Beyond Structuralism and Hermeneutics* (Brighton, 1986), p. 30.
41 Michel Foucault, *The Order of Things. An Archaeology of the Human Sciences* (London, 1974), p. 312.
42 Dreyfus and Rabinow, *Michel Foucault*, p. 28.
43 Mann, *Werke*, xi, p. 657.
44 See Franco Moretti, *The Way of the World. The 'Bildungsroman' in European Culture* (London, 1987); see also below, pp. 164–166.

1. *WILHELM MEISTERS LEHRJAHRE*

1 T. J. Reed, *Goethe* (Oxford and New York, 1984), p. 61.
2 Goethe, *Wilhelm Meisters Theatralische Sendung*, mit einem Nachwort von Wilhelm Voßkamp (Frankfurt am Main, 1984), p. 18. Cf. *Goethes Werke*, 'Hamburger Ausgabe', edited by Erich Trunz, 14 vols. (Hamburg then Munich, 1948–1960), vii, p. 21. All further references to *Wilhelm Meisters Lehrjahre* are to this edition. English translations adapted from: Wolfgang von Goethe [*sic*], *Wilhelm Meister*, translated by Thomas Carlyle, 2 vols. (London, 1912).
3 *Der Briefwechsel zwischen Schiller und Goethe*, edited by Emil Staiger, 2 vols. (Frankfurt am Main, 1977), i, p. 319 (28 November 1796).
4 'Über Goethes "Meister"', *Athenäum*, 1 Band, 2 Stück, 1798.
5 Beddow, *Fiction of Humanity*, p. 77.
6 See E. L. Stahl, *Die religiöse und die humanitätsphilosophische Bildungsidee und die Entstehung des deutschen Bildungsromans im 18. Jahrhundert* (Bern, 1934).
7 Cf. Guy Stern, 'Wieland and Goethe: a Study in the Development of the Novel' (PhD. thesis, Columbia University, New York, 1954), p. 186.
8 Werner Hahl, *Reflexion und Erzählung. Ein Problem der Romantheorie von der Spätaufklärung bis zum programmatischen Realismus* (Stuttgart etc., 1971), p. 11.
9 *Der Briefwechsel zwischen Schiller und Goethe*, i, p. 488.
10 See: Eric A. Blackall, *Goethe and the Novel* (Ithaca and London, 1976), p. 116; T. J. Reed, *The Classical Centre. Goethe and Weimar 1775–1832* (London, 1980), p. 101; Hildegard Emmel, *Was Goethe vom Roman der Zeitgenossen nahm* (Bern, 1972); Rosemarie Haas, *Die Turmgesellschaft in 'Wilhelm Meisters Lehrjahre'. Zur Geschichte des Geheimbundromans und der Romantheorie im 18. Jahrhundert* (Bern and Frankfurt am Main, 1975).

11 Reed, *The Classical Centre*, p. 113.
12 Friedrich Sengle, 'Der Romanbegriff in der ersten Hälfte des 19. Jahrhunderts', in *Arbeiten zur deutschen Literatur 1750–1850* (Stuttgart, 1965), 175–196, pp. 185–186; Georg Jäger, *Empfindsamkeit und Roman. Wortgeschichte. Theorie und Kritik im 18. und frühen 19. Jahrhundert* (Stuttgart, 1969), p. 79.
13 See Friedrich Sengle, 'Die klassische Kultur von Weimar, sozialgeschichtlich gesehen', *Internationales Archiv für Sozialgeschichte der deutschen Literatur*, 3 (1978), 68–86, pp. 80–81.
14 See Nicholas Boyle, 'Das Lesedrama: Versuch einer Ehrenrettung', *Kontroversen, alte und neue*, vol. VII (Tübingen, 1986), pp. 65, 67.
15 See Rolf-Peter Janz, 'Zum sozialen Gehalt der "Lehrjahre"', in *Literaturwissenschaft und Geschichtsphilosophie*, edited by Helmut Arntzen and others (Berlin and New York, 1975), pp. 320–340.
16 Hans H. Gerth, *Bürgerliche Intelligenz um 1800* (Göttingen, 1976), p. 42.
17 Hajo Holborn, *A History of Modern Germany* (Princeton, 1982), p. 305.
18 Rolf Selbmann, *Theater im Roman. Studien zum Strukturwandel des deutschen Bildungsromans* (Munich, 1981), p. 43.
19 See Georg Lukács, 'Wilhelm Meisters Lehrjahre', in Lukács, *Werke*, 17 vols. (Neuwied am Rhein and Berlin, 1962–1975), VII (1964), pp. 69–88.
20 See Giuliano Baioni, '"Märchen" – "Wilhelm Meisters Lehrjahre" – "Hermann und Dorothea". Zur Gesellschaftsidee der deutschen Klassik', *Goethe-Jahrbuch*, 92 (1975), 73–127.
21 See, for instance, Eagleton, *Ideology of the Aesthetic* and Bowie, *Aesthetics and Subjectivity*, and the related discussion in the Introduction above, pp. 6–9.
22 I am indebted to my colleague, Nick Boyle, for drawing my attention to this point.
23 Moretti, *Way of the World*, p. 64.
24 See, for instance, Lukács, *Werke*, II (*Geschichte und Klassenbewußtsein*, 1968), p. 236.
25 See Christa Bürger, *Der Ursprung der Institution Kunst. Literatursoziologische Untersuchungen zum klassischen Goethe* (Frankfurt am Main, 1977).
26 See Eagleton, *Ideology of the Aesthetic*, passim, especially pp. 112–119.
27 Moritz, *Schriften zur Ästhetik und Poetik*, p. 148.
28 Julian Roberts, *German Philosophy. An Introduction* (Polity Press, Cambridge, 1988), p. 65.
29 Lukács, *Geschichte und Klassenbewußtsein*, p. 317.
30 Cf. Stefan Blessin, *Die Romane Goethes* (Königstein/Ts, 1979), p. 14.
31 Baioni, 'Gesellschaftsidee', p. 79.
32 Ibid., p. 86.

33 Hahl, *Reflexion und Erzählung*, p. 87.
34 Ibid., p. 138.
35 David Roberts, *The Indirections of Desire. Hamlet in Goethe's 'Wilhelm Meister'* (Heidelberg,1980), p. 221.
36 Haas, *Die Turmgesellschaft*, p. 101.
37 See Roberts, *Indirections*, pp. 48–49, 150.
38 Roberts, *Indirections*, p. 161.
39 Ibid., p. 150.
40 See Friedrich A. Kittler, 'Über die Sozialisation Wilhelm Meisters', in Gerhard Kaiser and Friedrich A. Kittler, *Dichtung als Sozialisationsspiel. Studien zu Goethe und Gottfried Keller* (Göttingen, 1978), p. 100.
41 *Der Briefwechsel zwischen Schiller und Goethe*, I, p. 237 (8 July 1796).
42 Cf. Eagleton, *Ideology of the Aesthetic*, p. 41.
43 Paul Cantor, *Shakespeare, Hamlet* (Cambridge, 1989), p. ix.
44 Ibid., p. x.
45 Catherine Belsey, *The Subject of Tragedy. Identity and Difference in Renaissance Drama* (London and New York, 1985), pp. 40–42.
46 Ibid., p. 41.
47 Ibid., p. 42.
48 Ibid.
49 Roberts, *Indirections*, p. 28.
50 Belsey, *The Subject of Tragedy*, p. 42.
51 Roberts, *Indirections*, p. 215.
52 Ibid., p. 217.
53 Ibid., p. 128.
54 Ibid., p. 27.
55 See Otto Rank, *Das Inzest-Motiv in Dichtung und Sage. Grundzüge einer Psychologie des dichterischen Schaffens*, second edition (Leipzig and Vienna, 1926), 387ff.
56 See Cantor, *Hamlet*, p. 23.
57 Rank, *Das Inzest-Motiv*, p. 33.
58 Ibid., p. 19.
59 Roberts, *Indirections*, pp. 129–132, 203.
60 Ibid., pp. 34, 127.
61 Ibid., p. 61.
62 Ibid., p. 214.
63 Cf. Kittler, *Dichtung als Sozialisationsspiel*, pp. 14–28.
64 Roberts, *Indirections*, p. 49.
65 *Hamburger Ausgabe*, I, pp. 359–360.
66 Eagleton, *Ideology of the Aesthetic*, p. 41.
67 Ronald Gray, *Goethe the Alchemist. A Study of Alchemical Symbolism in Goethe's Literary and Scientific Works* (London, 1952), p. 231.

68 See Roberts, *Indirections*, and Cristoph E. Schweitzer, 'Wilhelm Meister und das Bild vom kranken Königssohn', *PMLA*, 72 (1957), 419–432.
69 Gray, *Goethe the Alchemist*, p. 221.
70 Ibid., p. 245.
71 Ibid., p. 227.
72 Ibid., p. 246.
73 Ibid., p. 227.
74 Ibid., p. 231.
75 Cf. Ibid., pp. 231–232.
76 Ibid., p. 245.
77 Ibid., p. 228.
78 *Der Briefwechsel zwischen Schiller und Goethe*, I, pp. 220–221 (2 July 1796).
79 'Kanzler Müller im Gespräch mit Goethe, 29 Mai 1814', *Goethe Gedenkausgabe*, vol. XXII, p. 273, quoted by Hannelore Schlaffer, *Wilhelm Meister. Das Ende der Kunst und die Wiederkehr des Mythos* (Stuttgart, 1980), p. 40.
80 From *Fragments, 1797–1798*, quoted in *Hamburger Ausgabe*, VII, p. 657.
81 See Bernd Peschken, *Versuch einer germanistischen Ideologiekritik. Goethe, Lessing, Tieck, Hölderlin, Heine in Wilhelm Diltheys und Julian Schmidts Vorstellungen* (Stuttgart, 1972), pp. 31–45.
82 Ibid., p. 40.
83 Ibid., pp. 40–41.
84 Karl Schlechta, *Goethes Wilhelm Meister*, mit einer Einleitung von Heinz Schlaffer (Frankfurt am Main, 1985), p. 12.
85 Peschken, *Ideologiekritik*, p. 45.
86 Bürger, *Institution Kunst* , pp. 110–118.
87 Quoted in *Hamburger Ausgabe*, VII, p. 618 (22 January 1821).
88 *Novalis, Schriften*, III, p. 639.
89 Peschken, *Ideologiekritik*, pp. 83–85.
90 Hannelore Schlaffer, *Das Ende der Kunst*, pp. 219–220; Schlechta, *Goethes Wilhelm Meister*, p. 11.
91 Schlechta, *Goethes Wilhelm Meister*, p. 62.
92 Quoted ibid., p. 157. See *Theatralische Sendung*, p. 96.
93 Schlechta, *Goethes Wilhelm Meister*, p. 26.
94 Hannelore Schlaffer, *Das Ende der Kunst*, p. 7.
95 Jochen Hörisch, *Gott, Geld und Glück. Zur Logik der Liebe in den Bildungsromanen Goethes, Kellers und Thomas Manns* (Frankfurt am Main, 1983), p. 15.
96 Ibid., p. 9.
97 See note 40 above.
98 Kittler, *Dichtung als Sozialisationsspiel*, p. 106.
99 Ibid., p. 71.

100 E.g. 'Der Dichter, die Mutter, das Kind. Zur romantischen Erfindung der Sexualität', in *Romantik in Deutschland*, edited by Richard Brinkmann, Sonderband der *DVjs* (Stuttgart, 1978), pp. 102–114; 'Die Irrwege des Eros und die "Absolute Familie"', in *Psychoanalytische und psychopathologische Literaturinterpretation*, edited by Bernd Urban and Winfried Kudszus (Darmstadt, 1981), pp. 421–470.
101 Beddow, *Fiction of Humanity*, p. 297.
102 Ibid.
103 Kittler, *Dichtung als Sozialisationsspiel*, p. 56.
104 Ibid., p. 102.
105 Ibid., p. 14.
106 Ibid., p. 87.

2. *AGATHON, ANTON REISER, HYPERION*

1 See the account of Wieland's sources in *Geschichte des Agathon*, edited by Klaus Manger (Frankfurt am Main, 1986 [Deutscher Klassiker Verlag]), pp. 937–938.
2 See Robert Spaemann, *Reflexion und Spontaneität* (Stuttgart, 1963), p. 10; Gabrielle Bersier, 'The Education of the Prince: Wieland and German Enlightenment at School with Fénelon and Rousseau', *Eighteenth Century Life*, n.s., 10 (1986), 1–13, p. 3.
3 Bersier, 'The Education of the Prince', p. 3.
4 Fénelon, *Les Aventures de Télémaque*, edited by Jeanne-Lydie Goré (Paris, 1968), p. 30.
5 Bersier, 'The Education of the Prince', p. 3.
6 Fénelon, *Télémaque*, p. 88.
7 Ibid., p. 185.
8 See *Agathon*, ed. Manger, p. 800.
9 Letter to Immermann, 5 December 1758, *Wielands Briefwechsel*, edited by Hans Werner Seiffert (Berlin 1963–), I, p. 392.
10 Fénelon, *Télémaque*, p. 391.
11 Ibid., p. 392.
12 Spaemann, *Reflexion und Spontaneität*, p. 208.
13 Wolfgang Paulsen, *Christoph Martin Wieland. Der Mensch und sein Werk in psychologischen Perspektiven* (Bern and Munich, 1975), pp. 161–162.
14 Stern, 'Fielding, Wieland and Goethe', p. 14; Werner Hahl, *Reflexion und Erzählung*, pp. 73–77.
15 Christoph Martin Wieland, *Werke*, edited by Fritz Martini and Hans Werner Seiffert, 5 vols. (Munich, 1964–1968), I, p. 376. Further references in the text are to this edition. Translations are adapted from *The History of Agathon* [translated by John Richardson] (London, 1773).

16 Stern, 'Fielding, Wieland and Goethe', pp. 14–15.
17 Paulsen, *Wieland*, pp. 139–142.
18 Friedrich Sengle, *Wieland* (Stuttgart, 1949), p. 198.
19 See Victor Lange, 'Zur Gestalt des Schwärmers im deutschen Roman des 18. Jahrhunderts', *Festschrift für Richard Alewyn*, edited by Herbert Singer and Benno von Wiese (Cologne and Graz, 1967), pp. 150–164.
20 See Lange, 'Zur Gestalt des Schwärmers', pp. 160–164; cf. Peter J. Brenner, *Die Krise der Selbstbehauptung. Subjekt und Wirklichkeit im Roman der Aufklärung* (Tübingen, 1981), p. 130.
21 Hahl, *Reflexion und Erzählung*, p. 43; see also Kurt Wölfel, 'Daphnes Verwandlungen. Zu einem Kapitel in Wielands "Agathon"', *Jahrbuch der deutschen Schillergesellschaft*, 8 (1964), 41–56, p. 42; Hans-Jürgen Schings, 'Agathon – Anton Reiser – Wilhelm Meister. Zur Pathogenese des modernen Subjekts im Bildungsroman', in *Goethe im Kontext*, edited by Wolfgang Wittkowski (Tübingen, 1984), 42–68, pp. 56–58.
22 Sengle, *Wieland*, p. 194.
23 Paulsen, *Wieland*, p. 78.
24 Ibid., p. 187; see too Wölfel, 'Daphnes Verwandlungen', p. 54, note 14.
25 Paulsen, *Wieland*, pp. 139–142.
26 Cf. Lessing's famous judgement: 'it is the first and only novel for the thinking reader of classical taste'. Cit. Sengle, *Wieland*, p. 199; Christian Friedrich von Blankenburg, *Versuch über den Roman*, 1774.
27 Wölfel, 'Daphnes Verwandlungen', p. 49.
28 'Sex and Sensibility: Wieland's Portrayal of Relationships Between the Sexes in the *Comische Erzählungen*, *Agathon*, and *Musarion*', *Lessing Year Book*, 12 (1980), 189–218, p. 196.
29 *The Fiction of Humanity*, p. 59.
30 Paulsen, *Wieland*, p. 259; see too Wölfel, 'Daphnes Verwandlungen', p. 45.
31 Paulsen, *Wieland*, p. 46.
32 See Hans Joachim Schrimpf, *Karl Philipp Moritz* (Stuttgart, 1980), pp. 52–53.
33 Martin L. Davies, 'Karl Philipp Moritz's Erfahrungsseelenkunde: Its Social and Intellectual Origins', *Oxford German Studies*, 16 (1985), 13–35, p. 30.
34 Karl Philipp Moritz, *Anton Reiser. Ein psychologischer Roman*, edited by Wolfgang Martens (Stuttgart, 1973), p. 13. All further references are to this edition.
35 Cf. Paulsen, *Wieland*, p. 38.
36 See Brenner, *Die Krise der Selbstbehauptung*, p. 96.

37 Cit. Ibid., pp. 96–7.
38 Günter Niggl, *Geschichte der deutschen Autobiographie im 18. Jahrhundert* (Stuttgart, 1977), p. 71.
39 Ibid., esp. pp. 6–38.
40 Ibid., p. 71.
41 Ibid.
42 See Roy Pascal, *Design and Truth in Autobiography* (London, 1960), p. 89; D. Stevens Garlick, 'Moritz's *Anton Reiser*: The Dissonant Voice of Psycho-Autobiography', *Studi germanici*, 21/22 (1983–1984), 41–60, p. 47.
43 See Niggl, *Geschichte der deutschen Autobiographie*, p. 72.
44 See Mark Boulby, 'Anton Reiser and the Concept of the Novel', *Lessing Yearbook*, 4 (1972), 183–196, pp. 185–186.
45 *Karl Philipp Moritz: At the Fringe of Genius* (Toronto, Buffalo, London, 1979), p. 39.
46 See, for instance, Eagleton, *The Ideology of the Aesthetic*, p. 55 (on Burke).
47 See Mark Boulby, 'The Gates of Brunswick: Some Aspects of Symbol, Structure and Theme in Karl Philipp Moritz's "Anton Reiser"', *MLR*, 68 (1973), 105–114.
48 See Stevens Garlick, 'Moritz's *Anton Reiser*'.
49 Selbmann, *Der deutsche Bildungsroman*, p. 58.
50 Boulby, *Karl Philipp Moritz*, p. 39.
51 Davies, 'Karl Philipp Moritz's Erfahrungsseelenkunde', p. 30.
52 Boulby, *Karl Philipp Moritz*, p. 108.
53 Karl Philipp Moritz, 'Über den "Tasso" von Goethe. Aus einem Brief an Goethe vom 6. Juni 1789', *Schriften zur Ästhetik und Poetik*, ed. Schrimpf, p. 326.
54 See Schings, 'Agathon – Anton Reiser – Wilhelm Meister'.
55 Letter to Charlotte von Stein, 14 December 1786.
56 Boulby, *Karl Philipp Moritz*, p. 176.
57 See Rudolf Lehmann, 'Anton Reiser und die Entstehung des Wilhelm Meister', *Jahrbuch der Goethe-Gesellschaft*, 3 (1916), 116–134, p. 126.
58 Cf. Boulby, *Karl Philipp Moritz*, pp. 49–50.
59 Ibid., p. 202; see too Schrimpf, *Karl Philipp Moritz*, pp. 111–112.
60 Boulby, 'The Gates of Brunswick', p. 114.
61 See H. Pfotenhauer, '"Des ganzen Lebens anschauliches Bild." Autobiographik und Symbol bei Karl Philipp Moritz', *Jahrbuch des Wiener Goethe-Vereins*, 86/87/88 (1982/83/84), 325–337.
62 Davies, 'Karl Philipp Moritz's Erfahrungsseelenkunde', p. 29, esp. the quote from Zimmermann.
63 *Schriften zur Ästhetik*, p. 148.

64 Ibid., pp. 73–78.
65 Ibid., p. 79.
66 'Michelangelo', Ibid., pp. 218–223.
67 Ibid., p. 79.
68 Ibid., pp. 91–92.
69 Ibid., p. 92.
70 Martin L. Davies, 'The Theme of Communication in *Anton Reiser*: A Reflection of the Feasibility of the Enlightenment', *Oxford German Studies*, 12 (1981), 18–38, p. 35.
71 Boulby, 'Gates of Brunswick', p. 114.
72 See Boulby, *Karl Philipp Moritz*, p. 200.
73 See H. Rudolf Vaget, 'Das Bild vom Dilettanten bei Moritz, Schiller und Goethe', *Jahrbuch des freien deutschen Hochstifts* (1970), edited by Detlev Lüders (Tübingen, 1970), pp. 1–31.
74 Schrimpf, *Karl Philipp Moritz*, pp. 98–99.
75 See Lehmann, 'Anton Reiser und die Entstehung des Wilhelm Meister'.
76 3 January 1789, cit. Boulby, *Karl Philipp Moritz*, pp. 186–187.
77 *Schriften zur Ästhetik*, pp. 142–148.
78 Pfotenhauer, 'Des ganzen Lebens anschauliches Bild', pp. 325–326.
79 See Eudo C. Mason, *Hölderlin and Goethe* (Bern and Frankfurt, 1975), p. 86.
80 See Hildegard Emmel, 'Hyperion, ein anderer Agathon? Hölderlin's zwiespältiges Verhältnis zu Wieland', in *Christoph Martin Wieland. Nordamerikanische Forschungsbeiträge zur 250. Wiederkehr seines Geburtstages 1983*, edited by Hansjörg Schelle (Tübingen, 1984), pp. 413–429.
81 Hölderlin, *Sämtliche Werke*, Beißner, III (1957), p. 297. All further references are to this edition.
82 *Das Erlebnis und die Dichtung*, third edition (Leipzig, 1910), p. 395.
83 Ibid., pp. 393–399.
84 Mason, *Hölderlin and Goethe*, pp. 95 and 114.
85 See Lawrence Ryan, *Hölderlins 'Hyperion'. Exzentrische Bahn und Dichterberuf* (Stuttgart, 1965), pp. 8–32.
86 English versions of quotations from *Hyperion* are taken, sometimes modified, from the translation by Willard R. Trask and adapted by David Schwarz in Friedrich Hölderlin, *Hyperion and Selected Poems*, edited by Eric L. Santer (New York, 1994).
87 Janz, 'Hölderlins Flamme – Zur Bildwerdung der Frau im "Hyperion"', *Hölderlin-Jahrbuch*, 22 (1980–1981), 122–142, pp. 135–137.
88 Mason, *Hölderlin and Goethe*, p. 54.
89 See Janz, 'Hölderlins Flamme'.
90 Ryan, *Hölderlins 'Hyperion'*, p. 188.

91 Janz, 'Hölderlins Flamme', p. 122.
92 Hölderlin, *Sämtliche Werke*, VI, 1, p. 370.
93 See Ryan, *Hölderlins 'Hyperion'*.
94 Ibid., p. 147.
95 Dilthey, *Das Erlebnis und die Dichtung*, p. 400.
96 Ryan, *Hölderlins 'Hyperion'*, p. 22.
97 Ibid., p. 235.
98 David Constantine, *Hölderlin* (Oxford, 1988), p. 93.
99 See Howard Gaskill, *Hölderlin's 'Hyperion'* (Durham, 1984), p. 7 and passim.
100 Constantine, *Hölderlin*, p. 93.
101 Gaskill, *Hölderlin's 'Hyperion'*, p. 55.
102 Constantine, *Hölderlin*, pp. 93–94.
103 Ryan, *Hölderlins 'Hyperion'*, p. 226.
104 Constantine, *Hölderlin*, p. 282.
105 Jean Laplanche, *Hölderlin und die Suche nach dem Vater* (Stuttgart and Bad Cannstatt, 1975); originally *Hölderlin et la question du père* (Paris, 1961).
106 Laplanche, *Hölderlin und die Suche nach dem Vater*, p. 120.
107 Ibid., p. 51.
108 Cit. Dilthey, *Das Erlebnis und die Dichtung*, p. 382.
109 Cf. Constantine, *Hölderlin*, p. 127.
110 'The Father's "No", Language, Counter-Memory, Practice', in *Selected Essays* by Michel Foucault, edited by Donald F. Bouchard (Ithaca, 1977), pp. 68–86; originally 'Le "non" du père', *Critique*, 178 (1962), 195–209.
111 Foucault, 'The Father's "No"', p. 86.

3. *DER GRÜNE HEINRICH*

1 See Karl Pestalozzi, '"Der grüne Heinrich", von Peter Handke aus gelesen', *Jahresbericht der Gottfried Keller Gesellschaft*, 43 (1974).
2 Hans Wysling, '"Und immer wieder kehrt Odysseus heim." Das "Fabelhafte" bei Gottfried Keller', in *Gottfried Keller. Elf Essays zu seinem Werk*, edited by Hans Wysling (Zürich, 1990), pp. 151–162.
3 See 'Kellers grüner Heinrich', in *Gottfried Keller. Der grüne Heinrich. Erste Fassung*, edited by Thomas Böning and Gerhard Kaiser (Frankfurt am Main [Deutscher Klassiker Verlag], 1985), pp. 901–1034, p. 961, where Hermann Hettner is quoted to this effect.
4 Adolf Muschg, *Gottfried Keller* (Frankfurt am Main, 1980), p. 103.
5 Gottfried Keller, *Gesammelte Briefe*, 4 vols., edited by Carl Helbling (Bern, 1950–1954), I, p. 382.
6 Ibid., I, p. 240.

7 Gottfried Keller, *Sämtliche Werke*, edited by Jonas Fränkel and (from 1944) Carl Helbling, 24 vols. (Erlenbach–Zürich and Munich, [after 1931] Bern and Leipzig, 1926–1949), XVI (1926), p. 45. All further references to the texts of *Der grüne Heinrich* are to this edition, page number preceded by volume number in roman numerals. English versions adapted from *Green Henry*, translated by A. M. Holt (London, 1960).
8 See 'Kellers grüner Heinrich', pp. 901–912.
9 Ibid., pp. 913–914.
10 Cf. ibid., p. 903.
11 Keller, *Gesammelte Briefe*, IV, p. 24.
12 Ibid., I, p. 382.
13 J. E. Toews, *Hegelianism. The Path Towards Dialectical Humanism 1805–1841* (Cambridge, 1980), p. 328.
14 'Kellers grüner Heinrich', p. 960.
15 Keller, *Gesammelte Briefe*, III.2, p. 17.
16 Ibid., III.1, p. 156.
17 See, for instance, ibid., III.1, p. 48.
18 See Kaspar T. Locher, 'Gottfried Keller and the Fate of the Epigone', *Germanic Review*, 35 (1960), 164–184. For the place of Immermann's novel in this context, see Michael Minden, 'The *Bildungsroman* and Social Forms: Immermann's *Die Epigonen*', *Ideas & Production*, 2 (1984), 10–27, and 'Problems of Realism in Immermann's *Die Epigonen*', *Oxford German Studies*, 16 (1985), 66–80.
19 Keller, *Gesammelte Briefe*, I, p. 353.
20 See Emil Ermatinger, 'Gottfried Keller und Goethe', *PMLA*, 64 (1949), 79–97.
21 Keller, *Gesammelte Briefe*, I, p. 416.
22 Cit. 'Kellers grüner Heinrich', p. 1021. For Keller's reception of this view of poetry see Keller, *Sämtliche Werke*, VI, pp. 203–204, and note, p. 383.
23 Gerhard Kaiser, *Gottfried Keller. Das gedichtete Leben* (Frankfurt am Main, 1981), p. 134.
24 'Kellers grüner Heinrich', p. 961.
25 Kaiser, *Gottfried Keller. Das gedichtete Leben*, p. 137.
26 See Muschg, *Gottfried Keller*, p. 101.
27 Renate Boeschenstein, 'Der Schatz unter den Schlangen. Ein Gespräch mit Gerhard Kaisers Buch *Gottfried Keller. Das gedichtete Leben*', *Euphorion*, 77 (1983), 176–199, p. 193.
28 Cf. Boeschenstein, 'Der Schatz unter den Schlangen', p. 191, where Alice Miller is cited on the link between landscape painting and narcissism.
29 The first version of the novel stresses the powerful masculine sexual element even more (XIX, pp. 23–24).

30 Keller, *Gesammelte Briefe*, I, p. 374.
31 See Kaiser, *Gottfried Keller. Das gedichtete Leben*, p. 134.
32 Keller's own words from notes for the novel, cit. 'Kellers grüner Heinrich', p. 923.
33 Cit. ibid., p. 912.
34 See Karl Moormann, *Subjektivismus und bürgerliche Gesellschaft. Ihr geschichtliches Verhältnis im frühen Prosawerk Gottfried Kellers* (Bern and Munich, 1977), p. 32, where Hegel's employment of this term is quoted, and Georg Lukács, *Die Theorie des Romans* (Berlin, 1920), p. 76.
35 See letter to Drachmann, Keller, *Gesammelte Briefe*, IV, p. 255.
36 Kaiser, *Gottfried Keller. Das gedichtete Leben*, p. 101.
37 Ibid., *passim*, esp. pp. 39–65.
38 Ibid., p. 129.
39 See Kaiser, ibid., pp. 61–62, and *passim*. Kaiser cites Freud, p. 54.
40 Georg Lukács, 'Gottfried Keller', in *Die Grablegung des alten Deutschland. Essays zur deutschen Literatur des 19. Jahrhunderts* (Hamburg, 1967), pp. 21–92, p. 72.
41 See also 'Stellenkommentar', in Böning and Kaiser, *Gottfried Keller. Der grüne Heinrich. Erste Fassung*, pp. 1044–1387, p. 1386.
42 Hartmut Laufhütte, *Wirklichkeit und Kunst in Gottfried Kellers Roman 'Der grüne Heinrich'* (Bonn, 1969), p. 373.
43 Kaiser, *Gottfried Keller. Das gedichtete Leben*, pp. 131–132.
44 Keller, *Gesammelte Briefe*, I, p. 357.
45 Boeschenstein, 'Der Schatz unter den Schlangen', p. 193.
46 Ibid.
47 Kaiser, *Gottfried Keller. Das gedichtete Leben*, p. 205.
48 Keller, *Gesammelte Briefe*, I, p. 397.
49 Ibid., I, p. 48.
50 See ibid., I, p. 240.
51 See ibid., III.1, p. 156.
52 'Kellers grüner Heinrich', p. 956.
53 Lukács, 'Gottfried Keller', p. 78.
54 As well as Kaiser and Muschg, see Jochen Hörisch, 'Gott, Geld und verunglücktes Dasein im "Grünen Heinrich"', in *Gott, Geld und Glück. Zur Logik der Liebe in den Bildungsromanen Goethes, Kellers und Thomas Manns* (Frankfurt, 1983), pp. 116–179.
55 Keller, *Gesammelte Briefe*, III.1, p. 448.
56 See ibid., IV, p. 227.
57 Muschg, *Gottfried Keller*, pp. 100–101.
58 Martin Swales, 'Reflectivity and Realism. On Keller's *Der grüne Heinrich*', in *Gottfried Keller 1819 -1890. London Symposium 1990*, edited by John L. Flood and Martin Swales (Stuttgart, 1991), pp. 41–52, p. 42.
59 Boeschenstein, 'Der Schatz unter den Schlangen', pp. 192–193.

60 Hörisch, *Gott, Geld und Glück*, p. 167.
61 Ibid., p. 139.
62 Muschg, *Gottfried Keller*, p. 104.

4. *HEINRICH VON OFTERDINGEN* AND *DER NACHSOMMER*

1 See Elisabeth Stopp, '"Übergang vom Roman zur Mythologie": Formal Aspects of the Opening Chapter of Hardenberg's *Heinrich von Ofterdingen*, Part II', *DVjs*, 48 (1974), 318–341, reprinted in *German Romantics in Context, Selected Essays by Elisabeth Stopp*, edited by Peter Hutchinson, Roger Paulin and Judith Purver (London, 1992), pp. 91–121.
2 *Novalis Schriften*, I, *Das dichterische Werk*, third edition (1977), pp. 335–355. All references are to this edition.
3 See Herbert Uerlings, *Friedrich von Hardenberg, genannt Novalis. Werk und Forschung* (Stuttgart, 1991), p. 406.
4 Jeffrey L. Sammons, 'The Mystery of the Missing *Bildungsroman*, or: What Happened to Wilhelm Meister's Legacy?', *Genre*, 14 (1981), 229–246, p. 256.
5 See Franz Baumer, *Adalbert Stifter* (Munich, 1989), p. 76.
6 Thomas Keller, *Die Schrift in Stifters 'Der Nachsommer'. Buchstäblichkeit und Bildlichkeit des Romantextes* (Cologne and Vienna, 1982).
7 Ulrich Stadler, *'Die theuren Dinge'. Studien zu Bunyan, Jung-Stilling und Novalis* (Bern, 1980).
8 See, for instance, Hans-Joachim Mähl, 'Novalis' Wilhelm-Meister-Studien des Jahres 1797', *Neophilologus*, 47 (1963), 286–305; Clemens Heselhaus, 'Die Wilhelm-Meister-Kritik der Romantiker', pp. 113–127; Hans-Joachim Beck, *Friedrich von Hardenberg. 'Oeconomie des Styls'. Die 'Wilhelm-Meister Rezeption im 'Heinrich von Ofterdingen'* (Bonn, 1976); Géza von Molnár, 'Wilhelm Meister from a Romantic Perspective. Aspects of Novalis' Predisposition that Resulted in his Initial Preference for Goethe's Novel', in *Versuche zu Goethe. Festschrift für Erich Heller*, edited by Volker Dürr and Géza von Molnár (Heidelberg, 1976), pp. 235–247; Ernst Behler, '*Wilhelm Meisters Lehrjahre* and the Poetic Unity of the Novel in Early German Romanticism', in *Goethe's Narrative Fiction*, edited by William J. Lillyman (Berlin and New York, 1983), pp. 110–127; Uerlings, *Friedrich von Hardenberg*, pp. 444–458.
9 Uerlings, *Friedrich von Hardenberg*, p. 445.
10 Ibid., p. 435.
11 See Manfred Frank, 'Die Philosophie des sogenannten "magischen Realismus"', *Euphorion*, 63 (1969), 88–117, p. 110.
12 Géza von Molnár, *Romantic Vision, Ethical Context. Novalis and Artistic Autonomy* (Minneapolis, 1987), p. 78.

13 See ibid., pp. 78–79.
14 See Ulrich Stadler, 'Novalis: *Heinrich von Ofterdingen*', in *Romane und Erzählungen der deutschen Romantik. Neue Interpretationen*, edited by Paul Michael Lützeler (Stuttgart, 1981), pp. 141–162, p. 160, note 72.
15 See Hermann Kurzke, *Novalis* (Munich, 1988), p. 89.
16 Behler, 'Wilhelm Meisters Lehrjahre', p. 114.
17 Oskar Walzel, 'Die Formkunst von Novalis Heinrich von Ofterdingen', *Germanisch–Romanische Monatsschrift*, 7 (1915–1919), 403–444 and 465–479.
18 See Nicholas Saul, *History and Poetry in Novalis and in the Tradition of the German Enlightenment* (London, 1984), p. 167.
19 Cf. Bernard E. Hauer, 'Die Todesthematik in *Wilhelm Meisters Lehrjahre* und *Heinrich von Ofterdingen*', *Euphorion*, 79 (1985), 182–206, p. 200.
20 Sammons, 'The Mystery of the Missing *Bildungsroman*', p. 235.
21 Adalbert Stifter, *Der Nachsommer. Eine Erzählung*, edited by Max Stefl (Augsburg, 1954), p. 243 and p. 258. All further references are to this edition.
22 See Margret Walter-Schneider, 'Das Licht in der Finsternis. Zu Stifters *Nachsommer*', *Jahrbuch der deutschen Schiller-Gesellschaft*, 29 (1985), 381–404, p. 397.
23 See, for instance, Walter-Schneider, 'Das Licht in der Finsternis'; and Peter Schäublin, 'Familiales in Stifters Nachsommer', in *Adalbert Stifter Heute*, edited by Johann Lachinger, Alexander Stillmark and Martin Swales (London, 1985), pp. 86–101.
24 Adalbert Stifter, *Sämmtliche Werke*, edited by A.Sauer, 24 vols. (to date) (Prague, etc., 1904–), XVIII, *Briefwechsel*, vol. 2, edited by Gustav Wilhelm, second edition (Hildesheim, 1972), No. 286, p. 225.
25 See, for instance, Uwe-K. Ketelsen, 'Adalbert Stifter: *Der Nachsommer* (1857). Die Vernichtung der historischen Realität in der Ästhetisierung des Alltages', in *Romane und Erzählungen des bürgerlichen Realismus*, edited by Horst Denkler (Stuttgart, 1980), pp. 188–202, p. 190; Peter Uwe Hohendahl, 'Stifters *Nachsommer* als Utopie der ästhetischen Erziehung', in *Utopieforschung. Interdisziplinäre Studien zur neuzeitlichen Utopie*, edited by Wilhelm Voßkamp, III (Stuttgart, 1982), pp. 333–356, p. 354.
26 See Karl Robert Mandelkow, 'Der Roman der Klassik und Romantik', in *Europäische Romantik*, I, edited by Karl Robert Mandelkow (Wiesbaden, 1982), pp. 393–428, p. 395.
27 See Saul, *History and Poetry in Novalis*.
28 See, for instance, Helmut Pfotenhauer, 'Aspekte der Modernität bei Novalis. Überlegungen zu Erzählformen des 19. Jahrhunderts, ausgehend von Novalis's *Heinrich von Ofterdingen*', in *Zur Modernität der Romantik*, edited by Dieter Bänsch (Stuttgart, 1977), pp. 111–142, p. 113;

Horst Albert Glaser, *Die Restauration des Schönen: Stifters Nachsommer* (Stuttgart, 1965).

29 Gail Newman, 'Poetic Process as Intermediate Area in Novalis's *Heinrich von Ofterdingen*', *Seminar*, 26 (1990), 16–33, p. 29.

30 See Anthony Phelan, '"Das Centrum das Symbol des Goldes": Analogy and Money in *Heinrich von Ofterdingen*', *German Life and Letters*, 37 (1984), 307–321.

31 Russell A. Berman, *The Rise of the Modern German Novel. Crisis and Charisma* (Cambridge, MA, and London, England, 1986), p. 127.

32 Uerlings, *Friedrich von Hardenberg*, p. 402.

33 Quoted in *Erläuterungen und Dokumente. Novalis (Friedrich von Hardenberg). Heinrich von Ofterdingen*, edited by Ursula Ritzenhoff (Stuttgart, 1988), p. 184.

34 See Helmut Pfotenhauer, 'Nachwort', in *Novalis. Hymnen an die Nacht. Heinrich von Ofterdingen*, edited by Helmut Pfotenhauer, fifth edition (Munich, 1991), pp. 212–228, p. 228.

35 Johannes Mahr, *Übergang zum Endlichen. Der Weg des Dichters in Novalis' 'Heinrich von Ofterdingen'* (Munich, 1970), p. 264.

36 Molnár, *Romantic Vision*, p. 118.

37 Stadler, 'Novalis: *Heinrich von Ofterdingen*', p. 142.

38 Adalbert Stifter, *Bunte Steine. Späte Erzählungen*, edited by Max Stefl (Augsburg, 1960), p. 122.

39 Uerlings, *Friedrich von Hardenberg*, p. 623.

40 Ibid., p. 402.

41 See Gunther Weydt, 'Ist der *Nachsommer* ein geheimer *Ofterdingen*?', *Germanisch-Romanische Monatsschrift*, 39 (1958), 72–81; Edmund Godde, *Stifters 'Nachsommer' und der 'Heinrich von Ofterdingen'. Untersuchungen zur Frage der dichtungsgeschichtlichen Heimat des 'Nachsommer'* (Bonn, 1960); Philip H. Zoldester, 'Stifter und Novalis. Ein Versuch, Wesensverwandtschaften zwischen Poetischem Realismus und Romantik aufzuzeigen', *Adalbert-Stifter-Institut des landes Oberösterreich. Vierteljahresschrift*, 22 (1973), 105–114; Raleigh Whitinger, 'Echoes of Early Romanticism in Adalbert Stifter's *Der Nachsommer*', *Monatshefte für deutschen Unterricht, deutsche Sprache und Literatur*, 82(1990), 62–72.

42 Uerlings, *Friedrich von Hardenberg*, p. 403.

43 See Molnár, *Romantic Vision*, pp. 101–115.

44 Gerhard Schulz, *Novalis in Selbstzeugnissen und Bilddokumenten* (Reinbek bei Hamburg, 1969), p. 139.

45 Gail Newman, 'The Status of the Subject in Novalis's *Heinrich von Ofterdingen* and Kleist's *Marquise von O ...*', *German Quarterly*, 62 (1989), 59–71, p. 66.

46 See Friedrich A. Kittler, 'Die Irrwege des Eros', p. 516.

47 Cf. Ritzenhoff, *Erläuterungen und Dokumente*, p. 66.

48 See Walzel, 'Die Formkunst von Novalis' *Heinrich von Ofterdingen*', p. 421.
49 Molnár, *Romantic Vision*, p. 72.
50 Ibid.
51 Sara Friedrichsmeyer, *The Androgyne in Early German Romanticism. Friedrich Schlegel, Novalis and the Metaphysics of Love* (Bern, Frankfurt am Main and New York, 1983), pp. 87–88.
52 Whitinger, 'Echoes of Early Romanticism', p. 67.
53 Baumer, *Adalbert Stifter*, p. 122.
54 Cf. Schäublin, 'Familiales in Stifters Nachsommer', p. 86.
55 See Godde, *Stifters 'Nachsommer'*, pp. 125–126.
56 Keller, *Die Schrift in Stifters 'Der Nachsommer'*, pp. 96ff.
57 See Christine Oertel Sjögren, 'Klotildes Reise in die Tiefe: Psychoanalytische Betrachtungen zu einer Episode in Stifters *Nachsommer*', *Adalbert-Stifter-Institut des Landes Oberösterreich. Vierteljahresschrift*, 24 (1975), 107–111.
58 Oertel Sjögren, 'Klotildes Reise in die Tiefe', p. 109.
59 Cf. Jürgen Scharfschwerdt, *Thomas Mann und der deutsche Bildungsroman. Eine Untersuchung zu dem Problem einer literarischen Tradition* (Stuttgart, Berlin, Cologne and Mainz, 1967), p. 24; Herbert Kaiser, 'Adalbert Stifter: *Der Nachsommer*. Dialektik der ästhetischen Bildung', in *Studien zum deutschen Roman nach 1848* (Duisburg, 1977), p. 150.
60 Cf. Godde, *Stifters 'Nachsommer'*, p. 98.
61 Kurzke, *Novalis*, p. 95.
62 Weydt, 'Ist der *Nachsommer* ein geheimer *Ofterdingen*?', p. 80.
63 Cf.Godde, *Stifters 'Nachsommer'*, p. 87.
64 For instance, J. M. Ritchie, 'Novalis' *Heinrich von Ofterdingen* and the Romantic Novel', in *Periods in German Literature II. Texts and Contexts*, edited by J. M. Ritchie (London, 1969), pp. 117–144, p. 135; Hannelore Link, *Abstraktion und Poesie im Werk des Novalis* (Stuttgart, etc., 1971), p. 170.
65 Kittler, 'Die Irrwege des Eros', p. 458.
66 Ibid., p. 453.
67 See also Kittler's 'Der Dichter, die Mutter, das Kind', pp. 102–114.
68 Kittler, 'Die Irrwege des Eros', pp. 464–465.
69 Ibid., p. 429.
70 See Dagmar C. G. Lorenz, 'Stifters Frauen', *Colloquia Germanica*, 15 (1982), 305–320.
71 See Schäublin, 'Familiales in Stifters Nachsommer', p. 95.
72 Ibid.
73 Ibid., p. 100.
74 Mahr, *Übergang zum Endlichen*, p. 264.
75 Molnár, *Romantic Vision*, p. 97.

76 Ibid.
77 Ketelsen, 'Die Vernichtung der historischen Realität', p. 195.
78 Ritzenhoff, *Erläuterungen und Dokumente*, p. 183.
79 See Walter-Schneider, 'Das Licht in der Finsternis', pp. 400–401.
80 Ketelsen, 'Die Vernichtung der historischen Realität', p. 194.
81 Christine Oertel Sjögren, 'Mathilde and the Roses in Stifter's *Nachsommer*', *PMLA*, 81(1966), 400–408, p. 400.
82 Ketelsen, 'Die Vernichtung der historischen Realität', p. 194.
83 See Molnár, *Romantic Vision*, Chapters Two and Three.
84 Berman, *The Rise of the Modern German Novel*, p. 133.
85 Marianne Schuller, 'Das Gewitter findet nicht statt oder die Abdankung der Kunst. Zu Adalbert Stifters Roman *Der Nachsommer*', *Poetica*, 10 (1978), 25–52, p. 34.
86 Kittler, 'Die Irrwege des Eros', p. 464.
87 Ibid., p. 465.
88 Cf. ibid., p. 447, but see also Uerlings, *Friedrich von Hardenberg*, p. 519.
89 Kittler, 'Die Irrwege des Eros', p. 469.
90 Pfotenhauer, 'Aspekte der Modernität bei Novalis', p. 135.
91 See J. P. Stern, *Re-Interpretations* (Cambridge, 1981), p. 288.
92 Pfotenhauer, 'Aspekte der Modernität bei Novalis', p. 130.
93 Erika and Martin Swales, *Adalbert Stifter. A Critical Study* (Cambridge, 1984).
94 For a discussion of Novalis as a precursor of deconstruction, see Uerlings, *Friedrich von Hardenberg*, pp. 615–627. See also, for instance, Alice A. Kuzniar, 'Reassessing Romantic Reflexivity – the Case of Novalis', *The Germanic Review*, 63 (1988), 77–86, p. 81. For a deconstructive reading of *Der Nachsommer* see Keller, *Die Schrift in Stifters 'Der Nachsommer'*.

5. *DER ZAUBERBERG*

1 This and all future references to Mann's works are, unless otherwise indicated, to the thirteen-volume edition of his *Gesammelte Werke*, published in 1960 and again in 1974 by Fischer. English quotations from *Der Zauberberg* are adapted from the translation of H. T. Lowe-Porter (Harmondsworth, 1960).
2 See T. J. Reed, *Thomas Mann. The Uses of Tradition* (Oxford, 1974), pp. 179–274.
3 See Scharfschwerdt, *Thomas Mann und der deutsche Bildungsroman*.
4 See Oskar Seidlin, 'The Lofty Game of Numbers: The Mynheer Peeperkorn Episode in Thomas Mann's *Der Zauberberg*', *PMLA*, 86 (1971), 924–939.
5 See, for instance, Ulrich Karthaus, '*Der Zauberberg* – ein Zeitroman

(Zeit, Geschichte, Mythos)', *DVjs*, 44 (1970), 269–305; Terence K. Thayer, 'Hans Castorp's Hermetic Adventures', *The Germanic Review*, 46 (1971), 299–312; Hanns-Werner am Zehnhoff, 'Mythologische Motive der Siebenzahl in Thomas Manns Roman Der Zauberberg', *Études Germaniques*, 33 (1978), 154–171.

6 Cf. Michael Beddow, *The Fiction of Humanity*, p. 241.

7 Quoted from Peter de Mendelssohn, 'Nachbemerkungen des Herausgebers', in Thomas Mann, *Der Zauberberg*, edited by Peter de Mendelssohn (Frankfurt am Main, 1981), pp. 1007–1066, pp. 1053–1054.

8 See Burghard Dedner, 'Entwürdigung. Die Angst vor dem Gelächter in Thomas Manns Werk', in *'Heimsuchung und süßes Gift'. Erotik und Poetik bei Thomas Mann*, edited by Gerhard Härle (Frankfurt, 1992), pp. 87–102.

9 Ibid., p. 98.

10 See Wysling, 'Thomas Manns Goethe-Nachfolge', pp. 510–511.

11 Bloom, *The Anxiety of Influence*, p. 54.

12 In a letter to Agnes E. Meyer, 12 January 1943, *Thomas Mann, Briefe 1937–1947*, edited by Erika Mann (Frankfurt am Main, 1963), p. 290.

13 See Wysling, 'Goethe-Nachfolge', pp. 541–542.

14 De Mendelssohn, 'Nachbemerkungen des Herausgebers', p. 1055.

15 Claus Sommerhage, *Eros und Poesis. Über das Erotische im Werk Thomas Manns* (Bonn, 1983), p. 118.

16 Diana Behler, 'Thomas Mann as Theoretician of the Novel. Romanticism and Realism', *Colloquia Germanica*, 7 (1974), 52–88, pp. 57–58.

17 Letter to Ernst Fischer, 25 May 1926, *Thomas Mann, Briefe 1889–1936*, edited by Erika Mann (Frankfurt am Main, 1961), p. 255.

18 See, for instance, Hermann J. Weigand, *The Magic Mountain. A Study of Thomas Mann's Novel 'Der Zauberberg'* (Chapel Hill, 1965), pp. 3–13; Scharfschwerdt, *Thomas Mann und der deutsche Bildungsroman*; Jeffrey L.Sammons, 'The Mystery of the Missing *Bildungsroman*', Helmut Koopmann, 'Zur Einführung', in Børge Kristiansen, *Thomas Manns 'Zauberberg' und Schopenhauers Metaphysik*, 2., verbesserte und erweiterte Auflage (Bonn, 1986), pp. ix–xxv.

19 Hans Wysling, 'Probleme der *Zauberberg*-Interpretation', in *Thomas Mann Jahrbuch*, vol. 1, edited by Eckhard Heftrich and Hans Wysling (Frankfurt am Main, 1988), pp. 12–26, p. 25.

20 Wysling, 'Probleme der *Zauberberg*', p. 24.

21 Cf. Jill Anne Kowalik, '"Sympathy with Death": Hans Castorp's Nietzschean Resentment', *The German Quarterly*, 58 (1985), 27–48, p. 28.

22 Mann was delighted to discover Georg Brandes's treatment of Novalis in *Die Romantische Schule in Deutschland*, precisely because Mann found

there such a perfect intellectual-poetic formulation of problematic subjectivity, and one which at the same time was available for construction as essentially German. See Steven Cerf, 'Georg Brandes' View of Novalis. A Current within Thomas Mann's *Der Zauberberg*', *Colloquia Germanica*, 14 (1981), 114–129.

23 De Mendelssohn, quoting Brandes, 'Nachbemerkugen des Herausgebers', p. 1031.

24 Cit. Friedrich A.Kittler, *Aufschreibesysteme. 1800. 1900*, second edition (Munich, 1987), p. 231.

25 Cf. Horst Fritz, *Instrumentelle Vernunft als Gegenstand von Literatur* (Munich, 1982), p. 153.

26 Weigand, *The Magic Mountain*, p. 5.

27 Letter to Hans Pfitzner, 23 June 1925, *Briefe 1889–1936*, p. 241.

28 Cerf, 'Georg Brandes' View of Novalis', p. 116.

29 Eagleton, *The Ideology of the Aesthetic*, p. 196.

30 Thomas Mann, *Tagebücher 1918–1921*, edited by Peter de Mendelssohn (Frankfurt am Main, 1979), p. 510 (27 April 1921).

31 Hörisch, *Gott, Geld und Glück*, p. 16.

32 Richard Exner, 'Das berückend Menschliche oder Androgynie in der Literatur. Am Hauptbeispiel Thomas Mann', *Neue Deutsche Hefte*, 31 (1984), 254–276, p. 268.

33 Karl Werner Böhm, 'Die homosexuellen Elemente in Thomas Manns *Der Zauberberg*', *Literatur für Leser*, 3 (1984), 171–190, pp. 171–176.

34 Böhm, 'Die homosexuellen Elemente', p. 182.

35 See, for instance, besides Böhm, Sommerhage, *Eros und Poesis*; Gerhard Härle, *Die Gestalt des Schönen. Untersuchung zur Homosexualitätsthematik in Thomas Manns Roman 'Der Zauberberg'* (Königstein/Ts, 1986).

36 *Tagebücher 1918–1921*, p. 303 (17 September 1919).

37 Cf. Jeffrey Weeks, *Sexuality and its Discontents. Meanings, Myths and Modern Sexualities* (London, 1985), p. 152.

38 Klaus Theweleit, *Männerphantasien* (Frankfurt am Main, 1977); cf. Sommerhage, *Eros und Poesis*, p. 281.

39 See Sommerhage, *Eros und Poesis*, p. 127.

40 Böhm, 'Die homosexuellen Elemente', pp. 184–186.

41 Kittler, *Aufschreibesyteme*, p. 207.

42 Jeffrey Meyers, *Homosexuality and Literature 1890–1930* (London and Atlantic Highlands, NJ, 1977), p. 43.

43 Böhm, 'Die homosexuellen Elemente', p. 186.

44 Cf. de Mendelssohn, 'Nachbemerkungen des Herausgebers', p. 1044.

45 Seidlin, 'The Lofty Game of Numbers', p. 932.

46 Karthaus, '*Der Zauberberg*', pp. 286–287.

47 Hörisch, *Gott, Geld und Glück*, p. 228.

48 For Mann's reponse to the Kaiser's abdication, see *Tagebücher*

1918–1921, p. 45. Mann uses the word 'Persönlichkeit' to refer to the Kaiser.

49 Martin Swales, *Thomas Mann* (London, 1980), p. 54.

50 Exner, 'Das berückend Menschliche', p. 273.

51 See Eckhard Heftrich, *Zauberbergmusik. Über Thomas Mann* (Frankfurt am Main, 1975), pp. 210–217.

52 See Winfried Kudszus, 'Peeperkorns Lieblingsjünger. Zu Thomas Manns *Zauberberg*', *Wirkendes Wort*, 20 (1970), 321–330, p. 322.

53 Heftrich, *Zauberbergmusik*, p. 210.

54 Metteer, *Desire in Fictional Communities*, pp. 49–50.

55 Cf. Wysling, 'Goethe-Nachfolge', p. 542.

56 Härle, *Die Gestalt des Schönen*, p. 144.

57 See Wysling, 'Probleme der *Zauberberg*', p. 19.

58 Sommerhage, *Eros und Poesis*, p. 127.

59 See, for instance, the seminal exposition in Weigand, *The Magic Mountain*.

60 Cf. Wysling, 'Goethe-Nachfolge', p. 511.

61 Wysling, 'Probleme der *Zauberberg*', p. 16.

62 Cf. Stephen Heath, 'Ambiviolences: Notes for Reading Joyce', in *Post-Structuralist Joyce*, edited by Derek Attridge and Daniel Ferrer (Cambridge, 1984), pp. 31–68, pp. 36–37.

63 De Mendelssohn, 'Nachbemerkungen des Herausgebers', p. 1018.

64 *Tagebücher 1918–1921*, pp. 200–201 (17 April 1919).

65 Letter to Paul Amann, 3 August 1915, cit. de Mendelssohn, 'Nachbemerkungen des Herausgebers', p. 1018.

66 Berman, *The Rise of the Modern German Novel*, pp. 279–280.

67 Kowalik, 'Sympathy with Death', p. 42 and *passim*.

68 Kristiansen, *Thomas Manns 'Zauberberg'*, p. 306.

69 Ibid., p. 390.

70 Cit. de Mendelssohn, 'Nachbemerkungen des Herausgebers', p. 1057.

71 Heftrich, *Zauberbergmusik*, p. 201.

72 Helmut Koopmann, *Die Entwicklung des 'intellektualen Romans' bei Thomas Mann. Untersuchungen zur Struktur von 'Buddenbrooks', 'Königliche Hoheit' und 'Der Zauberberg'*, third edition (Bonn, 1980), p. 6.

73 Cf. Exner, 'Das berückend Menschliche', p. 271.

74 See Wysling, 'Probleme der *Zauberberg*', pp. 18–19.

75 Cf. Philip Sicker, 'Babel Revisited: Mann's Myth of Language in The Magic Mountain', *Mosaic*, 19 (1986), 2, 1–20.

76 See Weigand, *The Magic Mountain*, p. 13.

77 XI, p. 609; for details of the novel's commercial success, see de Mendelssohn, 'Nachbemerkungen des Herausgebers', pp. 1051–1053.

78 Hartmut Steinecke, 'Die "repräsentative Kunstform der Epoche". Bemerkungen zu Thomas Manns Romanverständnis', in *Thomas*

Mann 1875–1975. Vorträge in München-Zürich-Lübeck, edited by Beatrix Bludau, Eckhard Heftrich and Helmut Koopmann (Frankfurt am Main, 1977), pp. 250–268, p. 259.

79 See Kittler, *Aufschreibesysteme*, pp. 181–270.

80 See Jochen Hörisch, '"Die deutsche Seele up to date." Sakramente der Medientechnik auf dem *Zauberberg*', in *Arsenale der Seele. Literatur und Medienanalyse seit 1870*, edited by Friedrich A. Kittler and Georg Christoph Tholen (Munich, 1989), pp. 13–23.

CONCLUSION

1 The phrase is Malcolm Pasley's in a lecture entitled 'Kafka's Ruhm', given on the occasion of the award of an honorary doctorate by the University of Gießen, cited here after *Die Zeit*, 2 October 1992, p. 63.

2 Franz Kafka, *Schriften Tagebücher Briefe*. Kritische Ausgabe, edited by Jürgen Born *et al.*, *Tagebücher*, edited by Hans-Gerd Koch, Michael Müller and Malcolm Pasley (Frankfurt am Main, 1990), p. 887. See Ritchie Robertson, *Kafka, Judaism, Politics, Literature* (Oxford, 1985), pp. 25–26.

3 *Tagebücher*, pp. 372–373.

4 Robertson, *Kafka*, pp. 21–25.

5 *Tagebücher*, pp. 313–315.

6 *Tagebücher*, p. 313.

7 Robertson, *Kafka*, p. 27.

8 Gilles Deleuze and Félix Guattari, *Kafka. Toward a Minor Literature*, translated by Dana Polan (Minneapolis, 1986), p. 26.

9 *Nachgelassene Schriften*, p. 127.

10 *Nachgelassene Schriften*, p. 140.

Bibliography

PRIMARY TEXTS

Blanckenburg, Christian Friedrich von, *Versuch über den Roman* (Leipzig and Liegnitz, 1774)

Fénelon, François Salignac de la Mothe, *Les Aventures de Télémaque*, edited by Jeanne-Lydie Goré (Paris, 1968)

Goethe, Johann Wolfgang von, *Werke*, Textkritisch durchgesehen und mit Anmerkungen versehen von E. Trunz, W. Kayser, J. Kunz *et al.* ('Hamburger Ausgabe'), 14 vols. (Hamburg then Munich, 1948–1960)

Gedenkausgabe der Werke, Briefe und Gespräche, edited by E. Beutler (Zurich, 1948–1954)

Der Briefwechsel zwischen Schiller und Goethe, edited by Emil Staiger, 2 vols. (Frankfurt am Main, 1977)

Wilhelm Meisters Theatralische Sendung, mit einem Nachwort von Wilhelm Voßkamp (Frankfurt am Main, 1984)

Goethe, Wolfgang von (*sic*), *Wilhelm Meister*, translated by Thomas Carlyle, 2 vols. (London, 1912)

Hebbel, Friedrich, *Werke*, edited by G. Fricke, W. Keller and K. Pörnbacher, 5 vols. (Munich, 1965)

Hölderlin, Friedrich, *Sämtliche Werke*, edited by Friedrich Beißner, 8 vols. (Stuttgart, 1946–85)

Hyperion and Selected Poems, edited by Eric L. Santer (New York, 1994)

Kafka, Franz, *Gesammelte Werke*, edited by Max Brod (New York and Frankfurt am Main, 1946–)

Schriften Tagebücher Briefe. Critical edition, edited by Jürgen Born *et al.* (Frankfurt am Main, 1982–)

Nachgelassene Schriften und Fragmente, edited by M. Pasley and J. Schillemeit, 2 vols. (Frankfurt am Main, 1992–1993)

Metamorphosis and Other Stories, translated by Willa and Edwin Muir (Harmondsworth, 1961)

Keller, Gottfried, *Sämtliche Werke*, edited by Jonas Fränkel and (from 1944)

Carl Helbling, 24 vols. (Erlenbach–Zürich and Munich, [after 1931] Bern and Leipzig, 1926–1949)
Der grüne Heinrich. Erste Fassung, edited by Thomas Böning and Gerhard Kaiser (Frankfurt am Main, 1985)
Gesammelte Briefe, edited by Carl Helbling, 4 vols. (Bern, 1950–1954)
Green Henry, translated by A. M. Holt (London, 1960)
Mann, Thomas, *Gesammelte Werke*, 13 vols. (Frankfurt am Main, 1960, reprinted 1974)
Briefe. 1889–1936/1937–1947/1948–1955, edited by Erika Mann, 3 vols. (Frankfurt am Main, 1961–1965)
Tagebücher 1918–1921, edited by Peter de Mendelssohn (Frankfurt am Main, 1979)
The Magic Mountain, translated by H. T. Lowe Porter, with an introductory essay by the author, 2 vols. (New York, 1962)
Moritz, Karl Philipp, *Anton Reiser. Ein psychologischer Roman*, edited by Wolfgang Martens (Stuttgart, 1973)
Schriften zur Ästhetik und Poetik, edited by Hans Joachim Schrimpf (Tübingen, 1962)
Novalis [Friedrich von Hardenberg], *Schriften*, second edition, edited by Paul Kluckhohn and Richard Samuel, 4 vols. + 1 Begleitband (Stuttgart, 1960–1988; a third edition of vol. 1 only was published in 1977)
Schlegel, Friedrich, *Kritische Friedrich Schlegel Ausgabe*, edited by E. Behler *et al.* (Paderborn, 1958–)
'Über Goethes "Meister"', *Athenäum*, 1, Part 2 (1798), 323–354
Stifter, Adalbert, *Sämmtliche Werke*, edited by A. Sauer, 24 vols. (to date) (Prague, etc., 1904–)
Bunte Steine. Späte Erzählungen, edited by Max Stefl (Augsburg, 1960)
Der Nachsommer. Eine Erzählung, edited by Max Stefl (Augsburg, 1954)
Wieland, Christoph Martin, *Werke*, edited by Fritz Martini and Hans Werner Seiffert, 5 vols. (Munich, 1964–1968)
Geschichte des Agathon, edited by Klaus Manger (Frankfurt am Main, 1986)
The History of Agathon, [translated by John Richardson] (London, 1773)
Wielands Briefwechsel, edited by Hans Werner Seiffert (Berlin, 1963–)

SECONDARY LITERATURE

Baioni, Giuliano, '"Märchen" – "Wilhelm Meisters Lehrjahre" – "Hermann und Dorothea". Zur Gesellschaftsidee der deutschen Klassik', *Goethe-Jahrbuch*, 92 (1975), 73–127
Bakhtin, M.M., 'The Bildungsroman and Its Significance in the History of Realism (Toward a Typology of the Novel)', in *Speech Genres and*

Other Late Essays, edited by Caryl Emerson and Michael Holquist (Austin, 1986), pp. 10–59

Baumer, Franz, *Adalbert Stifter* (Munich, 1989)

Beck, Hans-Joachim, *Friedrich von Hardenberg. 'Oeconomie des Styls'. Die 'Wilhelm-Meister Rezeption im 'Heinrich von Ofterdingen'* (Bonn, 1976)

Beddow, Michael, *The Fiction of Humanity. Studies in the Bildungsroman from Wieland to Thomas Mann* (Cambridge, 1982)

Behler, Diana, 'Thomas Mann as Theoretician of the Novel. Romanticism and Realism', *Colloquia Germanica*, 7 (1974), 52–88

Behler, Ernst, '*Wilhelm Meisters Lehrjahre* and the Poetic Unity of the Novel in Early German Romanticism', in *Goethe's Narrative Fiction*, edited by William J. Lillyman (Berlin and New York, 1983), pp. 110–127

Belsey, Catherine, *The Subject of Tragedy. Identity and Difference in Renaissance Drama* (London and New York, 1985)

Berman, Russell A., *The Rise of the Modern German Novel. Crisis and Charisma* (Cambridge, MA, and London, England, 1986)

Bersier, Gabrielle, 'The Education of the Prince: Wieland and German Enlightenment at School with Fénelon and Rousseau', *Eighteenth Century Life*, n.s. 10, 1 (1986), 1–13

Blackall, Eric A., *Goethe and the Novel* (Ithaca and London, 1976)

Blessin, Stefan, *Die Romane Goethes* (Königstein/Ts, 1979)

Bloom, Harold, *The Anxiety of Influence. A Theory of Poetry*, (London, Oxford and New York, 1973)

Boa, Elizabeth, 'Sex and Sensibility: Wieland's Portrayal of Relationships Between the Sexes in the *Comische Erzählungen*, *Agathon*, and *Musarion*', *Lessing Yearbook*, 12 (1980), 189–218

Boeschenstein, Renate, 'Der Schatz unter den Schlangen. Ein Gespräch mit Gerhard Kaisers Buch *Gottfried Keller. Das gedichtete Leben*', *Euphorion*, 77 (1983), 176–199

Bogue, Ronald, *Deleuze and Guattari* (London and New York, 1989)

Böhm, Karl Werner, 'Die homosexuellen Elemente in Thomas Manns *Der Zauberberg*', *Literatur für Leser*, 3 (1984), 171–190

Boulby, Mark, 'Anton Reiser and the Concept of the Novel', *Lessing Yearbook*, 4 (1972), 183–196

'The Gates of Brunswick: Some Aspects of Symbol, Structure and Theme in Karl Philipp Moritz's "Anton Reiser"', *MLR*, 68 (1973), 105–114

Karl Philipp Moritz: At the Fringe of Genius (Toronto, Buffalo, London, 1979)

Bowie, Andrew, *Aesthetics and Subjectivity: from Kant to Nietzsche* (Manchester and New York, 1990)

Boyle, Nicholas, 'Das Lesedrama: Versuch einer Ehrenrettung', *Kontroversen, alte und neue*, Akten des VII. Internationalen Germanisten

Kongresses, Göttingen 1985, edited by A. Schöne, VII (Tübingen, 1986), pp. 59–68

Brenner, Peter J., *Die Krise der Selbstbehauptung. Subjekt und Wirklichkeit im Roman der Aufklärung* (Tübingen, 1981)

Bürger, Christa, *Der Ursprung der Institution Kunst. Literatursoziologische Untersuchungen zum klassischen Goethe* (Frankfurt am Main, 1977)

Bürger, Peter, *Theory of the Avant-Garde*, translated by Michael Shaw (Manchester and Minnesota, 1984)

Cantor, Paul, *Shakespeare, Hamlet* (Cambridge, 1989)

Cerf, Steven, 'Georg Brandes' View of Novalis. A Current within Thomas Mann's *Der Zauberberg*', *Colloquia Germanica*, 14 (1981), 114–129

Cocalis, Susan L., 'The Transformation of *Bildung* from an Image to an Ideal', *Monatshefte für deutschen Unterricht, deutsche Sprache und Literatur*, 70 (1978), 399–414

Constantine, David, *Hölderlin* (Oxford, 1988)

Davies, Martin L., 'Karl Philipp Moritz's Erfahrungsseelenkunde: Its Social and Intellectual Origins', *Oxford German Studies*, 16 (1985), 13–35

'The Theme of Communication in *Anton Reiser*: A Reflection of the Feasibility of the Enlightenment', *Oxford German Studies*, 12 (1981), 18–38

Dedner, Burghard, 'Entwürdigung. Die Angst vor dem Gelächter in Thomas Manns Werk', in *'Heimsuchung und süßes Gift'. Erotik und Poetik bei Thomas Mann*, edited by Gerhard Härle (Frankfurt, 1992), pp. 87–102

Deleuze, Gilles and Guattari, Félix, *Kafka. Toward a Minor Literature*, translated by Dana Polan (Minneapolis, 1986)

Dews, Peter, *Logics of Disintegration* (London and New York, 1987)

Dilthey, Wilhelm, *Das Erlebnis und die Dichtung*, third edition (Leipzig, 1910)

Dreyfus, Hubert L. and Rabinow, Paul, *Michel Foucault. Beyond Structuralism and Hermeneutics* (Brighton, 1982)

Eagleton, Terry, 'Self-authoring subjects', in *What is an Author?*, edited by Maurice Biriotti and Nicola Miller (Manchester, 1993), pp. 42–50

The Ideology of the Aesthetic (Oxford, 1990)

Emmel, Hildegard, 'Hyperion, ein anderer Agathon? Hölderlin's zwiespältiges Verhältnis zu Wieland', in *Christoph Martin Wieland. Nordamerikanische Forschungsbeiträge zur 250. Wiederkehr seines Geburtstages 1983*, edited by Hansjörg Schelle (Tübingen, 1984), pp. 413–429

Was Goethe vom Roman der Zeitgenossen nahm (Bern, 1972)

Ermatinger, Emil, 'Gottfried Keller und Goethe', *PMLA*, 64 (1949), 79–97

Exner, Richard, 'Das berückend Menschliche oder Androgynie in der Literatur. Am Hauptbeispiel Thomas Mann', *Neue Deutsche Hefte*, 31 (1984), 254–276

Foucault, Michel, 'The Father's "No", Language, Counter-Memory, Practice', in *Selected Essays by Michel Foucault*, edited by Donald F. Bouchard (Ithaca, 1977), pp. 68–86; originally 'Le "non" du père', *Critique*, 178 (1962), 195–209

'The Subject and Power', in Hubert L. Dreyfus and Paul Rabinow, *Michel Foucault. Beyond Structuralism and Hermeneutics* (Brighton, 1982), pp. 208–216

The Order of Things. An Archaeology of the Human Sciences (London, 1970)

Frank, Manfred, 'Die Philosophie des sogenannten "magischen Realismus"', *Euphorion*, 63 (1969), 88–117

Friedrichsmeyer, Sara, *The Androgyne in Early German Romanticism. Friedrich Schlegel, Novalis and the Metaphysics of Love* (Bern, Frankfurt am Main and New York, 1983)

Fritz, Horst, *Instrumentelle Vernunft als Gegenstand von Literatur* (Munich, 1982)

Gaskill, Howard, *Hölderlin's 'Hyperion'* (Durham, 1984)

Gerth, Hans H., *Bürgerliche Intelligenz um 1800* (Göttingen, 1976)

Glaser, Horst Albert, *Die Restauration des Schönen: Stifters Nachsommer* (Stuttgart, 1965)

Godde, Edmund, *Stifters 'Nachsommer' und der 'Heinrich von Ofterdingen'. Untersuchungen zur Frage der dichtungsgeschichtlichen Heimat des 'Nachsommer'* (Bonn, 1960)

Gray, Ronald, *Goethe the Alchemist. A Study of Alchemical Symbolism in Goethe's Literary and Scientific Works* (London, 1952)

Gundolf, Friedrich, *Romantiker. Neue Folge* (Berlin-Wilmersdorf, 1931)

Haas, Rosemarie, *Die Turmgesellschaft in 'Wilhelm Meisters Lehrjahre'. Zur Geschichte des Geheimbundromans und der Romantheorie im 18. Jahrhundert* (Bern and Frankfurt am Main, 1975)

Hahl, Werner, *Reflexion und Erzählung. Ein Problem der Romantheorie von der Spätaufklärung bis zum programmatischen Realismus* (Stuttgart, etc., 1971)

Härle, Gerhard, *Die Gestalt des Schönen. Untersuchung zur Homosexualitätsthematik in Thomas Manns Roman 'Der Zauberberg'* (Königstein/Ts, 1986)

Hauer, Bernard E., 'Die Todesthematik in *Wilhelm Meisters Lehrjahre* und *Heinrich von Ofterdingen*', *Euphorion*, 79 (1985), 182–206

Heath, Stephen, 'Ambiviolences: Notes for Reading Joyce', in *Post-Structuralist Joyce*, edited by Derek Attridge and Daniel Ferrer (Cambridge, 1984), pp. 31–68

Heftrich, Eckhard, *Zauberbergmusik. Über Thomas Mann* (Frankfurt am Main, 1975)

Heselhaus, Clemens, 'Die Wilhelm-Meister-Kritik der Romantiker und die romantische Romantheorie', in *Nachahmung und Illusion*, edited by H. R. Jauß (Munich, 1964), pp. 113–127

Hohendahl, Peter Uwe, 'Stifters Nachsommer als Utopie der ästhetischen Erziehung', in *Utopieforschung. Interdisziplinäre Studien zur neuzeitlichen Utopie*, edited by Wilhelm Voßkamp, III (Stuttgart, 1982), pp. 333–356

Holborn, Hajo, *A History of Modern Germany* (Princeton, 1982)

Hörisch, Jochen, '"Die deutsche Seele up to date." Sakramente der Medientechnik auf dem *Zauberberg*', in *Arsenale der Seele. Literatur und Medienanalyse seit 1870*, edited by Friedrich A. Kittler and Georg Christoph Tholen (Munich, 1989), pp. 13–23

Gott, Geld und Glück. Zur Logik der Liebe in den Bildungsromanen Goethes, Kellers und Thomas Manns (Frankfurt am Main, 1983)

Jäger, Georg, *Empfindsamkeit und Roman. Wortgeschichte. Theorie und Kritik im 18. und frühen 19. Jahrhundert* (Stuttgart, 1969)

Janz, Marlies, 'Hölderlins Flamme – Zur Bildwerdung der Frau im "Hyperion"', *Hölderlin-Jahrbuch*, 22 (1980–1981), 122–142

Janz, Rolf-Peter, 'Zum sozialen Gehalt der "Lehrjahre"', in *Literaturwissenschaft und Geschichtsphilosophie*, edited by Helmut Arntzen *et al.* (Berlin and New York, 1975), pp. 320–340

Kaiser, Gerhard, *Gottfried Keller. Das gedichtete Leben* (Frankfurt am Main, 1981)

Studien zum deutschen Roman nach 1848 (Duisburg, 1977)

Karthaus, Ulrich, '*Der Zauberberg* – ein Zeitroman (Zeit, Geschichte, Mythos)', *DVjs*, 44 (1970), 269–305

Keller, Thomas, *Die Schrift in Stifters 'Der Nachsommer'. Buchstäblichkeit und Bildlichkeit des Romantextes* (Cologne and Vienna, 1982)

Ketelsen, Uwe-K., 'Adalbert Stifter: *Der Nachsommer* (1857). Die Vernichtung der historischen Realität in der Ästhetisierung des Alltages', in *Romane und Erzählungen des bürgerlichen Realismus*, edited by Horst Denkler (Stuttgart, 1980), pp. 188–202

Kittler, Friedrich A., 'Der Dichter, die Mutter, das Kind. Zur romantischen Erfindung der Sexualität', in *Romantik in Deutschland*, edited by Richard Brinkmann, Sonderband der *DVjs* (Stuttgart, 1978), 102–114

'Die Irrwege des Eros und die "Absolute Familie"', in *Psychoanalyse und psychopathologische Literaturinterpretation*, edited by Bernd Urban and Winfried Kudszus (Darmstadt, 1981), pp. 421–470

'Über die Sozialisation Wilhelm Meisters', in Gerhard Kaiser and Friedrich A. Kittler, *Dichtung als Sozialisationsspiel. Studien zu Goethe und Gottfried Keller* (Göttingen, 1978), pp. 13–124

Aufschreibesysteme. 1800. 1900, second edition (Munich, 1987)

Kontje, Todd, *The German Bildungsroman: History of a National Genre* (Columbia, 1993)

Koopmann, Helmut, *Die Entwicklung des 'intellektualen Romans' bei Thomas Mann. Untersuchungen zur Struktur von 'Buddenbrooks', 'Königliche Hoheit' und 'Der Zauberberg'*, third edition (Bonn, 1980)

Kowalik, Jill Anne, '"Sympathy with Death": Hans Castorp's Nietzschean Resentment', *The German Quarterly*, 58 (1985), 27–48

Kristiansen, Børge, *Thomas Manns 'Zauberberg' und Schopenhauers Metaphysik*, second edition (Bonn, 1986)

Kudszus, Winfried, 'Peeperkorns Lieblingsjünger. Zu Thomas Manns *Zauberberg*', *Wirkendes Wort*, 20 (1970), 321–330

Kurzke, Hermann, *Novalis* (Munich, 1988)

Kuzniar, Alice A., 'Reassessing Romantic Reflexivity – The Case of Novalis', *The Germanic Review*, 63 (1988), 77–86

Lange, Victor, 'Zur Gestalt des Schwärmers im deutschen Roman des 18. Jahrhunderts', in *Festschrift für Richard Alewyn*, edited by Herbert Singer and Benno von Wiese (Cologne and Graz, 1967), pp. 150–164

Laplanche, J. and Pontalis, J.-B., *The Language of Psycho-Analysis* (London, 1980)

Laplanche, Jean, *Hölderlin und die Suche nach dem Vater* (Stuttgart-Bad Cannstatt, 1975), originally *Hölderlin et la question du père* (Paris, 1961)

Laufhütte, Hartmut, *Wirklichkeit und Kunst in Gottfried Kellers Roman 'Der grüne Heinrich'* (Bonn, 1969)

Lehmann, Rudolf, 'Anton Reiser und die Entstehung des Wilhelm Meister', *Jahrbuch der Goethe-Gesellschaft*, 3 (1916), 116–134

Link, Hannelore, *Abstraktion und Poesie im Werk des Novalis* (Stuttgart, etc., 1971)

Locher, Kaspar T., 'Gottfried Keller and the Fate of the Epigone', *Germanic Review*, 35 (1960), 164–184

Lorenz, Dagmar C. G., 'Stifters Frauen', *Colloquia Germanica*, 15 (1982), 305–320

Lukács, Georg, 'Gottfried Keller', in *Die Grablegung des alten Deutschland. Essays zur deutschen Literatur des 19. Jahrhunderts* (Hamburg, 1967), pp. 21–92

Die Theorie des Romans (Berlin, 1920)

Werke, 17 vols. (Neuwied am Rhein and Berlin, 1962–1975)

Mähl, Hans-Joachim, 'Novalis' Wilhelm-Meister-Studien des Jahres 1797', *Neophilologus*, 47 (1963), 286–305

Mahr, Johannes, *Übergang zum Endlichen. Der Weg des Dichters in Novalis' 'Heinrich von Ofterdingen'* (Munich, 1970)

Mandelkow, Karl Robert, 'Der Roman der Klassik und Romantik', in *Europäische Romantik*, vol. 1, edited by Karl Robert Mandelkow (Wiesbaden, 1982), pp. 393–428

Martini, Fritz, 'Der Bildungsroman. Zur Geschichte des Wortes und der Theorie', *DVjs*, 35 (1961), 44–63

Mason, Eudo C., *Hölderlin and Goethe* (Bern and Frankfurt am Main, 1975)

Mendelssohn, Peter de, 'Nachbemerkungen des Herausgebers', in

Thomas Mann, *Der Zauberberg*, edited by Peter de Mendelssohn (Frankfurt am Main, 1981), pp. 1007–1066

Metteer, Michael, *Desire in Fictional Communities* (New York and London, 1988)

Meyers, Jeffrey, *Homosexuality and Literature 1890–1930* (London and Atlantic Highlands, NJ, 1977)

Minden, Michael, 'The *Bildungsroman* and Social Forms: Immermann's *Die Epigonen*', *Ideas and Production*, 2 (1984), 10–27

'Problems of Realism in Immermann's *Die Epigonen*', *Oxford German Studies*, 16 (1985), 66–80

Molnár, Géza von, 'Wilhelm Meister from a Romantic Perspective. Aspects of Novalis' Predisposition that Resulted in his Initial Preference for Goethe's Novel', in *Versuche zu Goethe. Festschrift für Erich Heller*, edited by Volker Dürr and Géza von Molnár (Heidelberg, 1976), pp. 235–247

Romantic Vision, Ethical Context. Novalis and Artistic Autonomy (Minneapolis, 1987)

Moormann, Karl, *Subjektivismus und bürgerliche Gesellschaft. Ihr geschichtliches Verhältnis im frühen Prosawerk Gottfried Kellers* (Bern and Munich, 1977)

Moretti, Franco, *The Way of the World. The 'Bildungsroman' in European Culture* (London, 1987)

Morgenstern, Karl, 'Bruchstück einer den 12/24 Dec 1810 zu Dorpat im Hauptsaal der Kaiserl. Universität öffentlich gehaltenen Vorlesung über den Geist und Zusammenhang einer Reihe philosophischer Romane', in *Dörptsche Beyträge für Freunde der Philosophie, Litteratur und Kunst*, edited by Karl Morgenstern, vol. 3 (Dorpat and Leipzig, 1817), 180–195

Muschg, Adolf, *Gottfried Keller* (Frankfurt am Main, 1980)

Nagel, Thomas, *The View from Nowhere* (Oxford, 1986)

Newman, Gail, 'Poetic Process as Intermediate Area in Novalis's *Heinrich von Ofterdingen*', *Seminar*, 26 (1990), 16–33

'The Status of the Subject in Novalis's *Heinrich von Ofterdingen* and Kleist's *Marquise von O ...*', *German Quarterly*, 62 (1989), 59–71

Niggl, Günter, *Geschichte der deutschen Autobiographie im 18. Jahrhundert* (Stuttgart, 1977)

Oertel Sjögren, Christine, 'Klotildes Reise in die Tiefe: Psychoanalytische Betrachtungen zu einer Episode in Stifters Nachsommer', *Adalbert-Stifter-Institut des Landes Oberösterreich. Vierteljahresschrift*, 24 (1975), 107–111

'Mathilde and the Roses in Stifter's *Nachsommer*', *PMLA*, 81 (1966), 400–408

Pascal, Roy, *Design and Truth in Autobiography* (London, 1960)

Paulsen, Wolfgang, *Christoph Martin Wieland. Der Mensch und sein Werk in psychologischen Perspektiven* (Bern and Munich, 1975)

Peschken, Bernd, *Versuch einer germanistischen Ideologiekritik. Goethe, Lessing, Tieck, Hölderlin, Heine in Wilhelm Diltheys und Julian Schmidts Vorstellungen* (Stuttgart, 1972)

Pestalozzi, Karl, '"Der grüne Heinrich", von Peter Handke aus gelesen', *Jahresberichte der Gottfried Keller Gesellschaft*, 43 (1974)

Pfotenhauer, H., '"Des ganzen Lebens anschauliches Bild." Autobiographik und Symbol bei Karl Philipp Moritz', *Jahrbuch des Wiener Goethe-Vereins*, 86/87/88 (1982, 1983, 1984), 325–337

'Aspekte der Modernität bei Novalis. Überlegungen zu Erzählformen des 19. Jahrhunderts, ausgehend von Novalis's *Heinrich von Ofterdingen*', in *Zur Modernität der Romantik*, edited by Dieter Bänsch (Stuttgart, 1977), pp. 111–142

'Nachwort', in *Novalis. Hymnen an die Nacht. Heinrich von Ofterdingen*, edited by Helmut Pfotenhauer, fifth edition (Munich, 1991), pp. 212–228

Phelan, Anthony, '"Das Centrum das Symbol des Goldes": Analogy and Money in *Heinrich von Ofterdingen*', *German Life and Letters*, 37 (1984), 307–321

Rank, Otto, *Das Inzest-Motiv in Dichtung und Sage. Grundzüge einer Psychologie des dichterischen Schaffens*, second edition (Leipzig and Vienna, 1926)

Reed, T. J., *Goethe* (Oxford and New York, 1984)

The Classical Centre. Goethe and Weimar 1775–1832 (London, 1980)

Thomas Mann. The Uses of Tradition (Oxford, 1974)

Ritchie, J. M., 'Novalis' *Heinrich von Ofterdingen* and the Romantic Novel', in *Periods in German Literature II. Texts and Contexts*, edited by J. M. Ritchie (London, 1969), pp. 117–144

Ritzenhoff, Ursula, ed., *Erläuterungen und Dokumente. Novalis (Friedrich von Hardenberg) Heinrich von Ofterdingen* (Stuttgart, 1988)

Roberts, David, *The Indirections of Desire. Hamlet in Goethe's 'Wilhelm Meister'* (Heidelberg,1980)

Roberts, Julian, *German Philosophy. An Introduction* (Polity Press, Cambridge, 1988)

Robertson, Ritchie, *Kafka, Judaism, Politics, Literature* (Oxford, 1985)

Ryan, Lawrence, *Hölderlins 'Hyperion'. Exzentrische Bahn und Dichterberuf* (Stuttgart, 1965)

Sammons, Jeffrey L., 'The Mystery of the Missing Bildungsroman, or: What Happened to Wilhelm Meister's Legacy?', *Genre*, 14 (1981), 229–246

Six Essays on the Young German Novel, second edition (Chapel Hill, 1975)

Sandkühler, Hans Jörg, *Friedrich Wilhelm Joseph Schelling* (Stuttgart, 1970)

Saul, Nicholas, *History and Poetry in Novalis and in the Tradition of the German Enlightenment* (London, 1984)

Scharfschwerdt, Jürgen, *Thomas Mann und der deutsche Bildungsroman. Eine Untersuchung zu dem Problem einer literarischen Tradition* (Stuttgart, Berlin, Cologne and Mainz, 1967)

Schäublin, Peter, 'Familiales in Stifters Nachsommer', in *Adalbert Stifter Heute*, edited by Johann Lachinger, Alexander Stillmark and Martin Swales (London, 1985), pp. 86–101

Schings, Hans-Jürgen, 'Agathon – Anton Reiser – Wilhelm Meister. Zur Pathogenese des modernen Subjekts im Bildungsroman', in *Goethe im Kontext*, edited by Wolfgang Wittkowski (Tübingen, 1984), pp. 42–68

Schlaffer, Hannelore, *Wilhelm Meister. Das Ende der Kunst und die Wiederkehr des Mythos* (Stuttgart, 1980)

Schlechta, Karl, *Goethes Wilhelm Meister*, introduction by Heinz Schlaffer (Frankfurt am Main, 1985)

Schrimpf, Hans Joachim, *Karl Philipp Moritz* (Stuttgart, 1980)

Schuller, Marianne, 'Das Gewitter findet nicht statt oder die Abdankung der Kunst. Zu Adalbert Stifters Roman *Der Nachsommer*', *Poetica*, 10 (1978), 25–52

Schulz, Gerhard, *Novalis in Selbstzeugnissen und Bilddokumenten* (Reinbek bei Hamburg, 1969)

Schweitzer, Cristoph E., 'Wilhelm Meister und das Bild vom kranken Königssohn', *PMLA*, 72 (1957), 419–432

Seidlin, Oskar, 'The Lofty Game of Numbers: The Mynheer Peeperkorn Episode in Thomas Mann's *Der Zauberberg*', *PMLA*, 86 (1971), 924–939

Selbmann, Rolf, *Der deutsche Bildungsroman* (Stuttgart, 1984)

Theater im Roman. Studien zum Strukturwandel des deutschen Bildungsromans (Munich, 1981)

Sengle, Friedrich, 'Der Romanbegriff in der ersten Hälfte des 19. Jahrhunderts', in *Arbeiten zur deutschen Literatur 1750–1850* (Stuttgart, 1965), pp. 175–196

'Die klassische Kultur von Weimar, sozialgeschichtlich gesehen', *Internationales Archiv für Sozialgeschichte der deutschen Literatur*, 3 (1978), 68–86

Biedermeierzeit, III, *Die Dichter* (Stuttgart, 1980)

Wieland (Stuttgart, 1949)

Sicker, Philip, 'Babel Revisited: Mann's Myth of Language in *The Magic Mountain*', *Mosaic*, 19 (1986), 2, 1–20

Sommerhage, Claus, *Eros und Poesis. Über das Erotische im Werk Thomas Manns* (Bonn, 1983)

Spaemann, Robert, *Reflexion und Spontaneität* (Stuttgart, 1963)

Stadler, Ulrich, *'Die theuren Dinge'. Studien zu Bunyan, Jung-Stilling und Novalis* (Bern, 1980)

'Novalis: *Heinrich von Ofterdingen*', in *Romane und Erzählungen der deutschen*

Romantik. Neue Interpretationen, edited by Paul Michael Lützeler (Stuttgart, 1981), pp. 141–162

Stahl, E. L., *Die religiöse und die humanitätsphilosophische Bildungsidee und die Entstehung des deutschen Bildungsromans im 18. Jahrhundert* (Bern, 1934)

Steinecke, Hartmut, 'Die "repräsentative Kunstform der Epoche". Bemerkungen zu Thomas Manns Romanverständnis', in *Thomas Mann 1875–1975. Vorträge in München–Zürich–Lübeck*, edited by Beatrix Bludau, Eckhard Heftrich and Helmut Koopmann (Frankfurt am Main, 1977), pp. 250–268

Stern, Guy, 'Fielding, Wieland and Goethe; A Study in the Development of the Novel', PhD thesis, Columbia University, New York (1954)

Stern, J. P., *Re-Interpretations* (Cambridge, 1981)

Stevens Garlick, D., 'Moritz's *Anton Reiser.* The Dissonant Voice of Psycho-Autobiography', *Studi germanici*, 21/22 (1983–1984), 41–60

Stopp, Elisabeth, '"Übergang vom Roman zur Mythologie": Formal Aspects of the Opening Chapter of Hardenberg's *Heinrich von Ofterdingen*, Part II', *DVjs*, 48 (1974), 318–341, reprinted in *German Romantics in Context, Selected Essays by Elisabeth Stopp*, edited by Peter Hutchinson, Roger Paulin and Judith Purver (London, 1992), pp. 91–121

Swales, Erika and Martin, *Adalbert Stifter. A Critical Study* (Cambridge, 1984)

Swales, Martin, 'Reflectivity and Realism. On Keller's *Der grüne Heinrich*', in *Gottfried Keller 1819 -1890. London Symposium 1990*, edited by John L. Flood and Martin Swales (Stuttgart, 1991), pp. 41–52

The German Bildungsroman from Wieland to Hesse (Princeton, 1978)

Thomas Mann (London, 1980)

Thayer, Terence K., 'Hans Castorp's Hermetic Adventures', *The Germanic Review*, 46 (1971), 299–312

Theweleit, Klaus, *Männerphantasien* (Frankfurt am Main, 1977)

Toews, J. E., *Hegelianism. The Path Towards Dialectical Humanism 1805–1841* (Cambridge, 1980)

Uerlings, Herbert, *Friedrich von Hardenberg, genannt Novalis. Werk und Forschung* (Stuttgart, 1991)

Vaget, H. Rudolf, 'Das Bild vom Dilettanten bei Moritz, Schiller und Goethe', *Jahrbuch des Freien deutschen Hochstifts* (1970), 1–31

Walter-Schneider, Margret, 'Das Licht in der Finsternis. Zu Stifters *Nachsommer*', *Jahrbuch der deutschen Schiller-Gesellschaft*, 29 (1985), 381–404

'Das Unzulängliche ist das Angemessene. Über die Erzählerfigur in Stifters *Nachsommer*', *Jahrbuch der deutschen Schiller-Gesellschaft*, 34 (1990), 317–342

Walzel, Oskar, 'Die Formkunst von Novalis Heinrich von Ofterdingen', *GRM*, 7 (1915–1919), 403–444 and 465–479

Weeks, Jeffrey, *Sexuality and its Discontents. Meanings, Myths and Modern Sexualities* (London, 1985)

Weigand, Hermann J., *The Magic Mountain. A Study of Thomas Mann's Novel 'Der Zauberberg'* (Chapel Hill, 1965)

Weydt, Günther, 'Ist der *Nachsommer* ein geheimer *Ofterdingen*?', *GRM*, 39 (1958), 72–81

Whitinger, Raleigh, 'Echoes of Early Romanticism in Adalbert Stifter's *Der Nachsommer*', *Monatshefte für deutschen Unterricht, deutsche Sprache und Literatur*, 82 (1990), 62–72

Wölfel, Kurt, 'Daphnes Verwandlungen. Zu einem Kapitel in Wielands "Agathon"', *Jahrbuch der deutschen Schillergesellschaft*, 8 (1964), 41–56

Wysling, Hans, 'Probleme der *Zauberberg*-Interpretation', in *Thomas Mann Jahrbuch*, vol. 1, edited by Eckhard Heftrich and Hans Wysling (Frankfurt am Main, 1988), pp. 12–26

'Thomas Manns Goethe-Nachfolge', *Jahrbuch des freien deutschen Hochstifts* (1978), 498–551

'"Und immer wieder kehrt Odysseus heim." Das "Fabelhafte" bei Gottfried Keller', in *Gottfried Keller. Elf Essays zu seinem Werk*, edited by Hans Wysling (Zürich, 1990), pp. 151–162

Zehnhoff, Hanns-Werner am, 'Mythologische Motive der Siebenzahl in Thomas Manns Roman *Der Zauberberg*', *Études Germaniques*, 33 (1978), 154–171

Zoldester, Philip H., 'Stifter und Novalis. Ein Versuch, Wesensverwandtschaften zwischen Poetischem Realismus und Romantik aufzuzeigen', *Adalbert-Stifter-Institut des Landes Oberösterreich. Vierteljahresschrift*, 22 (1973), 105–114

Index